CONSTRUCTING CURRICULUM

Alternate Units of Study

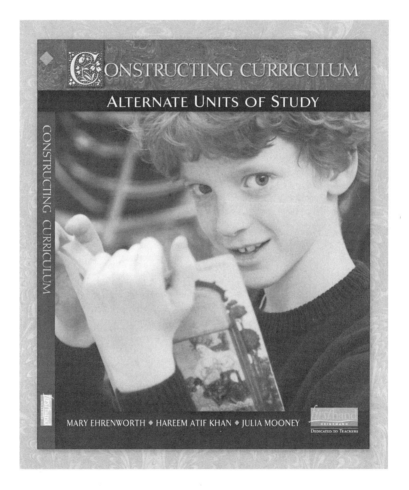

Lucy Calkins, Mary Ehrenworth, Hareem Atif Khan, and Julia Mooney

firsthand

HEINEMANN

DEDICATED TO TEACHERS

DEDICATED TO TEACHERS

firsthand
An imprint of Heinemann
361 Hanover Street, Portsmouth, NH 03801
www.heinemann.com

Offices and agents throughout the world

"Dedicated to Teachers" is a trademark of Greenwood Publishing Group, Inc.

The authors and publisher wish to thank those who have generously given permission to reprint borrowed material:

Excerpt from BECAUSE OF WINN-DIXIE. Copyright © 2000 by Kate DiCamillo. Reproduced by permission of the publisher, Candlewick Press, Somerville, MA.

Excerpt from EDWARD'S EYES by Patricia MacLachlan. Copyright © 2007 Reprinted with the permission of Atheneum Books for Young Readers, an imprint of Simon & Schuster Children's Publishing Division.

Excerpt from *The Lightning Thief.* Copyright © 2005 Rick Riordan. Published by Hyperion Books for Children.

Excerpt from *Thank You, M'am.* Text copyright © by Langston Hughes. Reprinted with the permission of Creative Co., publishers.

Excerpt from FANTASTIC MR. FOX by Roald Dahl, ILLUSTRATED BY Donald Chaffin, Text copyright © 1970, renewed 1998 by Roald Dahl Nominee Limited. Illustrations © 1979 by Donald Chaffin. Used by permission of Alfred A. Knopf, an imprint of Random House Children's Books, a division of Random House, Inc.

Photographers: Peter Cunningham and Melanie Brown
Cover and Interior Design: Jenny Jensen Greenleaf
Composition: Ed Stevens

Library of Congress Cataloging-in-Publication Data

CIP data on file with the Library of Congress

ISBN-10: 0-325-03070-7
ISBN-13: 978-0-325-03070-8

Printed in the United States of America on acid-free paper
14   13   12   11   10   ML   1   2   3   4   5   6

To Breshnay Atif Khan, A Little Girl of Big Words
—H. A. K.

To Rich Hallett, who makes so much of my work possible
—M.E.

To Aidan, my favorite character study
—J.M.

To Jackson Ehrenworth, an inspired fantasy reader
—M.E.

Contents

Lucy Calkins

PART ONE
ALTERNATE UNITS OF STUDY FOR TEACHING READING

Hareem Atif Khan

Our first job in September is to engage our students—in their reading and also in our teaching. This unit has been written with an eye towards engaging as well as teaching students with brief, spirited minilessons that welcome youngsters into a reading workshop. We recommend this unit for teachers of third graders in your second year of launching, after you have learned from teaching the foundational units. The unit takes the rollicking favorite, *Fantastic Mr. Fox* by Roald Dahl, as a touchstone text, although you could alter this, and teaches the habits, rituals, and skills that are especially important at the start of the year.

Mary Ehrenworth

This unit is designed for teachers and students who are both seasoned participants in a reading work-shop. The unit rallies students to adopt ambitious goals and to do this by drawing on all they have already learned during previous years in order to work with great personal resolve to read increasingly complex books with depth and sophistication. The unit expects that students will work with increasing independ-ence and resourcefulness, and helps them want to do this. It's written with an eye towards appealing to stu-dents who are on the brink of adolescence and are eager to be treated like they are practically experts. The unit is written with *Edward's Eyes* by Patricia MacLachlan as a touchstone text—but it relies only lightly on that book, and you could easily substitute another well-written novel. This unit will make the most sense when your students (and you) have experienced the foundational units.

Julia Mooney

In *Because of Winn-Dixie* by Kate DiCamillo, a scruffy, homeless dog turns a town into a community and begins to heal a young girl's old wounds. In this unit, you'll bring that dog, its owner Opal, and dozens of other characters from your children's own books to front and center in your classroom. The result will be not only a community, but a community of readers who grow theories about characters as they read. You'll use these relationship between readers and characters to propel your students into important work with skills such as envisioning, developing theories about characters, using story structure to support compre-hension, and inferring. The unit was written with the expectation that you might elect to teach it as a vari-ation on *Unit 2: Following Characters into Meaning,* so that students will have a chance to cycle through character work several times—once with *Because of Winn-Dixie* and perhaps a year later with *The Tiger Rising.* Kate DiCamillo's flawed and deeply loving characters are almost impossible not to embrace as real, and their struggles will help children address important lessons about loss and renewal.

This unit of study aims to get kids hooked on reading fantasy—hooked on the intense characters, the danger-filled narrative, and the underlying themes of the essential goodness and courage of mankind, even in the darkest of hours. The unit will help you launch experienced readers into this compelling genre, and it will help you be sure they emerge with increased confidence, better able to tackle more complex texts. The unit demonstrates some of the complicated intellectual work students can do in fantasy and any complex novel, using Rick Riordan's *The Lightning Thief* as a touchstone text.

PART TWO
FRAMEWORKS FOR ALTERNATE UNITS

There is a reason that fairytales, folktales, fables, and myths have stayed with us for centuries—evolving and changing over time and across cultures, but remaining crucial elements of our collective literary vocabulary. Not only are the types of stories presented in this unit unfailingly engaging and fun, but they also offer up a wealth of teaching material. In this unit, students will learn the characteristics and structures of each type of story, and learn to use their deeper understanding of these old tales in the context of their other fiction reading. Equally as important, they will learn to recognize the archetypical characters appearing in these tales as the antecedents of contemporary characters. They will be exposed to the idea of literary allusion, and come to understand that a little research into an unfamiliar allusion will yield deeper understanding, a process that has the potential to enhance and enrich their reading for the rest of their lives.

This unit teaches content area reading through a study of one topic—immigration. It aims to do this in ways that might allow you to adopt a different topic, if you like, while still leaning on this unit of study. You will help children understand that one way to learn about an era in history is to learn about its people. For a month or so, your reading workshop will provide students with a forum for reading nonfiction pertaining to the topic on hand, which in this case is immigration. Your emphasis will not be on the content of this topic but rather on the transferable skills of reading to learn. You'll help students learn from nonfiction books, articles, video, photographs, documents, and web-based sources as well as from fiction texts. You'll support your students' envisionment and empathy, questioning and critical reading, and interpretation.

This unit is designed not to invite readers to work with a kind of *text*, but instead to develop a kind of *skill*. Specifically, the unit shines a spotlight on the important skill of questioning. The real goal, of course, is not simply questioning—it is the thinking that results because readers are digging deep. You'll help students learn to ask deep, critical questions, first of texts, then of authors, and finally of themselves as readers and as people. In this unit, students question and mull over possible answers, discussing them with their book club members and writing to grow their thinking. The ultimate aim of this unit is that students carry the habit of questioning into their own lives.

The Teachers College Reading & Writing Project staff

This is an all-time favorite unit. The unit helps youngsters synthesize a text, following a single story line through the separate chapters as they read, seeing cause-and-effect relationships, predicting outcomes, and reading closely. It is natural to expect readers of mysteries to try to solve the mystery before the crime solver does—but to actually accomplish this goal is as complex as all of reading. The bar is set high! With support from book clubs, readers can learn to be attentive and constructive readers. Mystery readers need to be able to pull in to catch key details, and they need to be able to pull back to assemble those details and grow something out of them—a hunch, a suspicion, a prediction, a theory. And that is the art of reading.

Anna Gratz

This unit helps sharpen advanced readers' awareness of perspective. The unit first invites readers to study texts that clearly reveal two separate points of view, learning to think about who is telling the story and what that perspective involves. Readers then apply this understanding of perspectives to work with all fiction texts. Readers learn to consider how the story might go were it told from a different viewpoint, and, from this thinking, to develop big ideas about the characters, the events, and the power structures in the story.

Mary Coakley

As students prepare for sixth grade and begin to notice more cliques and bullying among their peers, a unit on reading books through a social issues lens could be called for, providing students with language and frames for examining texts and their own lives. This unit helps young people read critically and think deeply, together in book clubs, especially about power. The skills students use to improve their reading of texts can also help them improve their reading of the world—and, too, it can inform the way they live their lives.

(Please see *Resources* CD-ROM for this unit.)
Lauren Ciuffreda, Kyleen Davis, and Bethany Trench

This unit was born of wanting to bring more humor into a yearlong reading curriculum. Originally designed for third graders, the unit could also be adapted for younger or older readers. One important goal is to help readers laugh at the funny parts in books. This, of course, requires that they "get the joke," which requires far more comprehension and close reading than you might at first think! The unit supports readers in enjoying, sharing, enacting, and studying humorous texts. Readers learn to notice patterns in humorous texts and they see the signals authors give.

(Please see *Resources* CD-ROM for this unit.)

Marcie von Beck

How does the idea of *place*—the intersection of geography and time—affect who we are and who we become? What elements of the human spirit seem to cut across history, appearing in characters that live on the unbroken prairie and on Southern plantations, in the filthy, boisterous streets of medieval London and in the Oklahoma dustbowl? How are our characters shaped by the places in which they live? How do the power structures existing within various historical contexts affect characters' decisions? These are only some of the questions that this unit of study in historical fiction will help you to explore with your students. This unit was designed for fifth-grade students who are well into their year of reading workshop. It aims to build on students' prior knowledge of envisioning, empathizing, critical reading, and synthesizing in order to lift the level of the reading work students have been doing throughout the year within the more complex context of historical fiction.

PART THREE
A BLUEPRINT FOR DESIGNING YOUR OWN UNITS OF STUDY

Lucy Calkins

The book ends with a chapter that passes the baton to you, setting you up to be able to construct your own units of study. You'll learn the underlying principles, the predictable challenges, the tricks of the trade—that is, you'll receive the same sort of coaching that the co-authors of this book have received. The purpose of this entire volume is not just to triple the number of units that you feel confident to teach—the purpose is also to provide you with some scaffolding so that you co-author some units of study with our involvement, too. In this way, you'll receive the support that can help you develop state-of-the-art reading workshop curriculum that can, in turn, be shared with other reading workshop teachers. Perhaps, before long, there will be a sequel to *Constructing Curriculum!*

Acknowledgments

As these books come to a close, this seems a fitting time to acknowledge not just the people who contributed to this series directly but the larger community that informs these books and our work every day in countless ways. The Teachers College Reading and Writing Project community as a whole deserves a big thanks. Every year, as all the staff developers at the Project help hundreds of schools from across the world invent and refine and revise units of study for the reading workshop, we find ourselves becoming more and more adept at designing units, and our knowledge grows as we take in each other's expertise. That accumulation of knowledge is all part of this series.

Then there are individual members in our community who have inspired and contributed to some of these units—a special nod goes to Colleen Cruz, who first developed many of the Project's ideas about fantasy; to Stacey Fell-Eisenkraft, who helped to edit the units in the second half of this book; and to Kathy Collins and Rebecca Bellingham for contributing their ideas and voice to this and other books in the series.

We are, of course, ever grateful to the teachers and principals who try out, invent, and champion new units of study and who help us think about the best ways to be sure all kids develop the skills they need. How lucky we are to work with such an inspired and inspiring group of educators, whose collaboration is at the core of this work. In particular, our gratitude goes to the six teachers who contributed their ideas, enthusiasm, and humor at the end of a school day once a week as we put our heads together to imagine ways to deepen our children's reading work and these books. They let us into their classrooms, volunteered their time, and shared stories about their teaching and their students' wonderful reading work. Their footprints are all over the prior books in this series. Once again, a special thanks to Molly Feeney, Sarah Colmaire, Randi Bernstein, Kathy Doyle, Katie Even, and Erin Hanley Cain. Thanks as well to Kelly Boland, Ali Marron, and Torrin Hallett, whose zealous reading work inspired some of these lessons.

Last but not least, we thank the teachers who abbreviated their units so we could include at least the essence of those units in the final section of this book, and we thank the many whose units are not included here but might have been. We aimed for a variety of topics and grade levels. Of all these contributors, one, Anna Gratz, has been especially helpful with this volume and the series. Anna is now in Australia, and from that far-off place she helped create condensed versions of a few of these units. Mike Ochs, teacher extraordinaire, also helped not only with this volume but with many parts of this project. You'll see his work in the nonfiction articles on the CD, but his hand is elsewhere, too.

What's so special about this particular final volume is the wide range of backgrounds it represents. The teaching ideas within this book were developed for classrooms in New York City public schools, in rural Pakistan, in Montessori schools, in Catholic schools, in suburban New Jersey schools, in Seattle and Texas schools, and in many places in between. The hope is that you, the reader, will imagine ways you—in your corner of the world—can also author units of study. May these pages inspire you to author your own, unique units.

Introduction

My son Miles recently graduated from college and got himself a job clear across the country. I took him to the airport that final day. We needed to leave the house at 4 A.M. for a 6 A.M. flight to Seattle, but I was happy to be part of this final rite of passage. We found the sign for Alaskan Air, and as I waited for a space at the curb, I explained to Miles that because he had so much stuff with him, he should get a porter to help. Miles had never employed a porter, so he had frantic last-minute questions about where to find the porter and how to pay him. "I'll stay right here while you flag one down," I reassured him.

Miles got out of the car and, his back to me, successfully flagged his porter; then the two of them opened the back of the van and unloaded one suitcase, then another one and another, as well as a bike and a box. They piled all of it onto the porter's trolley, and then Miles and the porter walked away.

That was it—no wave and no good-bye, just Miles's receding back as he accompanied the porter into the terminal.

I sat at the wheel of the car, straining to see where he'd gone. Surely he was just taking his stuff somewhere and he'd be back to say good-bye. But no—that was it. He was gone.

I've come to believe that parenting has everything to do with letting go. It changes you when you see your son round the bend—you realize that you bring kids up for this moment when they head off to places you can't even imagine. Teaching, too, is all about letting go—and that is true whether we are teaching kids or teaching teachers. For a time, we run alongside the bike, holding the back of the seat, keeping it steady. And then we let go, and ahead of us, the rider grows smaller and smaller, pumping for her life until she rounds the bend and is off to places we can't even imagine.

This final book in the series *Constructing Curriculum: Alternate Units of Study* is part of the letting go. The book aims to help you get started authoring your own units of study. The principle that informs this is the same principle that has informed much of the teaching that we do with kids. Over and over, you have seen me demonstrate and then name what I have done in ways that I hope are transferable to another day, another situation, another person. Then you've seen me pass the baton to children, saying, "You try it," and you've seen me say to them, "I'll get you started, and then you carry on. You can do it."

In the seven units of study volumes in this series, the coauthors and I have demonstrated methods for constructing curriculum in reading. Across each book, I've repeatedly extracted the principles that undergird the units and the minilessons, explicitly naming the transferable lessons that I hope you learn. But I will not have done my job well if the time doesn't come for me to also say, "Now it's your turn. We'll get you started, and then you'll be able to carry on. You'll see."

That's the message of this book. In this volume, you'll be riding the bike—that is, inventing the curriculum—first with us keeping a strong grip and then just holding a finger on the back of your bike's seat. Yet we'll still be there to help you gain momentum, to protect you from falling into any big ditches, to make it likely that you have success. We do this both by providing you with units that aren't written in anything close to the detail you'll find in the foundational units but that still sketch out the main story line that your unit might follow and by providing you with a final chapter that teaches and coaches you in much the same way that I have taught and coached the coauthors of these units. You see, the whole point of this book is for you to leave it feeling as if you and your colleagues could also be coauthors of it in a sense, developing units of study that someday could be included in the new edition of this volume.

I've written about *Constructing Curriculum* as if it is all about providing you, the teacher, with something that supports *your* growth, but actually the book is equally important for the kids. This one volume more than triples the total number of units we pass along to you. This means that you and your colleagues will have many more possibilities and options when planning your curriculum—and it means you will be in a far better place to design a curriculum that supports your particular learners.

Don't get me wrong. You will absolutely be able to teach variations of the foundational units in the series, described in the seven volumes, to a class of children over several consecutive years. The minilessons in those units—such as the importance of pushing ourselves to read more or the need to predict not only what happens next in a text but how it happens—will pertain to third and fifth graders alike (and actually we've been teaching these throughout middle school as well). You or the class's teacher the next year(s) would want to switch the read-aloud book for the minilessons and personalize the unit so as to make it filled with your own stories and with the kids' stories. As always, you'll delete parts of the minilessons that don't sit right with you and add parts that do, as well as add new minilessons to address the needs you see in your classroom. As long as you are always improvising a bit on the units of study, you will find that across the years in a school, children will no doubt revisit these units at least a second time.

But you will also want to sometimes launch a class in a dramatically new way. For example, if you are teaching a fifth- or sixth-grade class that has cycled through the reading workshop for two or three years already, experiencing the launching unit in both its original form and in a varied form, and that has harvested from that book all the insights you can about this form of teaching, then you may decide in your second year that you want to coauthor a unit of study. In this case, you'll teach with the support of Mary Ehrenworth's *Intellectual Independence: An Ambitious Workshop for Experienced Readers,* and you'll convey to your class the message that they are now experienced readers and that they'll need to be engaged in different work. This unit invites you to teach in ways that expect readers are comfortable both inventing their own strategies and drawing from their repertoire of ways of reading. Don't try this simply because your readers are older; they (and you) will need to work through *Building a Reading Life* first. You'll find that even *Intellectual Independence* could be taught not just as a launching unit—tweak it, and it could be the final unit in the year, one that launches readers into their summer of reading or into the rest of their reading lives.

On the other hand, if you have taught *Building a Reading Life* one year (and in fact, used the entire series one year) and for your second year inside this curriculum decide you'd like to teach a leaner launch, one that places more emphasis on the rudiments of reading, you may launch using *Launching the Reading Workshop with Young Readers.*

In the same way, you will want to first teach *Following Characters into Meaning.* But a year later, once you have learned how to teach this unit through the main units in the series, you might decide that third-grade readers will work best in *Bringing Characters to Life and Developing Essential Reading Skills,* a unit that offers a different spin on a character unit and is a bit simpler, especially simpler than the final portion of *Following Characters into Meaning.*

The other units we offer in this book aren't variations on the ones contained in the original volumes but instead are meant to help you imagine and plan entirely new units, taking readers to brand-new terrain. Of these, only one has been written out in some detail, as the units described above have been, and that is *Learning from the Elves: A Genre Study of the Complexities and Themes of Fantasy,* a unit that harnesses the complexity of fantasy texts to increase the complexity of the reading work.

The other units that are included in the volume are frameworks—they provide you only with the goals, the unit overview, the teaching points, the bibliography of touchstone texts, and a few minilessons. You might think this is sparse support, and it is true that a great deal is still left in your hands. But let me assure you that far more than half the work of planning a unit is completed once you have planned the overall pathway of your unit and drafted the teaching points (which will probably change somewhat as you work on more detailed minilessons). These unit plans, or frameworks, have all been through well over ten drafts and have had the benefit of input from all sorts of mentors and colleagues. Most of the authors are experienced teachers, teaching in leading language arts departments in far-flung parts of the world, but you'll see that some of the coauthors are first-year teachers. This should help all of you have the confidence to also invent curriculum.

As I mentioned earlier, I close the book with a final chapter in which I have tried to share with you, as teachers, some ways to help construct your own units of study in reading (and this has huge implications for developing units of study in writing as well). In graduate courses and at summer institutes for the past decade, I've developed and refined ways of supporting curriculum development. I know from all of this work the predictable challenges that you will encounter, so the tips I tend to give pay off the most. This chapter is detailed and explicit, but if you look at the units in this book, you will see that this process of writing your own unit of study yields stunning curriculum.

Finally, let me urge you to send completed units of study to the Teachers College Reading and Writing Project's website so that we can share with others what you and your colleagues coauthor. I'm already imagining the sequels to this series!

LAUNCHING THE READING WORKSHOP WITH YOUNG READERS

By Hareem Atif Khan

PART ONE

Living the Life of a Reader

Dear Teacher,

Great teaching isn't all that different from good read-ing. Instead of chapters, our school years are divided into units; as we progress through these, we learn more about the kids entrusted to our care, learn their stories and their challenges. As our kids grow, so do we.

This unit is a very first chapter in the "book" of a school year. In this unit, you'll gather your students close and look straight into their eyes to say, "A reader is a great thing to be." And then, perhaps even more importantly, you'll whisper, "Let me show you how it's done." Students need explicit instruction and real support in reading. This unit is one way to take young readers through September—one possible beginning to the year's story.

Setting New Year's Resolutions for Reading

Dear Teacher,

It's hard to imagine a goal that could be more important for today than that of setting the tone for this new year. Your goal today is to issue a generous invitation to your children, telling them each that this year will be a special one for reading. You'll demonstrate your own love of reading. You'll convey that readers will be active participants in shaping the classroom culture.

You'll want to use running records to channel your students to text levels that are apt to be just right for them. Once you've done this, you can also establish partnerships consisting of two readers in the same level of text difficulty. You'll probably want partners to sit near each other in the meeting area so that they may support each other during the minilesson.

For today, you can set children up to read from troughs or bins containing picture books and chapter books that are high interest and short. You are not yet imagining children settling into a book that will last the week, although some will. You are instead imagining a day of grazing.

CONNECTION

Launch the classroom library, inviting children in.

"Students, can I have your eyes?

"In a minute, we're going to gather in our library corner. I was here for the last few days setting up this library, and I am so incredibly bursting with pride over it. I thought of one of those red ribbons that they hang around a new building and knew that we need to launch this year with our very own ribbon-cutting ceremony. In a minute, I'm going to call on all of you to stand on the perimeter of the library. We'll embark on a new year of reading adventures. So walk over, really silently, just taking in all the amazing sights."

After calling the children over, table by table, and gesturing so they stood as close to me as possible, I picked up the scissors and handed them to one child in the group, saying, "As this ribbon is cut, I want us all to say to ourselves, 'This is going to be the best reading year ever.'" After we cut the ribbon, I ushered the kids into the meeting area and sat down. Motioning for the kids to gather close, I brought forth a sealed box of books.

Open up a box of new library books, suggesting that a new library and new books mark the launch of a new year in reading.

"Today is going to be a really lucky day because when I arrived this morning, there was a box at the door of my classroom, and I realized we are getting new books! Don't you *love* it when you get a new book? Let's open this box together, okay?"

I now proceeded to open the new box of books, and as I took out one book or another, I smelled it, commenting, "Don't you love the smell of new books?" I imagined what one of the books might be like, suggesting perhaps it might be as good as another that I knew the children had probably heard in the preceding year.

"Today we not only have a new class and new books; we also have new reading lives. That is, we have a chance to start our reading lives all over again. This is the start of a new year, and that means that each one of us can start today to make a whole new reading life for ourselves—starting today.

"We've cut the ribbon to open up our new library and also to start our new reading lives. The way to start a new year of any kind is through New Year's Resolutions."

State your teaching point. Specifically, tell children that readers use the memory of times when reading has been really good to set New Year's Resolutions for ourselves.

"Today I want to teach you that just as athletes sometimes say, 'In this new year, I'm going to get really good at my game' and then set goals for themselves, so, too, readers sometimes say, 'In this new year, I'm going to...' and then set New Year's Resolutions for ourselves. And one way to do this is to remember the times when reading has been a really good thing for us, and then we say, 'In the year ahead, I'm going to have more times when reading is a really good thing for me.'"

Teaching

Make resolutions for a new year in your own reading life, sharing these with students.

"So right now, I'm going to show you how I go about making New Year's Resolutions for myself as a reader (because I'm the same as you—I'm definitely wanting this to be the best year in the world for me as a reader).

"So one thing I do is I try to set myself up for a good year. When I wanted to become a better cook—to start making fancy suppers—I told my family that I needed them to get me an island for my kitchen, or at least a new frying pan. *Then* I could become a good cook. Or when I began to really take my painting seriously, I cleared up a sunny spot for my easel and went out and got myself a new set of brushes.

"Well, when I think about how I can make sure to set myself up so the year ahead is a great reading year, I'm thinking that maybe I should figure out if there is an extra lamp somewhere in our house that I could move beside my bed so I'll have a good place to read. *And* I'm also going to try to buy one of those tasseled bookmarks that I saw the other day at the drugstore, because I think if I have a bookmark in my book, I won't lose my place. I might even think about making a special shelf for *my* books, away from everyone else's."

Prompt students into noting what you just did, and repeat an explanation of your process.

"Did you see how I thought about the way I could make a reading life for myself? I know I just talked about the stuff I needed—the lamp, the bookmark, the shelf—but I'm also thinking that this way I'll make *reading* a bigger part of my life."

Active Involvement

Invite students to make New Year's Resolutions in their own reading lives.

"Can you try doing the same sort of thing? Right now, will you think about whether there is something *you* could do to change your life, or to change your stuff, so that reading becomes a bigger deal for you? Just think to yourself, 'What could I do so reading is a bigger part of my life?'"

As children thought, I said, "You might be thinking about setting up a place in your home where you like to read, or about finding a reading friend who could help you get good books, or about setting aside a special time for reading. In a minute, I'm going to ask you to tell the person next to you what you think you could do to set this year up so it will be the best year in your reading life. Use a thumbs up (I made one, thumb held close to my heart) to show me that you are ready to tell someone how you'll set things up so this year will be a great reading year."

When many children signaled with a thumbs up, I said, "Turn and tell someone near you what your New Year's Resolution will be."

LINK

Send children off with the resolve to make this be the best reading year ever.

"Readers, I'm hoping you will think about what you can do at home tonight to set things up so you have the best reading year ever. And in a minute, I'm going to send you off to your tables, and you'll see that I've got a bin of unbelievable books that I'm going to put out on each of your tables.

"But before you go, I want to tell you one more thing. Bookmarks and bookshelves and reading lamps matter. But what really matters is that you and I decide to appreciate books, to appreciate reading."

Invite children to recall a time when reading was special, urging them to make all reading match up to this memory.

"Will you, right now, remember a time when a book was just *so* special to you? I'm thinking of a winter night when a horrible storm clapped around our house. I was four, maybe five. The rain came down in torrents that splashed against the windows, making me feel like I was in a sinking ship. What's worse, a falling branch had snapped the cord that provided our electricity so my bedside lamp wouldn't switch on. The only light came from the flashes of lightning outside. I was cold and terrified. That's when my grandmother walked into the room, carrying a lantern and holding *Ramona the Pest*.

"Readers, pretty soon I was wrapped up in a blanket, and my grandmother was reading *Ramona* by lantern light. I forgot all about the storm. In my mind, Ramona and I were walking down Klickitat Street on her first day of school, where she boinged the curls on Susan's head. That story taught me what great reading should feel like.

"Right now, think of a time when you absolutely *loved* a book, and tell the person beside you the story of that time.

"Let's all of us get the feeling of that one special time inside us. As we go off to read, let's try to let reading matter to us like it did during that one time we've just re-created."

SESSION II

Choosing a Just-Right Book

Dear Teacher,

Today's lesson will help you channel your children toward books that are just right or actually easy, and of course your efforts to conduct running records will help you do this as well. Once you determine the highest level of text difficulty that a child can handle with ease, you will move that child from reading out of a trough of books at the center of his or her table to reading from an individual bin or book baggie containing a small collection of books at the child's level (or at an easier level). Doing this for every child will presumably require the week. Because you'll be assessing during the actual reading time, you won't be able to confer with as many readers as you'd like or do book introductions for as many books as you'd like.

CONNECTION

Connect the previous day's talk about making reading a bigger part of our lives with a story that highlights the importance of being able to make good choices.

"Readers, our conversation yesterday about favorite reading memories got me remembering another dog-eared book I had when I was little that told the story of a slightly cheeky little girl with beautiful golden locks, named Goldilocks. Thumbs up if you've heard of her.

"You'll remember she walked into a small cottage one day, not knowing that a family of three bears owned it. She saw Papa Bear's porridge on the table, tasted it, and hollered, 'Too hot!' She tasted Mama Bear's porridge and gulped, 'Too cold.' But then she took a bite of Baby Bear's porridge and said, 'Mmm! Just right!' I see some of you nodding. I guess you've read that book about cheeky Madame Goldilocks, and you know she then sat on Papa Bear's chair and grumbled, 'Too hard.' Then she sat in Mama Bear's chair and grouched, 'Too soft!' But then she set herself down in Baby Bear's chair and said, 'Mmm! Just right!'

"Readers, we learn lessons from the books we read. Goldilocks taught me how to make choices. She didn't just settle for the first bowl of porridge or the first chair she found. She tested her options before settling down for the one that was, 'Mmm! Just right!' As a reader, I follow Goldilocks' model whenever I want to choose a book to read."

Name your teaching point. Specifically, teach readers that before we settle down with a book, it helps to "test" it by examining the cover and reading a few lines to see if it is "just right."

"Today I want to teach you that readers don't just pluck any ol' book off a shelf and settle down with it. Just as Goldilocks tested one bowl of porridge and another before she found the one that was just right, we test our books, looking at them carefully, opening them up, and reading a few lines, wondering, 'Is *this* just right for me?'"

TEACHING

Demonstrate that instead of forming a theory about the book from only its cover, you also read a small section. You might demonstrate with the book that you will read aloud to the class.

"Readers, what I want you to know is that avid readers don't just settle for any ol' book. No way! I try to figure out if my book is just right by doing a couple of things. Let me count them on my fingers. *First,* I look at the title and author, study the picture on the cover, and check the writing on the back cover. Usually this gives me clues for how the story might go. But Goldilocks didn't just *look* at the porridge, did she? She tasted it before deciding if it was just right. So a *second* thing I do (that all avid readers do) is I open the book to a random page. I read a little bit and ask, 'Can I read the words smoothly and easily, or are there too many hard ones that I don't know?'

"So let me show you how I use these two things to decide if the book *Fantastic Mr. Fox* is one I should read aloud to all of you." I held up the first finger and pointed to the covers, showing that I was studying them. "The title has me a little worried—it is about a fox, so I'm not sure if it is a book for us or if it is for littler kids. I don't want it to be the kind of bunny book you read in kindergarten. But readers don't just look at the title and picture.

We note the author. Whoa! The author is Roald Dahl. He's the guy who wrote *Charlie and the Chocolate Factory* and *Matilda.* I've read those books aloud to my class before, and we loved them! So the author's name is helping me think this might be great. Let me read the blurb on the back cover. Blurbs are great for helping me figure out if I'm going to like a book. Here it is:"

> Fat Boggis, squat Bunce, and skinny Bean have joined forces, and they have Mr. Fox and his family surrounded....

"Hmm, the blurb mentions characters who sound interesting, and I get a sense that this is a book with action in it right away. I'm getting a sense this might be a great book for us to read!"

Holding up a second finger, I said, "I remember that I'll have to test the book before choosing it. As I read, I want you to listen and see if the words are too easy (maybe like in a bunny book), too difficult, or just right." I opened to a random page and used my strongest read-aloud voice to read a bit aloud. "If the words are just right for me, I should be able to read them smoothly in a storyteller voice that makes it easy for us to think about the story:"

> At that moment they heard a woman's voice calling out in the house above them.
>
> "Hurry up and get that cider, Mabel!" the voice called. "You know Mr. Bean doesn't like to be kept waiting! Especially when he's been out all night in a tent!"
>
> The animals froze. They stayed absolutely still, their ears pricked, their bodies tense. Then they heard the sound of a door being opened.

"Readers, this didn't feel too easy or too hard—it was 'Mmm! Just right!' Thumbs up if you were looking through the words to the story without feeling as if hard words got in your way."

Reiterate the points you want children to remember from what they just saw you do.

"Readers, I hope you noticed the two steps I took before settling on the book that was just right. *First,* I checked the title and the covers. I noticed the author. I had ideas about how the book might go; it looked like an interesting book, but I wasn't really *sure* if the book would be just right. *Second,* I read a small bit of the book to test the words— whether they were too hard or too easy. These two steps also helped me get a sense of the story. I feel that it's an action-packed one and that it has funny characters, and I feel that it will be fun."

ACTIVE INVOLVEMENT

Set children up to choose books to read from the baskets around the meeting area, using the strategies you just demonstrated.

"Readers, I want you to reach into one of the book baskets that are lined up on the perimeter of the rug and try to test a book to see if it is just right. Remember to look at the covers but also to read a paragraph or so before you decide if it's just right. If a book isn't right, try another. If you find a just-right book, turn to someone sitting near you. On your fingers, count out the steps you took to decide if this is a just-right book for you, and tell that person what you did. You might look up at this chart to remember these steps."

To Figure Out If Our Book Is Just Right, Readers. . .

- Check the cover, picture, and author, and read the blurb to see if it looks good.

- Open up to a page in the book, and read the words to see if they are too hard, too easy, or just right.

Allow students about three minutes to rummage through book baskets before asking them to start talking to their partners about their choices. If you hear a student describing a different book-choosing strategy, acknowledge this publicly.

"Readers, eyes up here." I waited until I had their attention. "Derek was just telling John that he chose this book, *A Dinosaur Named Sue,* because the words sound just right (I pointed to the second bullet from the chart) but *also* because he loves reading anything he can about dinosaurs. So Derek has a new way for us to tell if books are a just-right choice. We can see the book reflects a life interest. That is a smart way to choose a book, and the best readers use it. In *addition* to looking at the covers and reading a paragraph or two, we might choose books on topics that interest us. We're going to add this to our book choice chart."

To Figure Out If Our Book Is Just Right, Readers...

- Check the covers, picture, and author, and read the blurb to see if it looks good.

- Open up to a page in the book, and read the words to see if they are too hard, too easy, or just right.

- Consider books on topics that interest us.

LINK

Remind children of the previous day's resolution to make reading special. Invite them to choose books that are just right as a step towards achieving their New Year's Resolutions.

"Yesterday we realized that New Year's Resolutions for reading don't just involve organizing books and setting up lamps and making reading spaces for ourselves. We can resolve to make this one of the best reading years ever by creating a *feeling* inside us that reading will be special this year. To make reading special, it is important to choose books that we can read easily and love.

"In a minute, you'll have time to read. Some of you will be selecting books. As you do, don't settle for any ol' book—remember Goldilocks. Remember, this is the start to a new year. Each of us can make New Year's Resolutions to make the year into a terrific year for reading. To do that, it helps to remember times when reading has been the best thing in the world and to expect reading to be nothing less than that now. It helps to read, knowing you can flag good parts to share, and it helps to bring the lesson Goldilocks has taught us into reading time. So select books that feel just right for you. You're going to leave a Post-it with your name on it on the book you start today, so tomorrow you can continue reading this book. It'll stay in the bin at the center of the table, but you'll sort of own it 'til you finish it and choose another."

SESSION III

Getting Better One Step at a Time— Logs and Goals

Dear Teacher,

Requiring kids to maintain a log of their reading is not a new idea; teachers across the world have systems whereby kids mark off how much they've read in a given time period. Too often, the practice is reductive—children engage in competitive reading marathons for some coveted prize or, worse, trudge through a minimum daily reading requirement. In many such cases, the carriage drives the horse, with children being controlled by their logs rather than having control over their logs. The important question to ask while introducing logs into your reading community is, "Why logs?"

In this minilesson, you'll provide kids with the opportunity to answer this question, recalling the New Year's Resolutions they made at the start of the unit. As you urge children to study their own and each other's progress, you'll emphasize the role of logging as a personal tool, one through which kids self-assess and chart their own growth versus logging as record keeping for some higher authority. Though you set this ball in motion today, you'll return and refer to logs throughout the year, helping kids see patterns in their reading habits and helping them become accustomed to reflecting on their own decisions and practices as active readers.

CONNECTION

Use an anecdote to illustrate that goal setting and continuous self-assessment are natural steps to improvement in a field other than reading.

"Some people think that the best basketball player who ever lived on this planet is a man named Michael Jordan. He could jump exceptionally high, and he had a special 'fade-away' jump, in which he jumped *backward* and *away* from the basket while he made a shot, making it hard for an opponent to block him. Well, when interviewers ask Michael Jordan how he got to be so good at basketball, he said he knew where he wanted to go and focused on getting there step by step. In other words, once he knew his goal, he focused on how to get there, using small steps.

"Readers, we have been talking and thinking about how to make reading a bigger part of our lives, and we have come up with New Year's Resolutions for our reading. We have talked about some steps that we can take to make our reading lives the best they can be—steps like setting up a reading place by moving a lamp or a bookshelf and like choosing books that are neither too hard nor too easy but just right. It is easy to stop here and let our resolution fizzle away, because that's what happens when we set goals or New Year's Resolutions but don't have any strategies to achieve them. Our resolutions fizzle away. In this classroom community, though, now that we've set our goal for making this the best reading year possible, we've got to put our heads together and figure out *how* to make that actually happen. We've got to figure out what we're doing in our reading that we should do more of—and also what we need to do better and the strategies that we should adopt to get us there.

"Do you know how basketball players decide what strategy *they* should adopt? They get together after a game and study their play. They notice what strategies worked and what they might have done differently. I can just imagine Michael Jordan thinking, 'Hey, this fade-away thing that I did here totally works for me. I gotta do more of it!' Or some other player thinking, 'I gotta figure out a strategy for countering Michael's fade-away shots. Let me figure out some action plan, some strategy of my own to deal with this challenge.' In other words, players study the records of their game and note their weak spots and their progress.

"Readers, I used to think, 'Well, it's easy for Michael Jordan. He can make a video recording of his game, and thousands of people watch him play, so he can get feedback from them or from his coach. But how do I make and study a record of *reading?* I mean, reading isn't like basketball—reading is *invisible* work, right? How could I possibly track it?'

"The truth is that readers do have many ways of tracking our reading progress. We can record not only how *much* we read in a day but also how *long* we read every day, or we can note the genre in which we've been reading. When we keep track of our reading, we can see when and where we slowed down, and we can troubleshoot the problem."

State your teaching point. Specifically, tell kids that when readers want to get better, it helps to keep and study records of our reading. One way that we may track our reading is through a reading log.

"Today I want to teach you that keeping a reading log helps us track our reading. Then when we want to get better at reading, we can study our records and think, 'Hmm, is my reading fizzling out or working? Is there a strategy I could try to get better with some aspect of my reading? What reading goal should I set for myself?'"

TEACHING

Demonstrate the use of an active system for tracking and monitoring past reading.

"Readers, I have on my bookshelf at home a special book. If you look closely, you'll see that it isn't like the other famous books by best-selling authors; it is a homemade kind of book—a book *log* actually—and the author is me! You could say that I use it to author my reading life. Inside, you won't find a story like other stories, but what you will find is the story of my own reading history, a story of my own reading goals, written in a kind of code language with lots of dated entries. It is the one thing that I use to prevent my reading goals from fizzling out. This morning I plucked it out of its spot on my bookshelf and brought it to show you." I took out my book log—one that I'd been meticulously keeping for the past few days—from my bag. (Alternately, you could do this using a previous student's book log.)

"Let me show you how it works." Holding the book open, I pointed to the various columns as I explained them. "In these columns, I record the title and author of the book, and I put in the page number where I started reading and the page number where I stopped. I note the time when I start reading (I glanced briefly at my wristwatch) and also the time when I stop. And I put in an H if I read it on my sofa at home and an SW if I read it on the subway (because those are two of my favorite reading spaces) and a SL for school. Of course, I date each entry so that I know how much reading I've done on any single day. Then I compare the reading I've done one day or week with reading I did on another day or week."

Date	Title of Book	Author	Start Page	End Page	Start Time	End Time	Total Time	H/S
8/28	The Prophet	Kahlil Gibran	01	19	10:20 A.M.	10:48 A.M.	28 min	SW
8/29	Fantastic Mr. Fox	R. Dahl	33	52	8:02 P.M.	8:30 P.M.	28 min	H
8/29	Newsweek	Misc.	2	4	10:15 A.M.	10:28 A.M.	13 min	SW
8/30	Three Cups of Tea	Greg Mortenson	142	172	10:30 P.M.	11:00 P.M.	30 min	H

"Let me show you how it works. Here is the book that I just started this morning; it's called *My Family and Other Animals* by the author Gerald Durrell. So I'll write out the title and the author's name in the first two columns, respectively." I proceeded to do this as the children watched. "Now I started this book on the subway on my way to work this morning, so that was at about 8:05 A.M., which I'm going to put down as the start time, and when the subway reached my station at 8:30, I had reached page 22. So I'll enter the starting page as 1 and the ending page as 22," I explained as I entered all these statistics into the appropriate columns. "Hmm, I'll have to do a little math here." I calculated and demonstrated my working on the board. "The total is 25 minutes, so I enter that, too. Finally I'll put in an SW to remind myself that I read this on the subway."

Date	Title of Book	Author	Start Page	End Page	Start Time	End Time	Total Time	H/S
9/3	My Family and Other Animals	Gerald Durrell	1	22	8:05 A.M.	8:30 A.M.	25 min	SW

Introduce the second part of your teaching point. Suggest that readers don't just enter and maintain records of our reading; readers study and use these entries to figure out action plans.

"Readers, did you see me make a log entry about this morning's reading session? Simple, right? But that's just a small part of what this log is about. The real reason this log helps me be a better reader—and this is really important, so listen up—is that I use it to study myself as a reader. I use it to look at my reading choices over the past few days, or sometimes over the past few months, to see, for example, *how much* I've read and whether I need to read more, to see if I'm spending *less time* reading this week than I was last week and why. Sometimes looking over my log lets me know that I've been reading nothing but fiction this month. Oops! I need to try balancing my reading life by picking up more nonfiction. Or another day, I may look over my log and note, 'Uh oh, it looks like the only time I'm getting any reading done these days is on the subway. What is distracting me from reading at home, and how can I fix it?' We note these patterns and histories that come up in our logs, and they help us know what to change in our reading lives."

Look over your own log, searching for a pattern or habit that needs to be addressed.

■ *Though you're using this minilesson to give a quick demonstration of the purpose the log serves, your children will just be starting out with their first entries, and it will take them several days to have enough material in their own logs to "study." Your demo here is merely to reinforce that in your classroom, logs won't be empty bureaucratic devices, that they can be personalized tools for growth. In future conferences or mini-lessons, you'll urge kids to refer to their own logs in the way you're teaching today.*

"Readers, although I've been entering my reading regularly in my book log, it's been a while since I've really studied it, so let me take a moment to see what I've been up to in *my* reading life. Here's the page from my reading log; let me take a look for some patterns I might need to fix."

Date	Title of Book	Author	Start Page	End Page	Start Time	End Time	Total Time	H/S
8/28	The Prophet	Kahlil Gibran	01	19	10:20 A.M.	10:48 A.M.	28 min	SW
8/29	Fantastic Mr. Fox	R. Dahl	33	52	8:02 P.M.	8:30 P.M.	28 min	H
8/29	Newsweek	Misc.	2	4	10:15 A.M.	10:28 A.M.	13 min	SW
8/30	Three Cups of Tea	Greg Mortenson	142	172	10:30 P.M.	11:00 P.M.	30 min	H
9/3	My Family and Other Animals	Gerald Durrell	1	22	8:05 A.M.	8:30 A.M.	25 min	SW

"Readers, I'm noting here, with some alarm, that I didn't sit down with a book for more than thirty minutes all of last week. I'm the kind of reader who sits for *hours* with a good book, so what's gone wrong with me? I even see two days where I didn't read at all. From 8/30, I jumped to 9/3, with no entries in the middle." After feigning shock, I paused as if to ponder this anomaly. "You know, looking at this log, I'm realizing that I've been so excited about setting up our classroom for this new school year that I put my reading on the back burner—and that is something I've got to fix! Tonight I'm going to settle down with a book and read for one uninterrupted hour *at least*. I'm going to shut my mobile phone and the television off so that there won't be a thing to distract me. I'll fluff up my reading pillow and read, read, read."

Summarize what you just did in a way that makes it easy for students to retain your point.

"Here's the thing to remember. This log is not just a fancy 'for show' kind of thing. It's a *tool* for making me a better reader. I don't just fill in this log; I *study* it. I can look at past entries and note that I am reading nothing but fiction. I should try having at least one entry for nonfiction each day, even if it is the newspaper. Or I can look across my entries and think, 'Am I reading more pages on the subway than at home? What's keeping me from reading at home? Maybe I have too many distractions and interruptions at home.' And I will try to fix that. But I'd never really be able to study the records of my reading without such a tool, such a log. So like Michael Jordan or some other basketball player, I too study my play and think of strategies to make my game better. That's how I will keep my goals from fizzling out."

ACTIVE INVOLVEMENT

Set children up with a premade log to study, inviting them to note any discrepancy or pattern that might need attention.

"Readers, before you begin your own book logs, I wonder if you could take a glance at another one of my book log pages and note any other pattern that might need my attention. It really helps to have fellow readers advising us—you might see something that I've missed." I opened my log to another page, one where eight or nine consecutive entries have me reading on the subway, with no reading at home at all in those days. I've deliberately crafted these entries, setting them up for kids to notice this detail after having described this in the Teaching section. It will take students just a minute to deduce this pattern. I know that the bulk of the Active Involvement is to follow, when students will write the first entry into their own reading logs.

Give students a minute to study the log and share what they noticed with partners. Then invite them to fill out their own first log entries.

"Readers, I've been watching you select books that are not too hard and not too easy but just right for you, and I've been watching most of you already diving into these books. Well, right now I'd like you to begin logging your reading life by entering the details of the book you've currently chosen to read. I'll pass out reading log sheets. When you receive yours, try filling out the columns the way I did mine. Note that your logs have an added column titled 'Level.' You'll look at the spine of your book, note the color of the dot, and write that down. Those dots are sort of like the code markers on ski trails. I see a blue square at Okemo Mountain, and I know I'll be able to cruise easily while skiing that. I usually ski those trails. I see double black diamond, and I know my friend Abe, who has been skiing all his life, will go there, but I'm not as experienced, so I'd be crazy to go on that trail. You'll someday notice if the books you travel through are changing from a blue square to a green circle (easier) or a black diamond (more difficult), so record the level."

LINK

Send children off with the understanding that logs are a tool that readers might use to meet personal reading goals.

"Readers, we're going to be doing a ton of reading this year and we're going to trace our reading paths in our logs. As we do, we'll try to look over our own reading like researcher-scientists with a magnifying glass, poring over our own logs and those of our reading friends, looking for patterns that might need fixing, looking for habits that might need to be broken, and thinking of strategies we might try out to make this the best reading year ever. As you enter the details of your reading into your log sheet today and every day, try asking yourself, 'Am I getting close to the resolution that I made for myself? Is there *another* resolution that I should be making? Is there some small goal I should set for *tomorrow*? What can I do to make this the best reading year ever?'"

Marking Our Spot—And Reading On

> *Dear Teacher,*
>
> *The start of any year in a classroom is a time for establishing the culture and habits that will carry you through the year. These initial minilessons reflect this purpose. Inserting a bookmark to note the spot in which one stops reading is, in itself, neither a skill nor a reading strategy. But in honoring this and other habits of readers, you're putting in place the culture you want your classroom to adopt, nudging students into constructing an identity of themselves as active readers. The message is simple. Just as a guitar player will own a pick and a painter will own a mixing palette, readers will develop systems to manage their reading with efficiency. A simple bookmark can be part of such a system.*

CONNECTION

Elaborate that watching DVDs might be a tedious experience if DVD players didn't have a built-in pause button.

"Readers, I am proud to announce that I managed to read for a full hour and eleven minutes in one stretch last night, just like I set out to do when I studied my log with you all yesterday, remember? Our goals in reading can be like that—small steps that we take daily. Thank you for helping me study my log yesterday. As you fill out your own logs, keeping records of your reading, I'll be coming around later to join you in studying what your reading records show.

"Now if you will all give me your full attention, there's a question I want to ask you—have you ever had to leave a movie in the middle of a very exciting part because you had to run to the bathroom?'Wait, wait, wait, don't watch the rest without me!'you yell to everyone else as you run out of the room, and they all groan as they push the pause button? Has that happened when you watch a DVD at home? Imagine if there was no pause button, so each time you left a movie in the middle, you had to rewind and start watching right from the beginning again to get to the part where you left off. Everyone else in the room would probably eat you alive if they had to do that for your bathroom trip. How frustrating, right? Not to mention a huge waste of time. God bless the person who invented the pause button!

"Today I want to tell you about the pause button in reading. No specific person invented it. It is something all readers invent for ourselves."

State your teaching point. Specifically, tell children that readers use bookmarks to pause when we leave off reading. Later we reread big parts quickly to pick up the trail of the story.

"Today I want to teach you that readers use bookmarks to hold the spot when we put our books down. When we return to read, we can open up to the spot. Often when we want to resume reading, we'll reverse to a page or two to reread the starting lines of a few paragraphs on the preceding pages, moving our eyes quickly down the page—just to recall what had been happening in the book when we left off in our reading—and then we settle down to read forward from that point."

Teaching

Provide a few examples that illustrate how real readers use personalized ways of marking our reading spots.

"We all have our own quirky ways of marking the spot in our reading. Some of us use a Post-it. Some of us buy or make beautiful rectangular cards called bookmarks; I like the ones with tassels. Some books have in-built bookmarks: a long red ribbon attached to the book spine. You might have seen one of these on ancient and important books like the Bible or the Quran. If you're a reader like me, your bookmark might be your subway metro card because I read on the train a lot. My friend, who's a mom, often uses a grocery receipt as her bookmark.

"Readers, when I was younger, I ate candy while I read—not the best habit—so my bookmarks would often be flattened candy wrappers! I'd keep sniffing the chocolaty smell from the wrappers as I read. You can sometimes tell the personality of the reader just by the bookmark he or she uses. I used to have a friend who'd *memorize* the page number of her last read, and she'd remember it, too! I usually forget the page number if I try that, so I don't know if that's such a good way."

Pull out a book that you're currently reading, and reveal how you've marked the spot where you left off.

"Readers, I'm going to reach into my bag and pull out the book I'm reading these days. It is called *City of Thieves,* and it's by a man named David Benioff. I am keeping a special reader's eye on this guy because he's climbed into the *New York Times* Best Seller List, so I want to see what the hype is about and if his book is really that great. Well, I haven't gotten far; here's the spot I've read up to. Can you see my metro card peeking out? Today, after leaving school, I'll hop on the subway and flip open to this *exact* page. I won't waste time rummaging through the whole book while wondering, 'Hmm, does this part look familiar? Does this feel like I've already read it?' If I were to do that, I'd reach my subway stop before I had a chance to read, and I definitely do not want to lose a major chunk of precious reading time!"

"What I *will* do, though, when I flip over to the correct page is use a system I've developed that helps me recall what I've already read. I reread the page before I left off very quickly, almost using my eye to scan the page. Watch me do this.

I read, "'But it's not even the right color' and then looked up, confused, and mused to myself, Huh? What's not the right color? I'm a little confused because I don't remember immediately. So I'll try reading the paragraph before this." As I started to do this, I said, "Hmm, readers, there are a lot of words here, but my eye is looking for a big word or two that will really hook me back into a memory of this part of the story."

I read, "'Counterfeit notes floating around.'" This time I looked up from the page to say, "I got it! I remember a bit! These men are walking through the woods outside a city called Leningrad, and they just found some fake money that's not even the right color and so obviously fake. This is during a war, by the way. Some of it is coming back to me. I'll read farther on the page."

I read, "'He speared the note on to a tree branch and set it on fire.'" And again, I looked up from the page to muse aloud. "Oh yes, Kolya, one of the characters, just set fire to the fake bill. I think this is where I can read on from; this must be about the point that I left off, since I can't remember what happens after this, only before.

"Readers, it took me about twenty seconds to find my spot and resume reading. Without this bookmark, I would have had to search 112 pages and probably gotten sidetracked or impatient. This is why, whenever I'm doing serious reading—really living a reader's life—I always have a system to mark my spot.

"I use bookmarks. Of course, there are sloppier ways of marking a book. Some people bend pages or lay a book face down to mark their page, but this will weaken—and sometimes damage—the book. As someone who loves books and likes taking care of mine, I try to avoid these ways."

Name what you have just done in a way that makes it easy for students to remember and replicate.

"Readers, you just saw me use my bookmark to jump back into my reading. I opened my book to the last page that I'd read from, and my eyes quickly scanned the text to see where it was that I left off. If the text looked unfamiliar, I moved my eye *back* a paragraph until I reached a part I do remember reading—and started from there."

ACTIVE INVOLVEMENT

Invite students to think of ways to devise personalized placeholders in their own books.

"Readers, since the first day of reading workshop, I've been watching you and I know you are serious about reading. Serious readers usually have bookmarking strategies.

"Turn and talk to each other about how you could possibly mark your spot in the book you're reading. Mention if you've ever used a bookmark before or if you've seen anyone else use one. Make a plan for the kind of bookmark or bookmarks you plan to use this year; if you plan to make your own, brainstorm ideas for what your bookmark could look like."

LINK

Send readers off with the thought that serious readers use bookmarks.

"As we define ways to make this the best reading year ever, choosing books that are just right for us and setting goals to build our reading energy, remember that readers have systems and habits for keeping our reading lives organized. One way we organize our reading lives is by keeping a bookmark to signal the spot where we last finished reading. Remember that we can quickly get back into the flow of our books without wasting precious reading time."

SESSION V

Parts Go Together to Make a Book Flow

Dear Teacher,

Readers read, expecting that the parts of a book should fit together. The paragraphs within a chapter go together to create one or more scenes, and chapters in a book go together to create a whole story. As we read, we think about how our books fit together to make a connected story. You'll be surprised at how many kids might still pick up a book and open to any random page rather than starting from the beginning. To many such kids, books are merely pages with pictures, with text thrown in to fill remaining spaces. "There is a method here," you're telling your kids. You're introducing them to text structure and sequence. Most of all, you're teaching that a book needs to make sense—and that something is drastically amiss if a reader can't figure out this "sense." Instead of children thumbing through books, we want readers who know how to maneuver the pages and anticipate the plotline— readers with noses buried deep into the pages.

CONNECTION

Relay an account of seeing the disparate parts of something, and only later realizing how those parts went together to create a coherent whole.

"My friend called me over to her place last week. 'I'm baking a cake for Adam's birthday party,' she said.

"Readers, Adam is her four-year-old son. A birthday party for Adam! At home!" I feigned horror. "Those of you who've ever attended a four-year-old's birthday party will know why I was a little like, 'Uh oh! She'll need all the help she can get.' I had a picture of absolute hullabaloo, of four-year-olds swinging from the curtains like monkeys, flashing in my head. So I rushed over to help her set up beforehand.

"She'd just taken the cake out of the oven when I got there. Readers, I saw emerging from the oven, one by one, a big circular cake, a small circular cake, two cupcakes, and four loaf-shaped cakes—all of which she was laying out on the table to cool.

"'What!' I exclaimed. 'This makes no sense! Why have you made so many odd-shaped small cakes instead of one big cake?'

"Well, she smiled as if my questions amused her. Then, right there before my eyes, she pushed the big circular cake next to the small circular cake, and suddenly they became a round head and a fat tummy! Then she arranged the cupcakes next to the smaller circle to make round ears; the four loaf cakes became the limbs. Voilà! In front of me, I suddenly saw a teddy bear cake! All the individual parts actually fit together to make a whole shape.' So that is how a teddy bear cake is put together,' I said in amazement.

"Readers, books are like teddy bear cakes. Oh yes." I nod and look around as I say this. "Books are made of parts that fit together in a very specific way to make a whole. Just like the circular cakes and the loaf shapes fit together in a specific way to make a teddy bear, paragraphs and scenes fit together to make chapters, and chapters fit together to make the whole book."

State your teaching point. Specifically, tell children that as readers go through a book, we develop a sense for how a book fits together to make a whole.

"Today I want to teach you that readers read *expecting* that the parts of a book should fit together."

Teaching

Explain that the beginning, middle, and end of a book go together.

"We know that this (I raise a book to show them) is not just a couple of papers stapled together; it's not just a gibberish of paragraphs mushed together in any odd way. If you removed pages 4 and 5 and put them somewhere later in the book, the book would stop working. Readers would go 'Huh?' because the story wouldn't make sense, just like the small cakes placed separately didn't make sense at first. If my friend had arranged them any ol' way, they wouldn't have looked like a teddy bear. They would have looked like some confusing shape!"

"When we start off reading, from page 1, the first thing that we can expect is that we'll learn who this story is about—that is, we'll learn about the main character, the hero or heroine of our story. Possibly we'll be introduced to some secondary characters, too, the people in the main character's life. Readers, this is usually at the *beginning* of a book.

"Next, this main character usually has some challenge—there's something that this character wants or some problem that needs solving. We read on, knowing that this want or this problem will become better defined or better explained as the book progresses. Readers, this is usually in the *middle* of the book.

"We have a feeling also that as we read along, we'll see how things work out for the character—how the want is met or the problem is eventually solved. This usually happens at the *end*. As a result of this want being met or this problem being solved, the character might learn something about himself or herself—or about life. So the beginning connects to the middle, which then connects to the end. We often use the blurb on the back of the book and the title of the book as well as the chapter titles to help us get a sense of who that book is about and what that character wants or is trying to do. The ending of the story will fit with the beginning and the middle, like pieces of a teddy bear cake!"

Demonstrate that the parts of a book go together using an easy-to-follow picture book.

"I'm going to pick up any old book and see if I can figure out the beginning, the middle, and the end to show you how they connect. Here's one—it's called *Duck* and it's by Randy Cecil. In the beginning, we're introduced to Duck, a carousel animal." (As an aside, in a coaching voice, I add: "That's the main character, I see.") "And then we learn that Duck, whose wings are wooden, longs to fly." (As an aside, I ask, "So that's the big want?") "In the middle of the story, Duck sort of adopts a small lost duckling and teaches it to fly, and then that duckling flies away, leaving Duck lonely again. Readers, I see the problem's getting worse—not only can't Duck fly, but his small duckling has flown away, leaving him lonely. At this point, though, I'm waiting for the problem to be solved, knowing that things should work out for Duck somehow. I'm going to flip the pages—and indeed, things do get better. Duckling's returned! On the last page, the duckling, who's now a strong grown-up duck himself, takes Duck on his back and gives him a ride in the skies. So Duck gets to fly after all—on the back of the duckling he raised!

"Did you see how the end goes with the beginning? At the start of the book, Duck wanted to fly. At the end, Duck's actually flying—not in the typical way, but he's getting a ride in the skies, finally knowing what it feels like to soar."

Summarize your teaching, revisiting the anecdote from your connection to drive home the point that parts of a book go together.

"Readers, remember the teddy bear cake? That teddy bear cake was made of smaller cakes, each of which fit together to make one big cake. Books, too, are made of words and paragraphs that are arranged in a way so that they connect to each other; they fit together in some specific design to create a book, a story. We might think, 'How does this paragraph connect to the next paragraph? How do these paragraphs fit together to make a story?' Just like I looked at the smaller circular cake and said, 'Oh, that's the head,' and looked at the rectangular cakes and said, 'Those are the arms and legs,' we can look at the parts of a book and identify the main character, the problem or challenge, and the solution to this problem or challenge, knowing that these make up the beginning, middle, and end of the book."

Add that not all books are built the same, that some are simple stories while others are chapter books, but even so, their parts fit together in some specific way.

"Readers, fiction books are built differently. Some are comprised of a single story, like this book *Duck* that we just looked at. Others are simple chapter books where each chapter is actually a small story about the same character or set of characters, like this one called *The Stories Julian Tells.* Each chapter has its own beginning, middle, and end, so it's like tiny little books about one character bound together. Then, of course, there are more grown-up chapter books, where the chapters fit together to tell one story, where each chapter builds off the previous chapter—so the first few chapters are the beginning, the next few chapters define the problem, the next ones build up as the problem becomes even more intense, and finally the last few chapters tell how things are working out or what lesson is being learned."

ACTIVE INVOLVEMENT

Nudge kids into noting how the beginning, middle, and end of their independent reading books fit together.

"Readers, right now, please look at the book you're reading and think about who the main character is and also about what this main character wants or about the problems this main character is facing, as well as the obstacles standing in his or her path. What do you think the ending will be like? How will this ending be connected to the problem introduced at the start of the book?"

Allow kids a minute or two to get their thoughts together before adding, "Turn to the person beside you, talk about the beginning of the book and the middle, and also share how you think the ending might go."

LINK

Send readers off with the advice to anticipate the structure of the text they're reading, expecting that it will flow coherently and make sense.

"So, readers, back to my story of that teddy bear birthday cake. When I saw those individual cake parts, I had no idea that they connected with each other, and I didn't even *expect* that the different cakes had anything to do with each other. But when readers read a book, we do *expect* that the parts will go together in some way, and we figure out *how* they connect. This helps us become expert readers—real *knowers* of books. Real readers don't just read books; we understand the architecture of books, and we know how books are put together.

"So as we go about making reading a bigger part of our lives, choosing books that are just right, remember that a reader expects that the parts of his or her book will fit together, that each sentence will pick up from the sentence that comes before, and that each paragraph will pick up from the paragraph before to create a scene. And these scenes will change across the various chapters, and each chapter will also pick up on the chapter that comes before it. Today as we read, we'll eventually come to the end of a part or a chapter. When readers come to places such as that, it helps to pause and think, 'How does this part fit into what I read earlier, and how does my whole book fit into one story line?'

"More than this, we know a whole book will tell a story, so all the chapters and all the parts will fit together into one story. We can look over a book before we read it, or glance back over a part of it that we've already read, and think of the book as a story with some characters who want something, who make steps toward their goal, and who end up somehow either getting what they wanted—or not getting it, but learning a lesson."

PART TWO

Making Meaning

Dear Teacher,

Now that you've set children up with goals and logs for the year ahead, it is time to pull them into the world of a good story, aiming for the spark—that special moment—when a book stops being a sheaf of papers in a kid's hands and instead becomes a world that envelops the reader. The upcoming bend in the road of this unit, then, is about comprehension—basic comprehension. You'll teach toward total immersion in the text, suggesting that reading narrative is actually all about picturing the story in the mind's eye and following the continuity of action as this story moves forward, retaining and adding to its meaning.

You'll hope that as children read, they develop visuospatial maps that approximate the physical settings of their stories, so that the two-dimensional print on the page translates into a three-dimensional world. Picking up the theme introduced in the very first minilesson, you'll suggest that this, in essence, is what reading feels like when it works!

SESSION VI

Stepping into the World of the Story

CONNECTION

Recall a fictional world from a book you read when you were younger, suggesting that this world feels as real to you still as the actual places you might have visited at that age.

"Do you recall the first day when we talked about what reading should feel like? I told you about the time when my grandmother and I read about a girl named Ramona Quimby as a thunderstorm clapped outside? Well, readers, the funny thing is, I haven't picked up a *Ramona* book in over twenty years, but I can still sort of remember what Klickitat Street felt like and what it looked like. Let's see—it had Ramona's house here (I gestured with my hands as I explained, almost as if I was reconstructing the street in the physical space of the classroom), and here, right next to it, was Howie's house, and a few blocks down was her school, which had a kindergarten on one side, and…..

"Readers, I guess you could say I haven't just *read* about Klickitat Street. I guess you could say I've sort of *been* there. That's what it feels like anyway. Twenty years later, I'm still carrying a map of it inside my head. That's what reading does; it takes you to another world, and that world becomes a part of you just like places you've visited—even long ago—become a part of you.

"We've set goals. We've begun the habit of keeping records of our reading in logs, and we've studied those logs. We're discovering books that are just right for us, and we're learning to manage our reading with bookmarks. We've learned that the parts of a book go together to make a whole. Readers, I think we're ready for this next thing—and it is big—so listen carefully."

State your teaching point. Specifically, tell children that as readers enter a new book, we notice what kind of world the author has created and we step into it.

"Today I want to teach you that every story has its own world. This world is set in a specific time and place; it has certain kinds of people with a certain lifestyle. When readers open a book, we pay attention to all the details our book provides about this world until we almost feel like *we've* stepped into the world of the book, leaving our own world behind."

Teaching

From your chosen read-aloud text, demonstrate how you flesh out setting details to imagine the world of the story until you feel transported to it.

"Remember *Fantastic Mr. Fox*, the book we selected as being just right for a read-aloud? Last night I reread the first bit of it. Although I was sitting in my armchair at home, after I read just a bit, I was—in my head—in the midst of a farm. Off in the distance, there was an enormously fat farmer, and next to him were two other farmers, one pudgy and short and one stick thin. Then, before I knew it, I was deep in a dark, dark tunnel, far underground, surrounded by a family of foxes.

"As you and I read this book together over the next few days, let's try to do what people talk about when they say readers travel on magic carpets to other worlds. Let's actually leave *this* world—our classroom, our rules—and jump into that farm, down that fox-hole.

"Listen while I read the beginning of the first chapter. Remember, we're leaving our classroom behind." I picked up the book and read the opening slowly, with expression:

> Down in the valley there were three farms. The owners of these farms had done well. They were rich men. They were also nasty men. All three of them were about as nasty and as mean as any men you could meet. Their names were Farmer Boggis, Farmer Bunce and Farmer Bean.
>
> Boggis was a chicken farmer. He kept thousands of chickens. He was enormously fat. This was because he ate three boiled chickens smothered with dumplings every day for breakfast, lunch and supper.

"Readers, already I'm miles away from our classroom, aren't you? I'm standing on flat farmland that's surrounded by hills. The farmland spreads out for miles and miles. Aha! (I muster maximum drama, using my body language to suggest that I am actually on the farm and can see it.) Who's there? Three nasty farmers! I have an image of one, Boggis, with his *hugely* fat belly and all those clucking chickens.

"Readers, do you see how I just entered the world of the story? I put myself right in the middle of those farms and saw them unfold around me. I don't yet know a lot about this world or these farmers, but I have the start of an image, and I know it will only grow from here."

ACTIVE INVOLVEMENT

Read aloud with expression, inviting students to imagine the world of the story. Later, ask children to exchange details of the world in which their independent books are set.

"Now it's your turn to try. I'm going to read from *Fantastic Mr. Fox,* just a few lines, and as I read, I want you to close your eyes and try to picture in your mind the world of the book."

As I resume reading, I use expression and pauses to help the listening children envision the world I'm reading about. It is essential that I am seeing the world I read about, because that is the single most powerful way to help listeners see the world as well:

> On a hill above the valley there was a wood.
>
> In the wood there was a huge tree.
>
> Under the tree there was a hole.
>
> In the hole lived Mr. Fox and Mrs. Fox and their four Small Foxes.
>
> Every evening as soon as it got dark, Mr. Fox would say to Mrs. Fox, "Well, my darling, what shall it be this time? A plump chicken from Boggis? A duck or a goose from Bunce? Or a nice turkey from Bean?"

"You may open your eyes now. If you saw a wood and a big tree or felt a forest around you, give me a thumbs up. If you saw a fox-hole far, far below an enormous tree, give me another thumbs up. As readers, we were able to travel down into that foxhole and see what's inside. There is a fox family of four little foxes and their parents—but not the kind we have in our world. These are talking foxes! If you felt like you were somewhere in that foxhole *with* the family, watching quietly as Mr. Fox asked Mrs. Fox whether he should get a chicken, duck, goose, or turkey, give me another thumbs up.

"Readers, this is something we can try with our own books. It takes imagination, and that's a muscle that develops like any other muscle—with use. Right now, I'd like you to turn to the person beside you and take turns describing the world of your independent reading books. What is the world of your book like, and who are the people in it? Describe it so that your partner can almost feel and see this world, too, so your neighbor practically feels like he or she is in that world."

As children talked, I gave them small tips, coaching through a series of voiceovers. "Sometimes it's easier to feel the world of our books when we know the kind of people who are in that world, so we need to mention the characters in our book and even what they do."

After a few minutes, I called out, "Okay, switch. Listening partners, it's your turn to talk. Talking partners, it's your turn to listen."

As children talked, I listened in on a few conversations. Then I reconvened the group.

"I've heard some fascinating conversations. Here I was, thinking that everyone is sitting in this classroom reading, when all the while you readers have actually been out visiting Junie B. Jones's classroom or sitting in China or playing in a backyard swimming pool in summer! That's what books do—they take us places! Literally!"

LINK

Send children off with the message that reading is equal to immersing oneself in the world of one's story.

"Readers, you'll be traveling this year. You'll travel to Oz, to Narnia, to Zuckerman's farm, to the Wild West, to outer space, to a small Himalayan village." I hold up the corresponding books as I list the settings, almost as if I'm doing the book talks. "You'll enter a different time, a different space, with each book you pick up. Even if you don't exactly see what the world of your book looks like, you will *feel* this world and what it's like to live in it. So today and every day, as you pick a book that feels just right, as you read and try to put the pieces together so that the beginning of the book fits with the upcoming part, will you also try to feel the world of that book? See if you can step into that world and imagine it."

SESSION VII
Reading Is Like Watching a Mental Movie

Dear Teacher,

It is hard to say where the previous minilesson on entering the world of a story ends and this one, on making mental movies, begins. Though both teach envisioning, they do so by approaching envisioning from different stances altogether. There's a good reason to teach both minilessons—some books describe settings in detail; others begin with action. Consequently, in books (or parts of books) that are description-heavy and where the setting is described in detail, it pays to teach children to picture the physical world of the story. Other stories, however, begin directly with action, with little (or belated) mention of the setting. Even so, as a reader envisions the action and dialogue unfolding before him or her, this creates a visuospatial three-dimensional sense of the book's "world."

In this minilesson, you'll use the familiar metaphor of a movie to suggest that active envisioning involves much more than a static image, that reading is like entering and living in the mental movie that a book inspires. In this session, as in the previous one, you're aiming to allow the book to come to life in readers' hands, pushing them to actively construct the world of their book as they envision and experience the unfurling action and story within.

CONNECTION

Describe for children a time when you brought a story to life in your mind.

"Readers, when I was your age, my cousins and I would take the cushions off all the sofas and build a fort or a ship. If it was a fort we'd built, we'd sit in it and shoot at an imaginary army galloping full speed toward us till it collided with the fort walls, sending the cushions flying. If it was a ship, we'd imagine ourselves in the middle of a sea storm, covering ourselves with sheets against the mountainous waves and sweeping rain. Inevitably, one of us would fall 'overboard' (off the cushions and onto the rug beneath), and we'd yell, 'Help! Man overboard! Sharks!'

"Readers, of course there was no army, no waves, no storm. But when we were in the middle of that action, our hearts would be racing and our adrenaline would be pumping, and we'd truly build up a battle or a storm in our imaginations."

"Yesterday we stepped into the world of our story by picturing what that world was like—that there were farms in a valley and a gigantic tree with a foxhole beneath it. We used all the details in the book, and maybe added some missing details from our minds, and we pictured the world of our story so well that it felt almost like we were in that world. But that's not all. To really step inside the book, we do *more* than just see a *picture* of that world in our minds—we actually see all the moving *action,* too, kind of like there is a mental movie being played in our minds."

Name your teaching point. Specifically, teach children that readers make a mental movie of a book, paying attention to the world and the characters of the story.

"Today I want to teach you that as we read, we make a mental movie of what is happening in our books. We think of the world of the story, the people in it and what they are saying and doing, and we get our cameras rolling."

Teaching

Demonstrate how to make a mental movie by reading aloud a scene from your read-aloud book and then telling children what you see and imagine in your mind.

"Let's revisit *Fantastic Mr. Fox.* This time let's try to make a movie in our minds. As I read, turn your movie cameras on, picturing everything:"

> Every evening as soon as it got dark, Mr. Fox would say to Mrs. Fox, "Well, my darling, what shall it be this time? A plump chicken from Boggis? A duck or a goose from Bunce? Or a nice turkey from Bean?"
>
> And when Mrs. Fox had told him what she wanted, Mr. Fox would creep down into the valley in the darkness of the night and help himself.

"I see Mr. Fox planning to go out each night to get his family a meal. How does he do it? Let's make our best fox faces." I became a watchful fox, looking cautiously to the right and to the left with wide-open eyes, and made my feet move slowly out from under my chair. I cajoled the students to become Mr. Fox as well. "I see you creeping along. You're moving slowly, trying not to be seen. You're a sly one, all right.

"Now that we're in the story, let's read on. What's next? Dahl tells us that Mr. Fox would 'help himself.' Help himself? To what? Oh! He helps himself to the farmers' birds! What a sneak! Mr. Fox, *fantastic* Mr. Fox, is a thief! Let's read on a bit and see if we can gather more details for our movie, so we'll leave the fox for now and imagine what's going on, meanwhile, in another part of this world:"

> Boggis and Bunce and Bean knew very well what was going on, and it made them wild with rage. They were not men who liked to give anything away. Less still did they like anything to be stolen from them. So every night each of them would take his shotgun and hide in a dark place somewhere on his own farm, hoping to catch the robber.

"And the plot thickens! Those farmers *know* that Mr. Fox is stealing from them. Look at the three of them perched on their farms, each with a shotgun." I look as if I'm seeing them on the horizon. "They look hungry, hopeful. I bet each is hoping to be the one to get that fox! They're not slumped, like this." I hunched my shoulders. "No way! They're sitting alert, with determined, mean looks on their faces." I sat up tall and glared at the children "Make your best nasty farmer faces." The children made mean, ugly faces. "Hold your rifle at the ready. Great! You all look so angry. Do you feel it?" The children nodded.

"Do you see how we just made a mental movie of our book? We got our cameras rolling down into that tunnel the Foxes call home, and our cameras were rolling as Mr. Fox crept out and poached a bird in the middle of the night. And then we saw the three angry farmers poised to get him! Now that we've got our movie rolling, let's not stop."

ACTIVE INVOLVEMENT

Set partners up to work together to make a mental movie of the next part of the class's read-aloud book.

"It's your turn to try. I'm going to skip ahead to where we left off yesterday and read a bit from there. As I read, it will be up to you to get your cameras rolling and make that movie! Yesterday we read just the beginning of Chapter 3, 'The Shooting.' Hmm, remember that Mrs. Fox has requested two fat ducks for dinner and that she's urged her husband to be careful. Mr. Fox doesn't know it yet, but Bunce, Boggis, and Bean have found his hole and are sitting right at the entrance! And the wind is blowing away from them, so there's no chance Mr. Fox will smell them out. I'm about to begin reading. As I do, get up close to Mr. Fox. Zoom in on him. Notice how he moves and what he feels, the shifting expressions he wears on his face. Here we go."

I leaned in and read the text slowly, with expression, letting it unfold bit by bit:

Mr. Fox crept up the dark tunnel to the mouth of his hole. He poked his long handsome face out into the night air and sniffed once. *["Do you have your cameras? See Mr. Fox. What does he look like? Show each other!"]*

He moved an inch or two forward and stopped. *[I smiled as some of the children scooted their bottoms forward on the rug.]*

He sniffed again. He was always especially careful when coming out from his hole. *[I paused for effect, while many of the children made a sniffing sound.]*

He inched forward a little more. The front half of his body was now in the open. *["Readers, what does that look like? Show me!" More scooting.]*

His black nose twitched from side to side, sniffing and sniffing for the scent of danger. He found none, and he was just about to go trotting forward into the wood when he heard or thought he heard a tiny noise, a soft rustling sound, as though someone had moved a foot ever so gently through a patch of dry leaves. *[I paused again. The children made scared, startled faces. Some of them shook a little. I gave them a thumbs up.]*

Mr. Fox flattened his body against the ground and lay very still, his ears pricked. He waited a long time, but he heard nothing more. "It must have been a field-mouse," he told himself, "or some other small animal."

He crept a little further out of the hole…then further still. He was almost right out in the open now. He took a last careful look around. The wood was murky and very still. Somewhere in the sky the moon was shining. *["What do you see now? Be Mr. Fox on the lookout!"]*

Just then, his sharp night-eyes caught a glint of something bright behind a tree not far away. It was a small silver speck of moonlight shining on a polished surface. Mr. Fox lay still, watching it. What on earth was it? Now it was moving. *["Uh oh! Show me Mr. Fox's reaction! What do you think he's feeling?" The children put on their best frightened faces. Some of them started shaking again.]* It was coming up and up…*Great heavens! It was the barrel of a gun!* Quick as a whip, Mr. Fox jumped back into his hole and at that same instant the entire wood seemed to explode around him. *Bang-bang! Bang-bang! Bang-bang! [The kids jumped in the air. Some of them played dead.]*

"Eyes on me, everyone. What a great scene you all brought to life. I saw Donovan put his nose in the air, sniffing the way Mr. Fox would. He said he imagined Mr. Fox getting cocky, and he puffed out his shoulders as he said this. But then he saw the bit of metal, the gun, and he got big, scared eyes. Great job! Zoe was really funny as a farmer. She made small, mean eyes, and she cocked her pretend gun in the air; then when Mr. Fox darted out, she pointed her finger right at him and let him have it. I got scared watching! Great movies!"

LINK

Remind children that they can make and roll movies in their minds anytime they read, so that the images in their minds become more detailed and one image flows into another, like in a movie.

"Readers, we've learned a lot this year about ways to get better at our reading. We know how to choose just-right books like Goldilocks, how to reflect on what we tend to do as readers, and then how to be goal setters, like Michael Jordan. And more recently we've learned that reading, when it's really good, means that there is a mental movie playing in our minds as our eyes scan a page. Today and every day, as you read stories, try to bring the world of your books alive in your minds, picturing the setting and the action."

Keeping Track of an Unfurling Plot

Dear Teacher,

The synchronicity with which various processes occur while reading makes it difficult to isolate and teach any single skill or strategy exclusively without feeling an urgent need to call attention to other accompanying skills. Even as we pull children into active envisioning, for example, we feel the demand to also ensure that while they are going deeper into the story, they keep the gist of the plot in mind, constructing a coherent story line. This minilesson introduces the simplest of prompts to ensure that our students hold the plot intact: "Who's in this book?" and "What is happening?"

CONNECTION

Compare the "previously on" phrase used to recap last week's episode of a television show to what readers do when we want to recall what we've just read.

"You know how on some television shows each episode begins with, 'Previously on…,' followed by a short clip of what happened the week before? There's a voice that says, 'Previously on *Hannah Montana*,' and then there are a few snippets of scenes that remind the viewer of what happened in yesterday's episode or last week's episode. It occurred to me the other day that we do something similar when we read. In order to recall the characters and the events, to reorient ourselves in our books, we do a kind of 'previously on' before we resume reading."

Name your teaching point. Specifically, tell children that readers sometimes pause in our reading to recap the main characters and events.

"Today I want to teach you that as we read, we keep an eye on the main character, where the book is set, and the general plot. Sometimes we pause in the midst of reading to remember what we have read so far, and when we do, it's almost like we are writing the story in our minds. We tell ourselves who the main character is and what he or she has been up to. We ask ourselves, 'Who's in this book?' and 'What is happening?'"

TEACHING

Demonstrate that you can read on in your book and then pause to recall what happened previously.

"Let's do this with our read-aloud book, *Fantastic Mr. Fox.* I'm not just going to pick up this book and march forward to the next page and the next without mental preparation. Before I begin reading from the point where we left off yesterday, I'll do a brief 'previously on,' that is, I'll quickly ask myself, 'Who's in this book?' and 'What's happening?' to remind myself who the characters are and what's going on.

"Previously in *Fantastic Mr. Fox,* the farmers discovered Mr. Fox's hole, and they gathered together to shoot him. When he emerged from his hole, they fired shot after shot, but all they got was his tail! Mr. Fox escaped back down his hole, tail-less but alive. But little did he know that the farmers at that very moment were plotting to dig him out with shovels. Meanwhile, back in the hole, Mrs. Fox licked her husband's wound.

"Readers, see how I just reminded myself of the important events that led up to this next part of Chapter 4? Notice I skipped the little details; instead, I recapped the big things that happened. Now that I'm reoriented in the text, I'm ready to read." I opened the book to Chapter 4, "The Terrible Shovels," and began reading:

> There was no food for the foxes that night, and soon the children dozed off. Then Mrs. Fox dozed off. But Mr. Fox couldn't sleep because of the pain in the stump of his tail. "Well," he thought, "I suppose I'm lucky to be alive at all. And now they've found our hole, we're going to have to move out as soon as possible. We'll never get any peace if we... What was *that?*" He turned his head sharply and listened. The noise he heard now was the most frightening noise a fox can ever hear—the scrape-scrape-scraping of shovels digging in the soil.
>
> "Wake up!" he shouted. "They're digging us out!"
>
> Mrs. Fox was wide awake in one second. She sat up, quivering all over. "Are you sure that's it?" she whispered.

"I'm positive! Listen!"

"They'll kill my children!" cried Mrs. Fox.

"Never!" said Mr. Fox.

"But darling, they will!" sobbed Mrs. Fox. "You know they will!"

Scrunch, scrunch, scrunch went the shovels above their heads. Small stones and bits of earth began falling from the roof of the tunnel.

"How will they kill us, Mummy?" asked one of the Small Foxes. His round black eyes were huge with fright. "Will there be dogs?" he said.

Mrs. Fox began to cry. She gathered her four children close to her and held them tight.

"Aha! It makes sense that the foxes must go to bed with no food. Mr. Fox wasn't able to get them dinner! Not a chicken, or a duck, or a turkey, or a goose! Of course, poor Mr. Fox can't sleep. His tail aches, and he's worried about his family! And then *scrunch, scrunch, scrunch*—oh no! Here come the farmers' shovels! I'd be terrified if I were the foxes. It seems like those kids certainly are! And Mrs. Fox is so afraid she'll lose her children!

"Readers, do you see how pausing for just a minute to do a 'previously on' allows me to remind myself of the big things that just happened and that this helped me as I read on? I was able to understand the next part, to envision the activity and to empathize with the characters."

ACTIVE INVOLVEMENT

Ask children to recall the characters and events of their books and to share these with their partners.

"Now it's your turn to practice. In a moment, you'll flip through your independent reading books to remind yourself who the main characters are, what events have taken place so far, and where the stories take place. Take just a few minutes to do that. When you're done, Partner 1, you will tell Partner 2 about your book. Remember as you do this to tell just about the big things and to do so in such a way that your partner can envision the people, places, and events."

I gave children a few minutes to review their books. As the children talked, I listened in on some partnerships. Then I reconvened the group.

LINK

Send children off with the advice to envision the mental movies of their reading and to recall exactly what is happening as the story unfurls.

"Readers, before you resume reading today and every day, it helps to pause to do a 'previously on.' When you do this, it helps to recall the characters and to recall what they've been doing. Get started on your reading."

SESSION IX

New Parts of Books Fit with the Old

Dear Teacher,

This minilesson achieves several purposes. On a basic level, you teach kids to monitor for meaning, suggesting that unless new events in the story lead on from past events, a reread is probably in order. On another level, you teach that there is interconnectedness within a story and unity within a plot. As kids find the links between what is happening now in the story and details from earlier in the story, they put the pieces of the story together in ways that allow them to anticipate. Simply put, you're teaching that new events in the story should make sense based on what's happened before.

CONNECTION

Relate an anecdote or example that illustrates how something in the present fits with something that occurred in the past, acquiring greater significance because of this.

"Readers, yesterday I ran into an old friend from school. It was fun to catch up on the past fifteen years. You could say we did a 'previously on' recap session.

"'You mean you're an engineer now?' I asked him excitedly. 'That makes total sense! You were always obsessed with taking gadgets apart and trying to fit them back together.'

"'And you're a teacher?' he laughed. '*Of course* you would be. I mean, you're the one who'd smuggle chalk home from school and pretend to teach an invisible class of students.'

"Readers, I realized that who we are *today* usually fits with experiences we had yesterday or the year before or when we were younger. Life is like that—today builds off of yesterday. Stories are like that, too, where what happens on a certain page builds from what happened in the pages that came before.

"Earlier we learned that a 'previously on' recap reminds readers of who is in the story and what they are doing. But a 'previously on' recap also reminds us of the story so far, and we keep the previous story in mind as we go forward. When we read, we find that the events unfolding in our books have a lot to do with whatever happened previously. We read *expecting* that what is happening right now will fit with whatever came before."

State your teaching point. Specifically, tell students that as readers move along in our books, we find links between what comes now and what came before in the text.

"Today I want to teach you that readers constantly ask ourselves, 'How does what I am reading now fit with what came before?' As the story grows and moves forward, readers find interesting links between what is happening now and what came before."

Teaching

Demonstrate by linking an event that unfurls in your current read-aloud with an earlier event.

"Readers, as I read *Fantastic Mr. Fox* aloud to all of you, I keep making the links between what I am reading now and what we read on previous days. Each chapter builds on previous chapters, almost like stepping-stones. When I can link what I'm reading to something that came before in the story, I have a mental 'Aha! This fits!'

"Let me share an example from Chapter 5:"

> Bean rubbed the back of his neck with a dirty finger. He had a boil coming there and it itched. "What we need on this job," he said, "is machines…*mechanical* shovels. We'll have him out in five minutes with *mechanical* shovels."
>
> This was a pretty good idea and the other two had to admit it.

"So what I'm understanding is that Bean has come up with a good idea. Does this fit with what I already know about Bean from the pages that came before? Let's see. I remember reading in a previous chapter that Bean was the *cleverest* of the three mean farmers. The fact that Bean is the evil genius behind the idea of the mechanical shovels—neither Boggis nor Bunce, but *Bean*—specifically fits with the impression that I already have of him. After all, earlier in the story, he was the one who thought of digging in the first place. In fact, even before that, it was Bean who discovered the foxhole under the tree in the woods.

"Readers, I realize that what I am reading about Bean right now fits with what I already know of Bean from what came before. In this case, what I'm reading now *confirms* the details that came before. But beware! Sometimes what you read doesn't always confirm what came before. Either the story could be taking a surprising turn or you might have misread something that came before. But the only way to find out is to be alert and keep asking ourselves questions like 'How does what I'm reading right now fit with what came before? Does it confirm and continue what came before, or does it go against something in previous pages?'"

ACTIVE INVOLVEMENT

Set students up to ponder with their neighbors how the passage you read aloud fits with earlier sections of the story.

"As we read on, we keep making connections between what is happening now in the story and what came before. I'm going to read a small bit of the story; when I stop, tell your neighbor how this fits with what came before. I'm going to read on from the part where Bean and Bunce have returned to the hill, driving two enormous tractors with mechanical shovels attached to them:"

> Down in the tunnel the foxes crouched, listening to the terrible clanging and banging overhead. "What's happening, Dad?" cried the Small Foxes. "What are they doing?"
>
> Mr. Fox didn't know what was happening or what they were doing.
>
> "It's an earthquake!" cried Mrs. Fox.
>
> "Look!" said one of the Small Foxes. "Our tunnel's got shorter. I can see daylight!"
>
> They all looked around, and yes, the mouth of the tunnel was only a few feet away from them now, and in the circle of the daylight beyond they could see the two huge black tractors almost on top of them.

I stopped for about two minutes to let neighbors confer about how this new development fits with previous events in the story before interjecting.

"Readers, many of you are saying that this noise that the foxes are hearing fits with what the farmers planned to do, which is to dig them out with mechanical shovels. Some of you noted that the terrible banging and clanging and shaking that made Mrs. Fox think of an earthquake fits with the noise that mechanical shovels make. Some of you noted that the small fox noticed that his tunnel was getting shorter. This fits with the fact that the mechanical shovels are digging and getting closer and closer. Now I'll read on:"

"Tractors!" shouted Mr. Fox. "And *mechanical* shovels. Dig for your lives! *Dig, dig, dig!*"

I paused again, allowing students to link Mr. Fox's decision to dig, dig, dig with what had happened previously in the story.

"Readers, thumbs up if you said Mr. Fox ordered his family to dig because that was how they had defeated the shovels the last time. This goes with what they did before, which was to outdig the mean farmers."

If you want an additional scaffold to show that any new turn in a story evolves from previous events, ask children to study the table of contents in a chapter book.

"Now that we're getting a sense that everything we read has a way of fitting with what came before in the story, let's take a quick look at the table of contents that we had looked at earlier in the month to see if the chapters are indeed like stepping-stones in the story:"

1. *The Three Farmers*
2. *Mr. Fox*
3. *The Shooting*
4. *The Terrible Shovels*
5. *The Terrible Tractors*
6. *The Race*

"Readers, even the mere titles of these chapters in the book's table of contents help us see how each new chapter sort of fits in with the one that came before. First, we find out that there are three mean farmers. Then we discover that there is a fox who steals from them. And to solve the problem, the farmers plan a shooting. So Chapter 3, titled 'The Shooting,' builds on the problem described in the previous two chapters. But the shooting doesn't solve the farmers' problem, does it? The title of Chapter 4 is 'The Terrible Shovels.' Can you imagine how that builds on Chapter 3? And the *next* chapter is 'The Terrible Tractors.' Can you imagine how that builds on Chapter 4? We left reading at a point where the farmers in their tractors are chasing the foxes, who are digging for dear life. And the chapter that follows is titled 'The Race.' How does this help us predict what will follow, building on what has come before?

"Readers, if you and your neighbor felt that each chapter builds from what happened in the chapter before it, give me a thumbs up. Everything that we read in our books builds off what we've read previously. Reading is about finding ways in which what we are reading at the moment fits with what we've read previously. In life, too, what happens today usually has a history in the past, like my being a teacher today can be linked to my love for scribbling on a blackboard in front of a pretend class when I was your age. These links help us make sense of life and of our books!"

LINK

As you send children off to their independent reading, add today's strategy to the list of other strategies you've taught in previous days.

"Readers, as we pick up our independent reading and find the spot where we left off, we might do a 'previously on' or a brief recap—of who's in the story and what is happening—in order to get our mental movie rolling again. But envisioning and remembering are not enough. Today and every day, we try also to ask ourselves, 'How does what I'm reading now fit with what came before?' Remember that it may not always fit if our story is taking a surprising turn or if we misread something that came before. Remember that readers are alert to when this happens!"

PART THREE

When Meaning Breaks Down, Readers Use Fix-Up Strategies

Dear Teacher,

When we see a child who is disengaged we need to assess whether the book is too hard or whether the learner needs strategies for fixing confusion and holding tight to meaning. This bend in the road helps provide those strategies. It is important to help fidgety youngsters still hold on to a book's story when this becomes a challenge. This part introduces a few fix-up strategies to use whenever meaning breaks down. This is the work of this next part, and it begins with the following minilesson.

Bringing a Blurred Mental Movie Back into Focus

CONNECTION

Relate an anecdote where you were confronted by a complicated series of links or events that muddled your understanding.

"Readers, I have a large extended family. Someone or other in my family is always getting married, so there's usually a wedding just around the bend. 'How's the bride related to me exactly?' I'll ask my mom or grandma if I ever actually attend one of these weddings."

"Why she's your aunt's sister-in-law's husband's cousin—the lawyer sister-in-law, *not* the one who underwent open-heart surgery last fall—and we *also* know her because her mother's side of the family used to be neighbors with us when we lived in our old house on Mall Road."

"'Huh?' I'll ask, totally confused. They usually lose me after mention of the first aunt, so my grandmother will sigh and begin again."

"'You know your aunt's sister-in-law?' She'll ask first and then pause till I nod yes, waiting for me to recall whom she's referring to. 'Remember her husband?' She'll pause again till I actually remember the exact person she's talking about before proceeding to the *next* link. In this way, link by link, she'll go over the entire chain of relations again, step by step, pausing to check that I follow whom she's talking about until I understand my family tree a whole lot better."

Connect this example to instances where readers lose track of the story while reading.

"I'm telling you this story because the plots in our books can sometimes feel as complicated as my large extended family tree. We'll be reading fast, long, and strong, and suddenly say, 'Huh?' The story will take a turn; some new development will occur, and all of a sudden it may feel like the mental movie of our reading that was proceeding so smoothly until now gets all blurry. We try to read on, but the details don't seem to fit or flow—it's like the story isn't making sense, but maybe we missed some link that broke our chain of understanding."

State your teaching point. Specifically, tell children that in order to reactivate the mental movie of our reading when it gets blurry, we return to the last part we remember understanding and retrace our steps, bit by bit, from that point forward.

"Today I want to teach you that whenever the mental movie of our reading gets blurry, we stop and search for the last place we remember really understanding. Then we reread from that point on, bit by bit, till we find the spot at which the blurriness started—and clear the confusion."

Teaching

Demonstrate how when a mental movie becomes blurry, readers go back to the last place we remember well and then reread, reorienting ourselves.

"Let me show you how I do this, using the book I'm reading. This book, *Don't Let's Go to the Dogs Tonight,* is a memoir set in Africa." I held it up for them to see. "It's full of gorgeous descriptions of the landscape, and it's easy to get lost in the scenery. Like all of you, I'm transported to the world of my story and the movie in my mind. But all that description can be dense, too. Listen to this part I read over the weekend:"

> It was breathtaking, that first drive into the valley, dropping off the sandy plateau of the denuded Zamunya TTL, where African cattle swung heavy horns and collected in thorny corrals for the evening and where the land was ribbed with erosion, and then banking steeply into the valley, the road now shouldered by thick, old, vine-covered trees with a dense light-sucking canopy and impenetrable undergrowth.

"All that dense description, whew! Suddenly I couldn't see my characters or their world. My head went totally blank. So you know what I did? I thought to myself, 'What is the last bit of my book that I remember really well?' First, I remembered the narrator and her sister drinking Cokes at a hotel. That part was really clear in my head. I felt thirsty reading it, like I wanted a Coke, too! So I went back to that part and reread slowly from there on. When I got to the part where my movie got blurry, I realized that the family was now in a car headed to their new house; the hotel had been a stop along the way. All this description, which I had to read slowly, was the author's way of telling her reader about the new place the family would now call home. This was the landscape leading to and surrounding that house.

"Readers, do you see how when our mental movie becomes blurry, it helps to go back to the part we recall and reorient ourselves? That scene with the Cokes in the hotel was really clear, and then all of a sudden my characters were on this elaborate journey and I got lost in all the description. But when I went back to the scene in the hotel and reminded myself that we were now back in the car headed to a new place, I was able to understand better. And do you know what? This time I saw that scenery like I was right there in that car. I saw the cattle swinging their horns low to the ground and the road heading down to a valley full of trees. Rereading bit by bit to make sure I got every little detail helped me clear my mental movie."

ACTIVE INVOLVEMENT

Allow students to revise the steps involved in clearing out the confusion from the mental movie of their reading. Note these steps on a chart for classroom display.

"Readers, when I was reading ahead of you in *Fantastic Mr. Fox* a couple of nights ago, in preparation for reading aloud to you this week, my mind must have wandered because there I was, nose in the book, and suddenly I encountered Badger and I literally started. 'This is a story about a fox family and mean farmers,' I thought. 'Where on earth did a *badger* drop in from? There's not supposed to be any badger in this book!'

"You could say that my mental movie didn't just get blurry—it stopped altogether and a little reading voice in my brain squeaked 'Help!'

"I want you to turn to your partner for a bit and pretend that you were me at that point. What might you have done if you suddenly came across something surprising and unexpected in your book without any idea how it connected to your story?"

I waited for partners to discuss the situation, listening in on their conversations before reconvening the group. Next to me, I had positioned an empty chart sheet on which I had printed the title "Mental Movie Has Gone Blurry! What to Do?"

"Readers, I heard lots of smart things. I heard someone say that I ought to have stopped immediately and returned to the point that I remembered reading from last. And in fact, that's what I did." I flipped open *Fantastic Mr. Fox,* and pointed to the start of Chapter 12. On the blank chart sheet, I wrote as point 1: "Return to the last point you remember understanding and reread onward carefully."

"Someone among you also said that I ought to have found the exact point where the confusion started, and that, by the way, is a brilliant suggestion." As point 2, I wrote out: "Locate the exact point of confusion." Then, holding *Fantastic Mr. Fox* open to Chapter 12 in a way that the class could see, I quickly scanned for the point at which Badger appeared.

Open up the read-aloud to demonstrate that these fix-up strategies work.

"Readers, here it is. This was my exact point of confusion." I began reading:

> "Badger," cried Mr. Fox.
>
> "Foxy!" cried Badger.

"Now that I've located the exact point at which my mental movie broke down, I'll reread the part just before this." I began reading:

> All of a sudden a deep voice above their heads said, *"Who goes there?"* They saw, peeking through a small hole in the roof of the tunnel, a long black pointed furry face.

"Oh, I think I get it! This is the part I must have missed—that this black pointed furry face that poked itself in suddenly through the roof of the tunnel is actually an unexpected character appearing in the story. *Now* I get how Badger literally entered the story.

"You know what, though? I'm still not so certain what Badger's *doing* in this story; he's popped in so suddenly without rhyme or reason, it seems. Rereading helps, but to get a clearer sense of how to clear this blurriness in my mental movie, I might just have to read on from here, paying attention to parts that mention Badger." On the board, I wrote point 3: "Reread the part of the text just before the point of confusion." Below this, I added point 4: "From this point, read onward carefully, paying special attention to parts that mention or address your first source of confusion."

"Readers, we have a fine chart here, one that I think I'll put up as a reference for our community." I stood back to survey the points written out on the chart:

Mental Movie Has Gone Blurry! What to Do?

1. Return to the last point you remember understanding and reread onward carefully.

2. Locate the exact point of confusion.

3. Reread the part of the text just before the point of confusion.

4. From this point, read onward carefully, paying special attention to parts that mention or address your first source of confusion.

"But, readers, I have to share an insider's tip—it's a writer's tip really, but one that readers should know. Sometimes writers set up confusion *on purpose.* They call it 'Adding a twist in the tale,' and they do it to create suspense in the story, to keep the reader guessing. I'm suspecting that Dahl, too, might have done that by popping Badger into this tale without warning. That's all the more reason to read forward with our minds alert."

LINK

Remind children that even just-right books can get blurry. When they do, one thing we can do is go back to the last part we remember and then reread.

"Readers, even when we pick just-right books, we will hit spots in which things get a little blurry at some point in our reading. Maybe it's a part with lots of description, like that passage in my book, or maybe it's a part with lots of characters and action, and all those faces and all that activity make it hard to hold on to a clear mental movie. When that happens, one thing we can do is go back to the last part we remember really clearly—a part we can see in our minds—and then we can reread, this time trying to hold tight to that image, letting it not fade. You may find other strategies for what to do when your mental movie fades, and if you do, make sure you share those with each other! Off you go."

We Read Chunks of Meaning, Not Single Words

Dear Teacher,

In this minilesson, you'll teach that words, when strung together, form small units of thought. If the flowing cumulative act of reading is to be broken down into basic units at all, words are not the units that support strong comprehension; rather, groups of words, when they complete a thought, form a unit or building block for larger compre-hension. Much like talking or oral story-telling, pauses come not after individual words but after thought units.

CONNECTION

Relate an anecdote that conveys frustration at approaching a task in too small or disjointed a way.

"When we were little, my sister always drove me crazy with the way she ate cereal. She'd eat one cornflake at a time or scoop up one single measly Cheerio with her spoon at a time. 'You're driving me nuts,' I'd say. 'You'll never finish the entire bowl in one sitting that way!' I love cereal; I respect it. To me, the way she ate cereal was an insult to the cereal. I'd say, 'How can you know the true taste of cereal till you take a proper mouthful!'

"Of course, now I realize my sister ate her cereal that way to get me all worked up. This was something *she* could control, and she'd flaunt that control in front of me. Little sisters can be like that, right?

"But sometimes I see people reading their books the way my sister ate her cereal—one word at a time. 'How can you know the real taste of the story if you don't eat proper mouthfuls of words?' I want to say, or 'You'll never finish a big chunk of your book in one sitting if you read it one word at a time.'"

Name your teaching point. Specifically, tell children that meaning is not in a word but in a group of words.

"Today, readers, I want to teach you that we read faster, longer, and stronger by reading groups of words at a time. When we set our goal to make this year the best reading year ever and to read faster, longer, and stronger, we *didn't* mean we'd read one word, the next word, and the next word and do *that* kind of reading faster. In order to make meaning from the text, we read a group of words, then another group of words, and then another group of words."

TEACHING

Demonstrate that fluent reading involves pausing after an independent and meaningful flow of words rather than after every word.

"Readers, when we're really into a story, we don't read a word at a time. We don't pause after each word. If we pause at all, we do so after reading a whole group of words that makes sense. I'm going to show you how."

"Here are two sentences from page 50 of *Fantastic Mr. Fox*:"

Mr. Fox grinned slyly, showing sharp white teeth. "If I am not mistaken, my dear Badger," he said, "we are now underneath the farm which belongs to that nasty little potbellied dwarf, Bunce."

"Let me tell you first how *not* to read these sentences:"

Mr. Fox *(Pause)* grinned *(Pause)* slyly, *(Pause)* showing *(Pause)* sharp *(Pause)* white *(Pause)* teeth. "If I am *(Pause)* not *(Pause)* mistaken, my *(Pause)* dear *(Pause)* Badger," he *(Pause)* said, "we *(Pause)* are now *(Pause)* underneath *(Pause)* the farm which belongs to that *(Pause)* nasty *(Pause)* little *(Pause)* potbellied *(Pause)* dwarf, *(Pause)* Bunce."

"Readers, could you see how the way I just read that made it feel like I was eating one or two Cheerios at a time? Wasn't it frustrating? Didn't you feel like saying, 'I need to hear not just *one* word, *one* word, *one* word but one *mouthful* of words, another *mouthful* of words if I'm going to understand!' This is because reading is like talking. We don't pause after every word we utter; we only pause after we've said a *group* of words that makes sense.

"Let me read the two sentences again, and this time, watch out for the pauses. Note that I don't pause after every word. I only pause after a group of words that makes sense:"

> Mr. Fox grinned slyly, *(Pause)* showing sharp white teeth. *(Pause)* "If I am not mistaken, *(Pause)* my dear Badger," *(Pause)* he said, *(Pause)* "we are now underneath the farm *(Pause)* which belongs to that nasty little potbellied dwarf, *(Pause)* Bunce."

Name what you have just done in a way that makes it replicable for students to do with other texts at other times.

"Did you see how I waited for a complete thought before I paused? I still paused often because it was a pretty long sentence; in some shorter sentences, I wouldn't pause at all. But in any case, I wait for a group of words to make sense before pausing so that I can reach across the group of words to grab meaning. It's almost like each word group is a complete thought. You see how meaning is in word groups, not in individual words?"

ACTIVE INVOLVEMENT

Set children up to read aloud in a smooth and fluent way with appropriately placed pauses.

"Right now, please find a passage you like in your own books—an important one, maybe one where there's some story tension. Signal to me when you've found the passage." I waited until many had signaled. "Try reading this passage to your partner, taking care to pause only at a spot where a thought has been completed. Try to make your reading smooth, like the read-aloud, so that your partner follows the meaning of the story clearly, and that your partner actually begins to have a mental movie from just hearing you.

"Here's a tip: You'll want to think about who is talking, too, even if the author doesn't tell you. You'll want to think about the character's feelings. Try reading the passage, then talk about the changing feelings of it, and then reread it to show those feelings."

LINK

Send children off with the advice to take in more words before they pause while reading.

"So today you will continue to work on reading faster, longer, stronger. But your reading is not like this: 'Mr. *(Pause)* Fox *(Pause)* grinned *(Pause)* slyly, *(Pause)* showing *(Pause)* sharp *(Pause)* white *(Pause)* teeth.' Instead, your reading is like this: 'Mr. Fox grinned slyly, showing sharp white teeth.' As you continue reading today, try to make the voice in your head work so you aren't just seeing the words but are also learning the story."

Reading with Momentum—Riding over a Hard Word

Dear Teacher,

This minilesson introduces a strategy for decoding difficult words. Recall that you showed children that in a fluent reading, meaning is contained not in any single word but rather in groups of words that complete a thought. Stated differently, no one word is so important that it contains within it the key to the meaning of the entire text. Consequently, the odd, unfamiliar, or daunting word that appears in your children's reading need not be a source of worry or confusion— you'll teach that sticking a synonym or placeholder in its stead will still permit children to take away meaning from the text as a whole.

Your aim here is to shatter the myth that proficient reading means knowing all the vocabulary within the text before-hand. When children are reading texts they can handle with 96% accuracy, the texts will still be peppered with words that are new. This should not deter readers. Instead, children must have up their sleeves a couple of strategies to tackle such words as they appear.

CONNECTION

Explain how speed and momentum allow a moving object to cross small hurdles or obstacles in its path.

"Readers, have you ever seen those cars that fly across ditches in action movies? I've always found that unbelievable, that a big, heavy thing like a car can fly over and not fall into a ditch. Recently I read that a man even jumped his car over one part of the Grand Canyon, starting from United States and landing in Mexico! You know me—I love to read up on stuff that intrigues me, so I did some more reading about those cars. I found that, among other things, the secret to jumping ditches and canyons is speed. The driver needs to be going at a fast enough speed for the car to take off. If he's driving too slowly, into the ditch the car will go. You need *speed* to get a certain energy that is called 'momentum.'"

Liken the metaphor to reading, suggesting that reading with speed and meaning gives us reading momentum.

"Remember yesterday when we were talking about training our eyes to read not one word, another word, and another word but a group of words, another group of words, and another group of words? Well, if you read chunks of text at a time and keep your mental movie going as you do it, you'll be reading faster. And your reading will begin to gather momentum.

"Readers, I'm a big fan of this thing called *momentum,* and I'll tell you why. Reading has its own ditches in the form of big, unfamiliar words, and you need momentum to cross them. If you are reading fast, engrossed in your story and seeing the movie of what is happening in the world of your book, a difficult word or two aren't going to frazzle you. You'll still be able to make perfect sense of what is going on if you're reading with speed, if you have the momentum to cross straight through the difficult words."

Name your teaching point. Specifically, tell children that readers don't let tricky words halt our reading—we sound out the word ourselves, figure out what it might mean, and generate a synonym.

"Today I want to teach you that because readers are reading groups of words and because we have momentum as readers, we can read tricky words. We sound them out while thinking, 'What must this mean?' and we come up with another word that means the same thing."

TEACHING

Demonstrate how creating a strong and continuous mental movie of a book allows readers to negotiate unfamiliar words along the way.

"We come across difficult words every day in our books. The best readers, the ones who read with speed and have the most power or momentum, can cross through these difficult words with hardly any trouble. Let me show you what they do." I reread a paragraph from Chapter 13 of *Fantastic Mr. Fox,* fumbling deliberately over the word "overwhelmed:"

> Quickly Badger and the three Small Foxes scrambled up after him. They stopped and stared. They stood and gaped. They were so *(Pause)* over *(Pause)* overwhelmed *(Pause)* they couldn't speak; for what they saw now was a kind of fox's dream, a badger's dream, a paradise for hungry animals.

"Readers, if someone were to wake me up from sleep and show me this word (I pointed to "overwhelmed" written on chart paper) and ask what it meant, I would stand and gape just like the little foxes. I wouldn't have the momentum to cross through this word. But when I come across the word in a text that I am reading with speed, I have plenty of momentum. *Fantastic Mr. Fox* is a just-right book for me, one that I read with speed; I have plenty of momentum.

"Let's see. The first thing I'm going to do is use my mental movie to help me figure out what is going on."

I shut my eyes and demonstrated that I was literally envisioning as I spoke. "Badger, Mr. Fox, and the little foxes are semi-starved, digging underground, hardly daring to believe Mr. Fox when he tells them he's found the spot where the storehouse for Bunce's ducks and geese is. They're in this dark tunnel; Mr. Fox suddenly taps some floorboards loose above their heads, and they climb out to catch their first sight of the most *dazzling,* the most *appetizing* array of fat ducks and geese that they could possibly imagine. Till now, they've probably never seen more than a couple of ducks or geese at a time because Bunce guards his stock. Suddenly they're right in the middle of his treasure after days of starvation! They're face to face with rows and rows of food. They can't believe their eyes. They are *overwhelmed.*

"Readers, when I use my mental movie, I can almost *feel* what the word means! I'm going to hold this *feeling* of what the word means. It's shock and awe—they're stunned—it's a happy kind of feeling."

Demonstrate that readers might break up a hard word into smaller parts to guess its meaning.

"The second thing I do is sound out the word and see if I can break it up into any smaller words that I recognize. Let's see. 'Overwhelmed'—'over' is a word I know! It means too much! 'Overwhelmed' is probably what you feel when you suddenly have too much of something that you weren't expecting or when you've never seen it before, because that's what happened to Badger and the little foxes at the sight of so much food."

Recapitulate the two strategies you just used before demonstrating a third—namely that readers cross a hard word by placing a synonym in its stead and reading on.

"Readers, I've used two strategies so far. I've used my mental movie to imagine or feel what the word might mean. Second, I've broken up the word into smaller words and found a word part that gives me another clue to the word's meaning. Now I'm going to try reading the sentence again, this time fitting another word in its place, and then keep reading:"

> Quickly Badger and the three Small Foxes scrambled up after him. They stopped and stared. They stood and gaped. They were so *(Pause)* they couldn't speak; for what they saw now was a kind of fox's dream, a badger's dream, a paradise for hungry animals.

"Readers, I'm thinking 'stunned' is a good word to use in place of 'overwhelmed.' If the little foxes couldn't speak at the sight of what they saw, they were probably *stunned*. The word 'stunned' also matches my feeling of the word 'over':"

> Quickly Badger and the three Small Foxes scrambled up after him. They stopped and stared. They stood and gaped. They were so *stunned* they couldn't speak; for what they saw now was a kind of fox's dream, a badger's dream, a paradise for hungry animals.

"That seems to make total sense. Readers, did you note that my mental movie helped me find a placeholder for the difficult word? In case I couldn't figure the tricky word out any other way, I could put another word in its place so I could read on. Breaking up the word into smaller pieces also gave me a sense of what the word meant. But remember that I could only use my mental movie and find a placeholder because my reading had momentum I was reading with speed; I wasn't allowing my mental movie to break down.

"If, on the other hand, I'd been reading slowly and haltingly, a word at a time, when I would come to a difficult word, I'd probably just fall into that ditch and fling the book aside or lose interest. Reading with speed and having our mental movie going help us tackle difficult words. We can put up on a chart what we'd do when we come across a difficult word in our reading:"

Strategies for Figuring Out Tricky Words

- We use our mental movies to imagine or feel what the word might mean.
- We break up the word into smaller word parts for a clue to the word's meaning.
- We try fitting another word in its place and keep reading.

Active Involvement

Set children up to practice these three decoding strategies with their partners.

"Readers, I'm going to continue reading the rest of the page, only this time I'm going to ask you to read along with me. You'll see that we will come to another tricky word. When we do, I'll be quiet and ask you and your partner to take over reading. You'll need to be like one of those monster cars, ready to get through the hard part. Rely on the strategies we've listed to do this."

I began to read the next passage from the book. I had copied this passage onto chart paper. I came to the word "proclaimed" in the next sentence after the one in Chapter 13 of *Fantastic Mr. Fox* that I'd just referenced and let children word solve the word with their partners. Note that the word "proclaimed" especially lends itself to the strategy of splitting a word into its root components—*pro* and *claim.* You will want to be alert and assist kids in seeing how these roots help in obtaining a sense of the word's meaning.

Link

Send children off with a revised list of decoding strategies that they might use in their independent reading.

"Readers, it doesn't matter if we don't read every single word exactly right. It doesn't matter if we do not know the exact meaning of each word. We're reading a story, which is much bigger than any single word. And when we read fast and with momentum, if we're not exactly sure what one particular word means, we use our mental movie to imagine what it could mean—we look at the word parts and stick in a substitute, a place-holder, a synonym—and we focus on taking in the whole mouthful of words after it. We focus on making sense. And sense, or meaning, comes in word groups, not in single words.

"As you go off and read your books today, keeping a mental movie of your reading going and training your eye to take in groups of words at a time rather than single words, try also to tackle any difficult word that appears by using the strategies we just put on this chart. Leave a flag near words that you've tackled so you can later share these with each other."

Teachers, please turn to the Resources CD-ROM for Part Four of this unit, "Reading in the Company of Friends."

INTELLECTUAL INDEPENDENCE

An Ambitious Workshop for Experienced Readers

By Mary Ehrenworth

PART ONE

Readers Develop Agency to Lift Their Reading Lives into a New Orbit

Dear Teachers,

If your readers have been in a reading workshop for a few years and have learned from many of the units of study in this series, as well as others that you and your colleagues have developed together, they are probably knowledgeable about the essential skills of reading. They know how to choose books they can read with ease, they pay attention to characters and to story elements in the stories they read, and they think deeply across books as they read. They also monitor for comprehension, and they have a repertoire of strategies to draw upon when the book gets hard.

When I encounter readers who are this experienced, I'll tend to think of two different directions to go with them. If these readers are moving toward books at text levels R/S/T and above, one way to continue challenging them is to devise curriculum that helps them tackle books that are increasingly complicated. Over the past few years, Lucy, my other colleagues on the Teachers College Reading and Writing Project staff, and I have been immersed in research projects in which we investigate ways we can bring readers into a world of stories that have multiple narratives, tangled plotlines, cohorts of unpredictable characters, atmospheric—even symbolic—settings, and so forth.

It is also helpful to show readers who are experienced with these units of study some ways in which they can use what they know in order to be more independent, thereby teaching them to draw upon their repertoire of strategies as they become increasingly independent, synthesizing a whole array of strategies toward increasingly big purposes.

This unit is designed to accomplish both purposes but to especially help readers who have experienced these units of study during previous years to draw upon all they have been taught with increasing independence. The unit invites readers to do all the things that are essential at the start of a yearlong reading workshop—selecting just-right books, recording their reading in a reading log, pushing themselves to read with more stamina, growing ideas about characters—and doing this work with new ambitiousness. In recognition that this unit will probably be taught to older readers and to readers who could enter a reading workshop with some fleeting sense of "This again?," the unit focuses more on inspiring readers to outgrow themselves and on promoting a sense of agency—which means that readers need to make significant decisions about how to work hard.

The tone of these lessons is all about wild pleasure in stories and a fierce determination to outgrow ourselves both in reading and in all our endeavors.

You can find Part Three, which supports literary conversations and writing about reading, on the Resources CD-ROM.

Yours,

Mary Ehrenworth

SESSION I

Taking Charge of Our Reading Lives and Becoming Active Learners

GETTING READY

- Have a story ready about a time when you learned to be more powerful at some endeavor.

CONNECTION

Tell your students that this year they'll be active learners of reading, and suggest that a sense of personal agency is important to any learning.

"Readers, I need all your attention because what I am going to say is really important. All eyes here.

"What I need to tell you is that this year, we—as a community—will be launching into new reading work. We will be active learners of reading. That work will be at the heart of everything we do together. I know, you're thinking, 'I already know how to read,' but you already know how to ride a bike, too. Yet I think we've all seen someone riding a bike, whether it's Lance Armstrong riding hundreds of miles in the Tour de France or a kid doing flips at the X Games, that makes us go 'Wow! There's biking, and then there's *biking!*' It's the same with reading. There's reading, and then there's *reading!*"

Channel students to recall when they learned to read with a tremendous sense of agency, anticipating that many will recall a time in their very first years of school.

"Right now, will you think back in your life to a time when you would say, 'Yes, that's when I learned about reading'? Now, in your mind, leaf through your reading memories and settle on a time when you would say, 'Yes, that's when I think I learned to read.'"

I did this thinking myself while sitting in front of the class, knowing that when I actually do some thinking at the front of the room, the students can literally see wheels turning in my mind. Then I went on: "Recall that time with some detail—focus in on one particular moment, one episode. Recall where you were sitting, what you were reading—that sort of thing."

Again I did the thinking that I wanted the students to do. "Will you turn and tell a person sitting near you what you are recalling?"

They did.

Tell the class that most of the times in which they grew dramatically as readers were when they were very young, and suggest that in fact this coming year can be another time for dramatic growth.

"Readers, can I stop you? I am fascinated. I overheard what a lot of you were saying, and you know what? For most of you, when you were asked to remember a time when you learned a lot as a reader, you went back in your memories all the way to kindergarten or to first grade! Readers, I understand that when we go from not reading to reading, our reading growth takes off like a rocket."

I moved my hands as if to show a rocket blasting off into space. "Rockets shoot up into space, and then when they're about to flatten out and slow down in their trajectory, a second set of engines kicks in, which gets the rocket into space and into a higher orbit. And that's what will happen to you this year with your reading—you're going to shoot into a whole new orbit. A year from now, when a teacher asks you, 'When did you take off as a reader?' you'll talk about this year."

State your teaching point. Specifically, teach your students that readers, like any kind of motivated learner, learn best if they bring a sense of personal agency to their reading.

I looked up, making my voice earnest: "The most important thing I can teach you today, then, is that whenever a person wants to really become more powerful at something—*anything*—the learner needs to consciously take hold of his or her own life and say, 'I can decide to work hard at this. I'm *in charge* of this. Starting today, I'm going to make deliberate decisions that help me learn this skill in leaps and bounds so that I can be as powerful as possible.' That's called having *agency*. People who have agency *strive*—they work independently and incredibly hard at something in order to achieve."

Teaching

Remind your students that they have had agency in other endeavors, and tell a story about a time when you had agency, when you really _strove_ to become more powerful at something you were learning.

"I bet that most of you can think of a time in your recent life when you were determined to learn something, and because you had _agency,_ which means you actively worked at it, you learned it in leaps and bounds. Maybe it was a game—I've seen some of you striving to get to the next level on the DS or X Box. Maybe it was a sport, like biking or skateboarding or jumping rope. Maybe it was playing an instrument.

"For me, it was learning to run the hurdles in track. My coach didn't even want me to compete in hurdles. But I wanted to do it, and I used to stay at the track after school to practice—that's _agency._ Nobody made me do it, and nobody else could do it for me. I could only get better by taking charge and working hard at it."

"Readers, we can tap into these learning experiences to help us become more active learners of reading as well. I think if you ask yourself, 'What did I do in order to become more powerful at that one thing?' you'll get some ideas for what you could do (and we all could do) to make this class into a community of readers who have agency, a community where all of us are becoming more powerful readers."

I leaned in a little closer as I prepared to tell a story. "Right now, listen to what I realize about myself as a learner as I think about my experience, and then I'm going to give you a chance to do a self-study, reflecting for a moment on yourself as a learner. We'll see if, together, we can come up with some ideas for ways we can have more agency as readers."

■ _I will tell about my learning by showing the parts of what I did. The learning points are generally common across any experience. If you learned to play chess or ride horses or play piano or type, you'll have participated in all of this work. I'll show that I had a vision of what I wanted to achieve, I practiced hard, I studied mentors, and I learned specific strategies. One teacher recently spoke of learning to jump with a parachute from a plane. Another spoke of learning to dance for a wedding, and he spoke of learning from an expert, practicing a lot, and having a vision of what he wanted to look like. You'll have your own story, from childhood or from a recent experience, that illustrates deciding to learn._

"When I learned to run the hurdles, I already knew how to run. I also knew how to jump over a hurdle. But I wanted to get really good at it."

I used my hands to mimic my running style as I went on. "So when I wanted to get good at the hurdles, at first I practiced. When I got near the hurdle, I would kind of hop over it. For a while I didn't seem to get better. One thing that helped was that I had seen other hurdlers running and jumping right over the hurdles. I could see that they were able to leap as they ran—they didn't slow down before the hurdles. So I practiced, with an image in mind of what good hurdlers do."

I looked off for a moment, as if pausing to remember, and then went on. "Another thing that helped me was that I watched how hurdlers trained. I didn't just watch them race. I watched them during practice, and I saw that they ran for long periods of time. I also noticed that they worked together, sometimes in partnerships, to watch each other and to teach each other strategies. These hurdlers were sort of mentors for me. I tried to do what they did, including getting my own partner for running."

I looked back, bringing the focus back to the present. "Let me think for a moment now. Can any of this help me with becoming a more active learner of reading? I'm going to think about that for a moment. I imagine that some of the ways I showed agency as a learner in the hurdles could help me as a learner in reading also."

ACTIVE INVOLVEMENT

Channel your students to reflect on a time when they worked hard to learn something, and then suggest that what they did to learn that one skill could apply also to reading.

"Would you reflect on a time when you worked hard and actively, with agency, to learn *anything* in leaps and bounds? Ask yourself: 'What did I do in order to learn and improve at that one thing?' When you remember this time, when you had agency over your learning, just give a thumbs up." I waited and then added: "Now think of some specific things you did."

I waited again, saying, "Give a signal when you have a couple of ideas."

After many signaled they had recalled specific things they did to become skilled, I said, "Will you jot down a few things you did in order to learn in leaps and bounds?"

After they worked for a few minutes, I voiced over that work, saying, "This matters, class, because you and I can do the same sorts of things that helped us in our other endeavors in order to take off as readers. For example, I said that to do well in running hurdles,

I had to hold on to a vision of what I wanted to achieve. If I want to become skilled in reading, might I do that same thing?" The children nodded. "Absolutely, this was transferable to reading. And I heard Jennifer say that one thing she did to learn to play piano was she made sure that she set aside a specific time every day to practice. So maybe we could set aside a time every day to read. Amber said that when she studies a dance move and gets stuck, she does the same move over again until she's unstuck. We could do that, right? We could reread when we're stuck and make sure we figure out the hard parts of our stories. Adrian said that one way he improved in soccer was to practice a long time. So maybe we'll try to watch the clock less and keep going in our books more, reading for longer periods of time.

"There are so many ways that you know how to be active learners, to have agency over your learning. I've seen you learn new dances and new songs and new technology. I can't wait to see you show this same agency in reading—you are going to be so, so powerful."

LINK

Send your children off to read, with an inspiring comment that reiterates the teaching point.

"In a moment you will go back to your desks to read. Think of yourself as a reader who has agency—someone who actively takes charge of his or her reading life to become more powerful. Put all your effort into activating your learning. I'll be coming around to watch and hear about what you're doing as readers. After school today, I am also going to write down on a piece of chart paper all your ideas for being active learners. Whenever you need a push, you can look up at this chart and see the things that you and your classmates have done before in order to take off in other endeavors. Off you go!"

SESSION II

Reading with Agency

CONNECTION

Explain that just as an expert on baseball sees more in a baseball game, so too, a knowledgeable reader sees more in a story.

"Come close, I want you to imagine something with me. Have you ever been to a baseball game with someone who really understands baseball? That kid will be alert to all sorts of things that are happening in the game. He knows that the catcher is new and worth watching, so he says, 'Let's see how he does,' and he gets you to suddenly pull your eyes away from the pitcher and the batter—the guys with the ball—to a guy who doesn't even have the ball yet. Or he will be alert to signs that a man on base may be about to try to steal. He knows what will happen before it happens. He may have goose bumps sometimes at something that seems invisible to someone else who is less expert. Those are called *nuances*—small subtle details. It's almost as if he is at a different game—because he knows more, expects more, and sees more."

I shake my head as if I'm in awe. "And here's another thing. If that boy who knows a lot about baseball is also trying to *become* a terrific player, he may even watch and think, 'I've gotta do that,' or 'How'd he do that?' Either way, whether he likes to engage as a fan or as a player, this boy is watching a richer, more exciting game than many of the rest of us. My point is that reading can be like that for us, too. It can become a project we become more expert at so that when we read a story, we are getting all the details, the nuances of the story, the way this boy gets the nuances of the baseball game.

"I'm thinking we can learn to read the way someone who adores and studies baseball watches a game. If we harness everything we know and love about stories, like the way some people use everything they know and love about baseball, we'll be more alert."

Name your teaching point. Specifically, teach students that readers with agency rely on our knowledge of how stories go in order to be more alert readers.

"Friends, today I want to teach you that one way we can read actively and with agency is by relying on our knowledge of how stories go. Because we know a lot about stories, we know it is important that as we read, we get to know our characters and look for the problems they face, including the nuances of these problems. We also know we need to be aware of how problems are resolved and how characters change."

TEACHING

Demonstrate what it means to read alertly, using knowledge of how stories go to be alert to details and nuances in the story. Alternate between reading aloud and thinking aloud.

"Let's practice reading this way—reading on the edge of our seats as active participants. Just like that boy watching a baseball game, we're going to be eagerly witnessing the story unfold."

I sat up straighter and motioned to the students to do the same. "You know what? Let's actually get our bodies ready to really read like active participants. Let's sit up really tall, with our backs straight and bodies showing that we're alert and engaged. There have been a lot of scientific studies that show that when you change your posture or your expression, it can actually affect your whole attitude. (I was reading this book called *Blink* the other day, and it showed that if you put your mouth into a smile, you'll start having more pleasant emotions.) So let's start actively taking charge by sitting in ways that suggest we'll be active readers of this text.

"I'm going to read the first part of the story aloud. I'm going to use what I know about stories to really be an active participant in this story. So, hmm, what does what I know about stories tell me to watch for first? I'm thinking that first I'll get to know the characters—I'll really be alert for details that give me information about them."

I picked up the story and began:

She was a large woman with a large purse that had everything in it but hammer and nails. It had a long strap, and she carried it slung across her shoulder.

I looked up: "Already, because I know stories, I realize that this woman *is* the main character. It's not just that she has been introduced first; it's that there is something compelling about her. A woman who carries a purse that has everything in it but a hammer and nails! I'm actively picturing this large woman with her enormous purse, and I'm really getting to know her in my imagination."

I read on:

It was about eleven o'clock at night, and she was walking alone, when a boy ran up behind her and tried to snatch her purse.

I looked up alertly: "Oh my gosh." I put my hands to my face. "This is one of those stories where the problem comes up fast! I remember that we were going to start by getting to know characters and then we were going to be alert to the nuances, or small details, of the problems they face. So far, let's see, the woman has a problem: she is being assaulted. Let me really think hard, actively trying to construct this story. What else can I say? Well, she seems brave, to be walking alone so late at night. And it's possible that the boy is poor or really needs money if he's stealing her purse. He must be young, too, because the author doesn't say 'man' or 'young man.' He says, 'a boy.'"

Name what you did in a way that is transferable to other texts on other days.

"Readers, I'm going to stop here for a moment. Did you notice that as I was reading, I was thinking about how stories go, noticing details about the characters, inferring about their traits, and considering their problems right away?" I ticked these off on my fingers as I spoke. "And just like that boy at the baseball game, I didn't let things pass me by without noticing them, did I? That's what I mean when I say that we can read a story the way that boy reads a baseball game."

ACTIVE INVOLVEMENT

Organize your students to try what you have just demonstrated. Continue reading aloud, and set them up to talk to partners about what their knowledge of stories allows them to see in the story.

"Let's keep reading this way. Remember to use what you know about how stories go to be extra alert, the way that boy at the baseball game recognized the signs that a player was going to steal a base. Because we're skilled readers, we know, for instance, that at the start of the story we expect to find out a lot about the characters—we expect to notice every detail and put those details together rapidly in our mind as we read. When we get more to the middle of the story, we expect to know more about the characters' problems. And by the end, we know to be alert to how the main problem, at least, is resolved and how characters may be changing."

■ *Teachers, you'll probably just tick these reading strategies off on your fingers for now, but later you may jot them down on an informal chart as a reminder for students, giving them a visual cue as they read. Some students benefit from having visual cues to help activate their reading work and their academic language.*

I picked up the story again. "Are you ready?"

> The strap broke with the single tug the boy gave it from behind. But the boy's weight and the weight of the purse combined caused him to lose his balance so, instead of taking off full blast as he had hoped, the boy fell on his back on the sidewalk, and his legs flew up. The large woman simply turned around and kicked him right square in his blue-jeaned sitter. Then she reached down, picked the boy up by his shirt front, and shook him until his teeth rattled.

"Readers, I saw some of you almost fall off your seats there, and I agree, my sense of how stories go tells me this scene is important—we're really getting to know this woman better. Let me read that again:"

> … the boy fell on his back on the sidewalk, and his legs flew up. The large woman simply turned around and kicked him right square in his blue-jeaned sitter. Then she reached down, picked the boy up by his shirt front, and shook him until his teeth rattled.

"What is your expert story sense telling you about her? Turn and tell your partner."

After readers talked, I convened the group and said, "I heard some readers saying they think this woman is really strong and big. And some of you said that she's strong inside as well—she's not intimidated by this thief. She's assertive! Some of you said already that you admired how she's not going to let that boy get away with trying to steal her purse. Let's keep these descriptions of her in our mind, and our feelings about her in our hearts, as we keep on reading. And that's what active reading is, what you are doing now—it's reading using everything you know about how stories go to help you read with extra alertness."

Celebrate your students' observations about the story, and then suggest that the quality of their work prompts you to teach one more thing—the value of jotting as a way to grow ideas. Ask them to do this.

I put the story aside and said, "Readers, I need to just mention that I am moved by how deeply you are engaged with this woman in the story. I feel like you are really honoring her and doing justice to the writer who brought her into being. Because you are doing such wise work, I'd like to squeeze one more thing into this minilesson. Another thing that helps some readers be more active as they read is to sometimes jot down ideas or responses, often phrases or words, that feel important. These quick jottings are just one more way of actively engaging with the story. So I'm just going to pause for a moment and jot what I'm thinking about this woman right now, and I'm hoping you'll do this, too."

I jotted my thoughts on the piece of chart paper as if it were my notebook. "I'm going to read more and I may continue my jottings as I do. You can do this as well, if you want." I continued reading:

After that the woman said, "Pick up my pocketbook, boy, and give it here."

She still held him. But she bent down enough to permit him to stoop and pick up her purse. Then she said, "Now ain't you ashamed of yourself?"

Firmly gripped by his shirt front, the boy said, "Yes'm."

The woman said, "What did you want to do it for?"

The boy said, "I didn't aim to."

She said, "You lie!"

By that time two or three people passed, stopped, turned to look, and some stood watching.

"If I turn you loose, will you run?" asked the woman.

"Yes'm," said the boy.

"Then I won't turn you loose," said the woman. She did not release him.

"I'm very sorry, lady, I'm sorry," whispered the boy.

"Um-hum! And your face is dirty. I got a great mind to wash your face for you. Ain't you got nobody home to tell you to wash your face?"

"No'm," said the boy.

"Readers, this feels like another part where we are learning more about the problems characters face, doesn't it? I love how in good stories things are complicated. I see you're on the edge of your seats here. I'm just going to read that last line, and then you go ahead and start your conversations." I read again:

> "And your face is dirty. I got a great mind to wash your face for you. Ain't you got nobody home to tell you to wash your face?"

> "No'm," said the boy.

■ *Teachers, your students will probably surmise that the boy is lonely or neglected. This is actually a big reading move, to realize that characters have reasons for their behaviors, that those reasons are complicated, and that those who may seem flawed or even evil at first may, in fact, be more nuanced. As your students move to higher levels in their reading, they'll encounter more characters who have complicated emotional lives and experience multiple pressures in their stories.*

Restate overheard bits of partner conversations as a way to reteach and to crystallize what it is you hope students will take with them to another text on another day.

"Readers, turn this way. I heard you say that the boy might not have someone at home to take care of him. And that maybe he's too young to take care of himself. You were really thinking harder about the nuances, or details, of this problem of stealing, and realizing that the boy might have trouble, too. I love the way no one had to tell you to keep on working to know the characters—you took cues from the story. I could see the wheels in your mind turning. Readers, that's it! That's what it means to read with agency. You used everything you know about how stories usually go to learn everything you could about the characters and to understand their problems."

■ *Students will want to finish reading the story and talk about it. You can use your read-aloud time to keep going with the story and to keep going with this skill of using what they know about stories to be active readers. You may remind them to use what they know about stories to notice how the main problem is resolved and how characters change, but, for now, students need time for their own reading.*

■ *Teachers, we focus here on the structure of a single problem and a solution. If you have already been working with higher-level readers on how more complicated stories often have some problems in them that don't get resolved by the end of the story (like* Fly Away Home *or most stories at level R/S/T and above), your students may be alert to those details as well, noting that the boy is still poor at the end of this story but that he no longer is hungry and has made a friend.*

LINK

Send your students off to read, reminding them that great texts merit this kind of expert reading and praising them for lifting their reading into a new orbit. Stir them up!

"Readers, we spoke before about how you and I, like rocket ships, can lift ourselves out of one orbit so that we zoom into a higher one. I feel as if we did that today. We lifted ourselves out of one orbit (and that's hard because there's great inertia to just stay the same, doing the same thing, because it's safe and predictable and it's a habit), and we actively propelled ourselves into another orbit, one where we are seeing more in stories.

"This is so moving, especially because Langston Hughes is an incredibly beautiful writer. He brings these characters into the world, and today it felt as if he were writing just for us. I imagined he would have loved to watch you read his story, to see you on the edge of your seats, to listen to what you had to say about this woman and this boy, to look over your shoulder at your jottings.

"Readers, as you go off to read, remember that all good stories deserve this kind of attention and that as we become more and more expert readers this year, we can get more and more out of the stories we read. Be like that boy at the baseball game; be the kind of readers you just were today. Off you go."

SESSION III

Choosing Books Wisely

GETTING READY

- Prepare a stack of books to use for modeling during the teaching. You can use the ones listed in this lesson; for an even more authentic experience, grab your own stack.

- Decide if your students, at the start of the year, are choosing from baskets on their tables or from the open library. Some teachers prefer to cluster students around baskets that contain books they are apt to be able to read so that students are not up and browsing the library until the teacher has done the assessment necessary to guide their selections.

CONNECTION

Tell an engaging story that demonstrates the value of research. For example, you could tell about the research that is done on baseball players when making up a professional team.

"Readers, I've been fascinated with a story recently that I want to share with you. It's about a man named Billy Beane, the general manager of the baseball team called the Oakland A's. The Oakland A's are famous because even though they don't have a lot of money to hire star baseball players, the team does really, really well. It turns out that the reason they do so well is that Billy Beane knows how to find really good players before they are stars. Billy Beane can tell if they have the essential qualities that make a good ballplayer. He knows how to make such smart choices because he knows how to research a player. He's not fooled by star looks or put off by someone who seems different. Billy's the kind of general manager who would have hired Jackie Robinson in his first draft because Billy knows how to weigh a player's statistics, his performance, and his potential."

- *Teachers, the story I used in the connection about Billy Beane and the Oakland A's is from Michael Lewis's* Moneyball. *This is a well-known, much-discussed baseball legend. Billy Beane was one of the first general managers to bother to research players, using a lot of Bill James's statistics on college players rather than just sending a scout to look at high school players. He showed the baseball world the value of research, of numbers, of records. If you use this Billy Beane example, you could hold up a picture of the Oakland A's or of Billy Beane or of* Moneyball, *just to give a tangibility to these names and people.*

"For example, once Billy was watching this baseball player, Jason Giambi, whom a lot of other teams had passed over. The other general managers thought this one player wouldn't turn out to be that good because he didn't *look* the way they expected a pro ballplayer to look. He didn't look that strong, and he didn't hit that hard. But Billy, remember, saw things that others might not have seen. When Billy researched this kid, he saw that Giambi had the patience to wait for good pitches, and had a great attitude—he worked hard and wanted to improve. Billy knew then that this was a player he wanted. Jason Giambi became a famous heavy hitter on the Oakland A's. It was the same with a shortstop named Mark Kiger. Other scouts thought he was too small to play pro-ball. Billy saw smallness, but he also saw agility and an awareness of where the ball would go. He drafted Kiger, who became a famous shortstop. You see, Billy Beane knew how to really research a player. It's why he's built such a great baseball team."

I had been using my hands and body to mimic the motions of a baseball player. I continued, more quietly: "Friends, building a reading life is a little like building a baseball team. It takes an expert to be in charge, someone who works hard to make smart choices about reading the way Billy Beane does about players."

Name your teaching point. Specifically, teach your students that one way to make smart choices about what to read, and to build an extraordinary reading life, is to research books wisely.

"Today I want to teach you that we need to work hard to make smart choices about what we read so we can build an extraordinary reading life. One way we work at making smart choices is to research the books we plan to read so that we choose wisely."

TEACHING

Demonstrate how to use your expertise about books to research and choose wisely.

"Readers, I am going to show you how I work hard and use my reading expertise to research the books I choose. As I demonstrate, I want you to practice being reading researchers. Really watch hard, and be ready to jot down any strategies you see me using as tips you could give other readers about how I make wise choices. Remember that story I just told about Billy Beane? Well, his success as a researcher of baseball players has inspired general managers of all the great baseball teams. The Red Sox, Yankees, and Mets began to use his methods to look at players. They saw Billy having success and paid attention. See if you can watch me in the same way and pay attention."

I laid out a stack of books in front of me, picking up the first one in the pile. Then I continued: "Oh, here's a book by Judy Blume. That's definitely one way to research a book—look at the author and use my expertise to seek authors that I've read before and loved. I've read a bunch of other Judy Blume books and really enjoyed them."

I put my finger on the author's name, and then I opened the book to the inside page where it listed all her other books. I ran my finger down the list of titles. "Hmm, let me use this list of titles to remind me of what I know about this author. Yes, I read this one, and this one, and this whole series. What does this list of books tell me about what this book will be like if I choose it? Well, now I remember Judy Blume's books are usually about building friendships and fitting in."

I put down the book. "Let's see, how else can I research a book and choose wisely? If I read a few books in a series and enjoyed them, I try to find the rest of that series. Some series make it really easy to find the books—they all have the same cover design, and the title of the series is huge because you know right away that it's a book from that series. *Dragon Slayers' Academy* is like that—you can tell from far away that it's a DSA book, which is maybe why I read every single book in that series. But let me work harder now to research books by noticing series that are harder to identify. Hmm, what's this?"

I picked up the book, scanning the front cover and reading the title aloud: "It's *The Last Olympian.* Hmm, the cover looks a little familiar, but I don't see the name of the series on it. Let me look at the author. It's Rick Riordan. I think, yes, that's who wrote *The Lightning Thief.* I loved that book and heard it was a series, but I haven't found the others yet. Now I see why—the series title isn't that obvious on the cover. Way over here on the side, now I see that it says *Percy Jackson and the Olympians.* But wait, this is Book 5 and I only read Book 1. Whoops! I better seek out Book 2 next. I know it's worth researching to find the books and read them in order."

I looked inside the cover. "Book 2 is called *The Sea of Monsters.* So I can go to the library and look for that one if I want to continue this series, which I do."

ACTIVE INVOLVEMENT

Give partners a chance to share the tips for researching books that they jotted, and then recap what you hope they know about choosing books wisely.

"Readers, I saw you jotting down a lot of tips. Just show them to your partner for a minute."

I paused for just a moment and let them share a couple of their tips. "Readers, what's important here is not any of the small things I did as a reader to choose books wisely. You may or may not choose a familiar series or a familiar author. What's important is that I used my *expertise as a reader* to research books carefully before I chose. I tried to be like Billy Beane choosing baseball players. I looked carefully and considered before committing myself.

"You know a lot about choosing books wisely. You know how to look for familiar authors and series. You know how to use the cover and the blurb on the back to find stories you'll enjoy. You know how to use your knowledge of the sorts of books that you can read easily to choose books that are just right for you and then to open the book up and give it a quick try in order to double-check that it's not too hard. What matters now is that you use your reading expertise to take charge of your reading life."

LINK

Restate how important it is to research books thoughtfully and choose wisely, praising students' efforts.

I motioned to the baskets and the library. "Let's get started, readers. At your tables are some bins of books. Some of you need a new book, as you have finished your most recent one. All of you need a book or two to have 'on deck'—smart readers know that even as they read one book, they usually keep a list of what they want to read, so they don't waste a lot of time looking around for new choices when they could be reading. Why don't you practice researching these books and choosing books wisely. Remember to really use your expertise and work hard to research the books. Readers, keep in mind that many of the books have dots on them, or the level written on them, and that information will be helpful, too. As you try to really zoom ahead as readers and do powerful reading work, this is a good time to make sure you are in books you can read with ease. So use all you know and take charge!"

■ *Teachers, you can restate the comment about levels to match how you organize your library. Assuming that your students know their most recent reading levels, they'll probably know that they can read books on that level or ones that are easier. Eventually you may decide to set up a structure in your class so that if a reader wants to read a book that is a level or two higher than the one he or she usually reads, the reader checks with you and the two of you make a game plan for ensuring that the reader secures some extra support and doesn't spend more than a set amount of time—say, a week—with that book. But for now, you'll probably channel readers to books they can read with ease.*

As students looked over the books, I said: "I like the way Sam researched the books to find a series he already knew, and I see Isaac is checking the front and back covers.

"Readers, I love the way you've all done such smart research, and I can tell by how you're settling in to read that you're making wise choices. I want to let you get right to reading, so I'm just going to say that I know this hard work is going to make an enormous difference for you!"

Using the Reading Log as an Artifact to Help Us Reflect On and Improve Our Reading

GETTING READY

- Prepare a log for two different weeks. One should show that reading went well. It should document reading times at night and in the morning, long stretches and a rapid rate, short chunks of time reading throughout the day, and steady progress through books.

- The second log should have more fragmented time periods: perhaps an abandoned book, reading time at night that was cut short (as if one fell asleep), no time for reading for pleasure, short chunks of time and a slow rate, and some rereading (as if one had to go back).

- Bring the books your logs refer to so you can hold them up as you teach.

- Students will need to bring their reading logs for the first week or two of school.

CONNECTION

Suggest that throughout life, when we want to learn a lot, we often record data on our progress and study our data to help ourselves grow. Share an example.

"Readers, when we were thinking back to a time in our lives when we really took off as learners of any activity, and we recalled what strategies and habits we developed, I was struck by one thing in particular that some of us mentioned. It was that idea of keeping track of our progress with records or statistics. When people want to change their eating habits, for instance, they may write down everything they eat or keep track of their calories or carbohydrates or proteins. And marathon runners keep track of how much they run every day, and they build up distances across time. For runners, this data matters because it's the relationship between time and distance that can be interesting— they can see, as they run more, how their rate may also be getting faster. Swimmers keep track of their times, and baseball players watch their statistics.

"In fact, in a lot of sports we watch statistics to gauge success and progress. I know players, coaches, and fans count the number of assists an NBA player might make in a basketball game, for instance. Players, coaches, and fans keep track of these statistics, but when players are deeply involved in something, it's hard to really see it sometimes. In the middle of a game, it's probably hard for an NBA guard to know how he's doing. But later, a basketball player can look at his numbers and analyze his playing in that game and across games. These records are an artifact that lets him reflect."

Name your teaching point. Specifically, teach your students that powerful readers use artifacts to keep track of how reading is going for them.

"Readers, today I want to teach you that powerful readers use artifacts to help us reflect on and improve our reading lives. One artifact that is incredibly useful as a tool for reflection is the reading log, which helps us keep track of how reading is going for us. It's concise, it's easy to sustain, and it has tons of information that lets us reflect wisely on ourselves as readers."

TEACHING

Demonstrate how you use a record of your learning—in this case, your reading log—to reflect on how reading is going for you.

"Readers, I want to show you how useful this artifact is for a reader who wants to actively study his or her reading life. It's amazing how much information you can glean by looking at an accurate reading log. It really lets you know how reading is going for you."

I showed a log that had a few lines filled in and said, "There's nothing tricky about filling in a reading log. I imagine a lot of you have been doing this for years, and if you haven't, you can see just by looking at one that at the start and end of reading workshop we take a few seconds to jot down how long we read and the pages we completed. There's a simple space to mark home or school. We'll bring our logs between home and school; as we start reading workshop, we'll take a few seconds to fill them in accurately with the page we're starting on, and we'll finish each reading period by filling in what we read that day and how long we read. If any of you feel unfamiliar with this or want to practice filling in the log together, signal me at the end of the lesson, and we'll practice this together for a few days. It gets easy really fast, so after a day or two, you'll find it only takes a few seconds to complete."

■ *Teachers, you'll notice I didn't give a lot of instruction about how to fill in a log. Also, I made it implicit that we assume that filling in a log is easy, that it takes almost no time, and that it is a basic expectation. In classes where I see students resisting keeping a log, it's because it has become a system of discipline instead of a means by which readers reflect on their reading lives. You can't discipline kids into becoming passionate readers. It's not the log we care about—it's that readers reflect on how reading is going for them, and generally they need artifacts in order to do that well. It's hard to keep track of progress in any activity without records. Sometimes, students want to invent their own form of a log. Middle- and high-school students, for instance, have been using goodreads.com, which lets them keep their reading log online as a social network. I feel about that as I do about eBooks—as long as you're reading, I don't really care about what whether it's electronic or paper. In the case of a log, the form needs to be one that kids and teachers can look at quickly to assess how reading is going for each student. That's why I generally have one simple paper log so that it only takes a second to fill out and a minute to look across.*

I looked at the log and added, "What's really interesting about this artifact is how it lets us reflect on how reading is going for us. I have a log here for two different weeks of my reading life. Remember how we've been reading on the edge of our seats, noticing what there is to be noticed in a story because we are using our expertise to read alertly? Well, you can read a reading log this way. Use what you know about how reading goes—how we try to read at home and at school, how we try to choose books that keep us reading passionately, how we do our best but sometimes we falter. In a way, we read a reading log like a detective. Watch me do this work."

I had one log on chart paper—just sketched—for four days. It included the date, the title, the time, and the pages. This log showed that I was reading a series and was devouring the books, reading avidly, tucking reading in at night and in the morning, and sometimes even reading in the afternoon on the bus or in the car. There were long stretches late at night and fifteen minutes when I woke up. Also, I both read for long periods of time and got a lot of reading done in that time. My rate was strong; I moved rapidly through books.

■ *I chose to use* The Lightning Thief *in this class because it was a book that a lot of other students were devouring, one that I knew they would love and read with ease. In another class, I might have used* Diary of a Wimpy Kid *or a book from another popular series.*

"Hmm, let's see. I'll start here, on this Saturday. It looks as if I was reading *The Lightning Thief,* which is the first Percy Jackson book. I started it in the morning, and wow, right away I read for over an hour, and I got all the way to page 89! Later that night I picked up the book again, and I read from 10:30 at night until after midnight! And I was squeezing extra reading time in, too. I'm thinking this information tells me that reading was going really well for me—I was reading a lot, I seemed to love this book, and it kept me up late at night. I also got a lot of pages read when I did read."

I looked up from the log and said, "Readers, do you see how I looked at details such as when I was reading, how much I got done, and whether I chose to make extra reading time? I even looked to see whether the book put me to sleep or kept me awake at night."

ACTIVE INVOLVEMENT

Contrast this example with a vastly different one in order to emphasize what the process of reflecting on learning can reveal.

"I'm going to show you a few other days of my log."

This second log was also for just a few days, this one showing that I read at night but fell asleep after a few pages, that I got only few pages read in one sitting, that I seemed to be doing a lot of rereading, that all week I was barely moving through the book, and that I didn't choose to squeeze in extra reading time. It's helpful if the students can see both logs at the same time to compare the details—it encourages them to value these details.

■ *It's in the dramatic difference in these statistics that your readers will see how valuable statistics are. I'm a strong reader, but it doesn't mean that reading is always going well for me or that I'm in a book that is helping me get a lot of reading done. You'll want to invent a page for your log that shows a time when reading wasn't going so well for you.*

"I'm going to give you a chance to try this now. Really read the way you know how, with extra alertness, like a baseball expert watching a game, like a detective visiting a crime scene, like an expert reader being engaged in a story. Tell your partner what you surmise as you read these logs. What can you say about how reading was going for me when you use these artifacts as tools?"

■ *Teachers, this activity really galvanizes students to reconsider how much information you get from a reading log. Also, they like looking at our reading lives for a change. In writing workshop, we often show them how to revise our writing by showing them our own work; here we show them our reading life, and we consider how to revise it. They leaned forward, pointing eagerly to different parts, just as they would with a nonfiction text. Some began to say that I must have really liked the Percy Jackson series. Some said it had been just like that for them when they read it. Some noticed that on a few days, I read more than once. They were horrified as they looked at my second week. They suggested the book was really hard, maybe too hard. They noticed that I fell asleep quickly, that the book didn't keep me awake.*

Pull your readers together and share insights that you hope will help the class see the value of mining reading logs for information on their own reading life.

"Readers, let's come together again. Wow! I listened to you use these artifacts to reflect on my reading life, and it's incredible how much detail you came up with and how much you had to say about how reading was going for me. All of you surmised that reading was going really well for me on this first week. The log gave you a lot of important clues—that the books seemed to be keeping me awake, that I was really devouring them, that I was making extra reading time whenever I could to read more. Readers, that's what this artifact does—it tells us how reading has been going for us. You're right about that week. I loved this series, I was reading all the time, and I got a ton of reading done. I remember looking at my clock on Saturday night and telling myself, after midnight, that I needed to stop reading and turn the light off—but then I looked at the book and said, 'Just a little, little more!' Then I chose the book *Anathem*, which is by an author I love who writes these huge, long books. A lot of you noticed that every night I seemed to only read for a few minutes, and for a few pages, and then I went to sleep. That's sometimes how you know a book is too hard—you feel tired as you read."

I held up the books as I was talking. Then I added: "Readers, I have to say that during this whole week of reading, I didn't really feel any different than I had during that first week. After all, I was still the same reader, the same person. It's only when I use this artifact to reflect, the way a basketball player would look at his numbers after the game, that I see that reading wasn't going so well for me this week. In fact, when I compare different weeks on my log, I find that for this one week, I was barely reading. All sorts of things seem off when I look at my numbers. It's not just that I was reading for short amounts of time; I also seemed to be reading really slowly and getting just a few pages done. Yikes! I'll really have to think more about why that is happening and what I can do about it."

LINK

Remind them of all the information they just gleaned from studying that log, and send them off to analyze their own logs before getting started with reading.

"Readers, I hope that you can see that keeping reading logs as an artifact of our reading lives can really help us do more reflection and have more agency as readers. We used this artifact to compare how reading was going during different times. Learners use records of their work in all sorts of areas—that's one way we help ourselves grow! In this case, it was really smart how you thought about the possible reasons for what was happening for me as a reader. It was also incredible how many details you gleaned about my interest, my reading rate, and my habits as a reader across time.

"I think for us, as readers who are becoming increasingly powerful, the important thing about these logs will not be filling them in—that's a given, and we can do that in two seconds—but about how we read them in order to reflect. I'm picturing you in a few weeks, poring over your logs the way you pored over mine, really reading these artifacts as an expert so you can take charge of your reading life. With that in mind, as you go off to read, I'll be admiring all the important statistics you keep in your log, and I'll be ready to listen to anyone who suggests smart systems for doing this quickly and well each day. Off you go!"

SESSION V

Making Purposeful Choices About Our Methods for Retelling

CONNECTION

Tell your readers about times when you've listened to them retell stories or films, or retell one yourself, suggesting that there are lots of different ways to retell a story.

"Readers, recently I've been listening in during some of your casual conversations when you are talking about movies or television shows you've seen or about really favorite books you want to share with a friend. And here's what I noticed: you have different methods for retelling. Sometimes you retold the big events; other times you zoomed in on certain characters and told what they wanted and what got in their way. So interesting. Your conversations have reinforced my theory that there are a lot of different ways to retell a story. I think that if we consider the method of retelling as an important choice, this will be a significant way to have more agency as readers. Making informed and purposeful choices about our retelling method will be another way for us to do more powerful reading work."

Name your teaching point. Specifically, teach your readers that retelling is one way to make sense of and hold on to story elements.

"Readers, today I want to teach you that telling someone else, or ourselves, what has happened so far in our story is a crucial way to make sense of and hold on to that story. It may be some of the most important reading work we do because we have to think back over the parts of the story, decide what's important so far, and then make decisions about what to share. One way we can work harder at this important work is to make *conscious decisions* about *how* to retell a story—it's part of having agency as a reader, matching our *method* for retelling to the reading work we want to do."

TEACHING

Demonstrate one method for retelling a book—doing a sequential event-based retelling. Organize your readers to study your method for retelling and to share observations of it.

"Let me show you how this works. I'm going to demonstrate a few different ways readers can retell a story. Research the way I do this, okay? Ready?"

I held up a book I was reading. "Let's see. Imagine this: I'm in a book club that is reading *The Lightning Thief.* It's a complicated book. It can get confusing fast. So this week, I'm thinking of starting our club conversation with someone just retelling what happened so far. It's worth it to do this because the story gets confusing, and I don't know yet what's important and what's not. Hmm, that means I need to remember the big events, put them in order (or sequence), and retell what actually happened.

"Let's see. *First,* we meet Percy Jackson, the narrator, and he is riding a bus into New York City to go to the Metropolitan Museum on a field trip." I used my fingers to emphasize "First, Next, Then, And then, Finally" as I retold across my fingers. "*Next,* we find out that he's been kicked out of lots of private schools because strange things happen to him. *Then* Nancy Bobofit, a bully, torments Percy's best friend, Grover, who doesn't walk well. *And then* Percy somehow causes her to end up in the fountain in front of the museum. *Finally,* when they are in the museum, Percy's teacher, Mrs. Dodds, turns out to be a demon and attacks him! Whew! It's a lot to keep track of because so much happens in just the first chapter.

"Did you catch on to the way I was trying to retell the story? Did you notice my method for retelling?" I put down the book and said, "Quick, tell your partner how I retold that story and perhaps why I chose that way."

Recap what you hope students noticed about that sort of retelling; then set them up to observe and talk in partners about a different sort of retelling, this one being an idea-based retelling, where you recap the parts of the story that go with an idea you are growing.

"Nicely done, readers. It makes sense to choose the step-by-step method to retell the big events of the story in some detail when the book is complicated and there is a lot going on."

I picked up the book again and began: "Here's another method. Imagine this. I've read farther in *The Lightning Thief*. I've finished Chapter 3, and I'm getting ready to retell it to my partner. I'm thinking I'll use a different method. Ready to research how I go about it? Okay, hmm, I'm at the end of Chapter 3. I've read enough now to have an idea of something that seems really important in this story. One idea I have so far is that there is magic—that the kids are not actually completely human and that their world has magic in it. That's what feels important so far. So let's see. I could retell the parts that show that there's magic. Hmm, in Chapter 1, the big thing that feels important is that Percy's teacher turns out to be a demon and attacks him. Yes, that feels like the most magical and most important thing that happened in the beginning. Then in Chapter 2, the most important magical thing is that Percy sees three old ladies and that one of them takes out scissors and cuts the yarn she is holding, snipping the thread, which turns out to mean someone is going to die—it's a magical life thread. Then in Chapter 3, Grover reveals that he is a satyr. He is Percy's best friend, and he has cloven hooves. Let's see, yes, when I think about what's important so far, I think those are the most magical and most important parts."

■ *You'll want to repeat the phrase "what's important so far" to differentiate from a sequential event-based retelling.*

"Researchers, quick, turn and share your research. What did I do this time, and how was this method different from the first method for retelling?"

■ *I'm tempted to do a third kind of retelling but decide to save it for a teaching share. You might want to do the same. After asking students to research me, I do a retelling that is meant to be promotional. For example, I say, "So I'm reading this incredible book called* The Lightning Thief. *It starts with this boy, named Percy Jackson, who is always in trouble at school, and he doesn't know why. But here's the unusual thing about Percy." I made my voice low and full of suspense. "His father is Poseidon, the god of the sea. That makes Percy a half-blood. It also makes Percy prey for demons, who want to destroy him and all half-bloods. It starts with Percy going to the Metropolitan Museum in New York. But New York is an unpredictable, dangerous place. Percy is preoccupied with the bullies in his class, especially this girl named Nancy Bobofit, who torments Percy and his friend Grover. But little does Percy know that Nancy is nothing compared to the demons he'll encounter that day. You never know who is human, who is a god, and who is a demon, nor does Percy know yet that he has special gifts, one of which is a sword, which he'll use today." I put the book down again.*

■ *When students talk about this third kind of retelling, they'll note that this method involved telling the story in a storyteller's voice, really making it dramatic. Some noticed how I included enough information to set the scene but withheld information about what happens next to build tension. I didn't wreck the story by giving it all away. When you do this, picture that you're making a movie trailer or that you're doing the kind of "book sale" that you probably do often in your classroom.*

ACTIVE INVOLVEMENT

Summarize the methods of retelling you've demonstrated, and give your students a chance to try them.

"Friends, I love how closely you observe. What skilled researchers you are becoming! Being able to really *see* what someone does well, analyze it, and then attempt to do it yourself is an incredible skill to develop in any endeavor. It's one way that athletes and gamers and musicians and mathematicians get better. In fact, some researchers focus just on the research part, and they become coaches or scientists or authors. So from your research, I heard you describe two different methods so far that we might employ for retelling."

I counted on my fingers. "The first method was retelling the main events in sequence. This helped me untangle all the parts of this complicated story so that I wouldn't miss anything. The second method was just retelling the parts related to an important idea I was developing. This was a good method once I had started to have some clear ideas about what seemed important to me as a reader."

"Here's the thing, readers. I prepared slightly differently when I chose these different methods. As I retold the story in my head—and even flipped back through the chapters I had read so far—I was using different lenses. The first time I looked through the book bit by bit, trying to remember everything that had happened. The second time I thought of the biggest idea I have about the book and then quickly flipped through my Post-its to find parts that related to that idea.

"Let's give you a chance to try this now. We're not going to retell our stories—we'll do that at the end of reading workshop when you have time to talk to your partner. Right now, why don't you pick up your book and then think about what method might make sense for you as a reader of this story." Once students had made this choice, I said, "You'll actually do this retelling at the end of today's workshop, but meanwhile you can read with this in mind."

Link

Send them off to read, reminding them that retelling gives readers an important way to hold on to a story and that they'll always want to think "How will I retell?" before just launching into a retelling.

"Readers, off you go. I'll be curious to listen in to your retellings later. From now on, remember that retelling gives us an important way to hold on to our stories, and remember too that it is important to consider the method for retelling that you'll use and to make a smart choice about matching this method to your reading work."

PART TWO

Reading Between the Lines and Coauthoring the Text

SESSION VI

Reading Between the Lines

GETTING READY

- You'll probably want to use a story that you've already introduced in read-aloud. We'll use the first few pages of *Edward's Eyes*.

- It could be, however, that you are not intending to read the whole text aloud and that you will be using just the first page or two of any book from your classroom library to demonstrate how to read between the lines at the start of any book. Good texts for this are *Edward's Eyes, Freak the Mighty, Maniac McGee, Hatchet,* and *Because of Winn-Dixie.* They are all productive texts for this work because they will reward the intense inferring of reading between the lines.

- You will want a piece of chart paper up so that you can record main points from your teaching.

- Students will need to bring their independent reading books to the meeting area.

CONNECTION

Recall the metaphor of a watching a baseball game with someone who really understands baseball, and compare reading a game to reading a book.

"Readers, I've been thinking more about the comparison between watching a baseball game and reading a story. Several times, I've found myself at Yankee Stadium. Picture this: we're at Yankee Stadium. We've been there for three hours. The game is still going on. There have been some hits but only a few runs. Here's the thing. Unless there are lots of runs, I think nothing is happening. I'm missing the nuances (the subtle details) of the game. And you know what I end up saying after a while? I say that I'm bored!

"My friend, meanwhile, finds the same game fascinating—because he's a better reader of baseball than I am. He has seen all this drama and tension in between plays that I missed. I say, 'Nothing has happened!' He says, 'Are you kidding? Have you seen how that pitcher is dominating? Isn't it beautiful how he keeps preventing those stolen bases, too? Don't you think that the guy on third right now is incredibly gutsy and frustrated and that he's probably going to run soon?' It's like he's at a different game than I am. He knows how to read between the runs in baseball. I would love to be able to read baseball like that.

"Here's what I realized. I realized that baseball games, like books, have a *text* and a *subtext*."

I wrote those two words on a piece of chart paper and went on. "The *text* of a story is what happens—what the words say. The *subtext* is what those words suggest or imply— the secrets of the story. Let's imagine these words applying to baseball. At a baseball game, there's the score—it is easily visible to everyone in the audience. So the score is like the text of the game, and the obvious moves are also part of the text of the game. I can read that text! I get the score, I see when someone makes a hit, and I read the text of the game.

But meanwhile there's also a *subtext*—a kind of secret meaning in the details of the game that is only available to baseball fans who know what these details suggest. I say, 'Oh, he is stepping away from the base.' That's what is happening—the text of the game. My friend reads the game and says, 'He is stepping away from the base and leaning low, which *suggests* that he is the kind of baseball player who thinks about stealing bases.' My friend can read the subtext—the secret meaning of the game within the game—as well as the text. If I decide to work hard on becoming better at understanding baseball, one of the first things I want to work at is learning to read between the runs."

Name your teaching point. Specifically, teach your students that powerful readers read for the text but also for the *subtext*—for the subtle and secret meanings hidden between the lines.

"Readers, today I want to teach you that one way to lift our reading to the next level is to concentrate on reading for *subtext* as well as for *text.* One way to do this is, at the start of a story, is to work really hard to read between the lines, to imagine what the details *suggest,* or imply, about the characters or the place. Stories tend to start by giving lots of details either about the characters or about the place."

Teaching

Demonstrate reading for subtext by reading between the lines and thinking hard about the details we learn about the characters in the read-aloud text.

"Let me show you what this looks like. I'm going to read the first part of Chapter 1 of *Edward's Eyes*. It's the part where the narrator, Jake, is telling us about his family. And that's it, readers. That's the *text*: Jake tells us about his family. That's what happens. But the subtext is what the details suggest, or imply. In this case, the story starts with lots of details that Jake gives us about the characters in his family. So watch me work hard at reading between the lines, to really see what these details suggest, or imply, about these characters. I'm going to be working hard to build a 'subtext,' which means to use my imagination and infer what these details suggest. Ready?"

I slowly read aloud the first few lines of the story:

> *My earliest memory begins with Edward, as if somehow I have no life to remember before him. The memory comes to me often, mostly at night, but more often during the day now, surprising me.*

"Let me just say that line again:"

> *My earliest memory begins with Edward, as if somehow I have no life to remember before him.*

I looked up from the book and said slowly, "So the narrator, whose name we don't even know yet, clearly has this incredible love for Edward. Just think of saying that: "as if somehow I have no life to remember before him." I'd be thrilled if someone felt that way about me! It seems such an overwhelming force, this love. It's not a small love; it's something gigantic. And maybe there is something so memorable about Edward, as well, that everything that came before him gets put in the shadows and is never remembered again, once he comes into the narrator's life. Wow! So far, these words suggest that there is something amazing about Edward and something incredible about this love. What else?"

I paused and read the lines again, as if mesmerized by them. (And I am—I love these lines. I adore the way they imply this *overwhelming* love.) "He could have said, 'I don't remember much before Edward.' But he doesn't; he says that it's 'as if somehow I have no life to remember before him.' That makes me think that the narrator is poetic. He uses words beautifully. He is expressive.

"Let me move to the next line:"

The memory comes to me often, mostly at night, but more often during the day now, surprising me.

"When I read that again, it feels as if the narrator is almost haunted by these memories of Edward. Yes, that's the right word, haunted, and the dreams of Edward come at night and during the day."

I lowered the book.

Tell your readers what you are doing, how you are building up the meaning as you read—you are reading for the subtext.

"See how I did that, readers? The story doesn't say that the narrator is poetic and very loving and that he is haunted by memories of Edward. That's a subtext that I am building as I read. I assumed that in good books, details matter, and I tried to imagine and infer to read between the lines of the story."

I picked up the book again.

"I'm going to keep going just a little bit farther, so you can get even more of a feeling for how hard you can work at this and how much you can elevate your reading to new levels. I'll read slowly, and if you're having ideas as I read, go ahead and jot them down if you'd like, or give a thumbs up, or look at your partner."

I read:

It is a very early memory. Not as early as the artist, Salvador Dali, my sister Sola tells me. He could remember when he was inside his mother, Sola says, where the world looked flat, like squashed egg.

But this is my memory:

Maeve and Jack have just brought baby Edward home from the hospital. Maeve and Jack are our parents, but we don't call them Mom or Dad, except for Edward, who when he learns to talk will speak to them in a formal manner, a bit English. "Motha and Fatha," he will say in his little tin voice.

Here's the scene:

Maeve and Jack walk in the front door, Maeve carrying baby Edward in his green blanket, packed tightly like a pickle in plastic. I am only three years old, but I can tell from their faces that Maeve and Jack want us to love Edward. They look a little happy, but

not too happy; a little fearful as if they are adding an unwanted puppy to our large lit-
ter. Sola, the oldest, is used to this. Edward is the fourth baby they've brought home to
her. Will, seven, is interested for only the barest moment, then he goes off to read a book
in the corner, to spend the day happily in his own head. Wren, not yet five, reaches out
to brush Edward's face with her hand. Maeve and Jack like this, a physical sign of affec-
tion. They look at me then.

I pondered and paused as I read, and the students watched closely, sometimes putting a thumb in the air or nudging their partner or jotting. I nodded to them quietly but kept up the intensity of my own mind work, striving to give them a model of a reader working really hard to make meaning. I knew I needed to inspire them to lift the level of their reading, and I had to give a mesmerizing performance. I read once and then kept my eyes on the lines as I talked, saying some lines aloud and commenting, constructing this subtext aloud.

"The memory is not, he says, as early as the artist Salvador Dali, his sister Sola says. Let's see, so the narrator has a sister named Sola, and she is the kind of kid who knows the names of famous artists—and the narrator remembers, too. In fact, I'm starting to wonder if the narrator is the kind of kid who remembers everything! So let's see. The text says that he has an early memory of Edward. The subtext I've built is that he is poetic, extremely loving, incredibly attached to Edward, and observant. What next? He calls his parents Maeve and Jack, which is unusual. Then the next part of the text is Maeve and Jack bringing Edward home. What's the subtext here? Hmm, the narrator says that he is only three but he 'can tell from their faces that Maeve and Jack want us to love Edward.' What an unusual thing to say. So even at three, he was really perceptive. He could read people's faces. And it seems as if his parents were unsure if the kids would love Edward. I guess the next line explains that—there are already a lot of kids. Then I had to read just for the text for a minute. There was so much information. I learned that there was Sola, the eldest, and then Will, then Wren, then the narrator, and now Edward. Let's see, any subtext here? Hmm, Sola seems uninterested in another baby. Will likes to read and seems to live in his own imagination."

Name what you have done in a way that is transferable to another text on another day.

I looked up. "Okay, readers, see how much I've constructed as I read between the lines? In the story *I'm* reading, the narrator is poetic, loving, observant, perceptive, and incredibly attached to Edward. His parents seem unsure about bringing another child home. There's an elder sister, who is pretty much bored by more kids, and another brother, who lives in his imagination. In fact, even as I retell it this way, I realize that maybe the narrator was lonely, even with all these other kids around. That's the story I'm reading! And we're only a few paragraphs in. One reason I wanted to show you the beginning of the story was that I know we don't have any more information yet—all the words we have to build from are right here, and look how much reading work we can do! When you work hard to read between the lines, it's like you're reading a different story, a richer, denser, more intriguing one, where every detail has implications. In fact, it's almost as if you are coauthoring the story, building up the meaning as you construct this subtext from the words the author gives you."

ACTIVE INVOLVEMENT

Summarize what will happen in the upcoming passage, suggesting that the sequence of events is not all that dramatic. It's the subtext that will matter, and you hope they listen for it as you continue reading. Channel students to stop and jot and later to share.

"I could see, readers, that you were already having ideas as I reread that last part of the story. Some of you were looking at your partner or jotting or nodding as I read. In fact, some of you seemed as if you were on the edge of your seats. That means so much to me, to see you read that way. It's an entirely different way to read. Let's keep going a bit. I'm going to reread a bit more of the story aloud. We're still just in the first few pages. I'll tell you already what the text is—it's where his parents put Edward in his arms. That's the text. That's what happens. But let's see what else you have to say based on how the narrator explains things, what words he chooses, what details you notice that seem to suggest ideas about the characters. Let's see you read between the lines for the subtext of this part of the story. Ready?"

I waited until all eyes were on me, and I reread slowly, sometimes repeating a line when I saw they were excited about it, such as "Sola, having heard years of this talk, unscrews the top of her fingernail polish calmly. Will goes back to his book" and "His eyes are the dark mud-blue of the night sky, but there are surprising little flecks of gold in them:"

"Jake?" says Maeve.

They wait. I peer down at Edward, my face close to his.

"He will poop all day long. And throw up," Will says.

Wren bursts into laughter at the sound of the word, "poop." Sola, having heard years of this talk, unscrews the top of her fingernail polish calmly. Will goes back to his book. He turns a page.

"Jake?" repeats Maeve.

And when I don't say anything she hands me Edward. Just like that. As if he were a bundle or a book. I remember sitting very still, so scared I can't move. And then it happens. Edward opens his eyes and looks at me. His eyes are the dark mud-blue of the night sky, but there are surprising little flecks of gold in them. They stare right into my eyes. My heart begins to beat faster. I try to say something. I want to say that Edward is so beautiful…the most beautiful thing I have ever seen. I want to say that I love him more than anything or anyone I know. But I am only three, and when I try to talk I can't say all those words.

"His eyes," I begin.

As I read, the students jotted or whispered to each other. I gave them a chance to jot for a moment as I finished reading or to think hard, quietly, about what they had heard.

"Readers, I can tell you've been working hard to read between the lines. Why don't you compare your ideas with those of your partner? What subtext have you constructed from this part? What do these details imply or suggest about the characters? I'm going to listen in as you compare your ideas."

They talked eagerly. They compared Sola, who turns to nail polish, to Will, who turns to a book. They noted that Wren seems young and still silly—she laughs at the word "poop." They were struck by the words Jake uses to describe Edward's eyes and the force of Jake's love for him.

■ *This section of the book is good for this work because it gives so much implicit information about the characters—it's easy for kids to read between the lines here.*

Name what you heard partners saying in a way that elicits more insights, especially insights that are transferable to another day and another book.

"Readers, I'd like to pull you back, even though I hate to interrupt the intense literary analysis you are doing. Yes, that's what it's called when you read like that. When you assume that every word matters and you work incredibly hard to read between the lines, you are reading and analyzing at the same time. I heard you saying that the words suggested that Sola and Will are very different and that they reinforced the notion that Jake, the narrator, is poetic and observant, that he feels love very, very deeply for Edward. In fact, he loves Edward more than any other member of his family.

"That's subtext, readers! Nowhere in the text does it say that Sola and Will were different or that Jake was lonely. As the books you read get more complicated, they demand an imaginative reader, a reader who honors the words, works hard to read between the lines, and thus has access to the subtext the words create. That was incredible reading work you were doing."

LINK

Use the link to help your readers consider *when* this strategy might be useful.

"Readers, eventually this kind of reading becomes automatic. You'll be the kind of readers who are reading between the lines, being alert to details and constructing subtext, right from the first moment of the story. But when you are working hard to improve at something, it's often helpful to have someone tell you when you should strive particularly hard at this difficult work. I hope to become the kind of baseball fan who can read between the lines all the time, but in the beginning, I may need someone to nudge me and say, 'Watch right now! It will be worth it!' So that's what I'm saying to you, I guess. It's worth it to read this way at the very start of a book. You can do it anytime in the book, of course, but if you are a plot junkie, reading to find out what happens, and you want to know places to make yourself practice this work, go back and reread the first pages of your book or look really closely at the first pages of your next book."

SESSION VII

Imagining the Scenes in Our Stories

GETTING READY

- Read *Edward's Eyes* through Chapter 4. You'll read two scenes from this chapter during this minilesson.

CONNECTION

Ask students to recall a time when a vivid scene from a film or show stayed with them. Point out that this happens to readers with books, as well.

"Readers, have you ever seen a film that was perhaps too frightening, and you wished later that you hadn't seen it because there's one image, or scene, that stays in your mind and you can't forget it?"

I paused and quietly shivered, thinking of Freddy Kruger and Jack Nicholson or that awful, unforgettable shower scene Hitchcock gave us, to haunt us forever whenever we are alone and hear noises while the water runs hot. Some of the students nodded and shivered, too. You could see this struck a chord. Then I went on: "That's happened to me a few times, and I stay far, far away from horror movies now because I know that some image might haunt me forever—that's called an 'indelible' image or memory. On the other hand, sometimes you leave a movie with an image that is incredibly beautiful, and then it's like this gift that stays with you. I'll never forget this one image from *Up*, for instance, when the house rises in the air, with the thousands of balloons lifting it over Manhattan, and the little Boy Scout clinging to the porch.

"Just give a nod if you can think of an image, right now, that you loved in a movie."

Slowly, the students began to nod, and some whispered to their partner. I said, "Readers, this can happen with books also. I know this has happened for you. Imagine this: you are reading a story, and perhaps you're thinking about how the characters feel or about what their relationships are, but suddenly what you begin to see in your head is a vivid picture of a scene, with all the details, maybe with even with the smells and the sounds. It's as if you were brought into the scene—that's how detailed it is. Often, friends, those images, or pictures, will stay with you long after you close the book. So many of us can close our eyes and picture the 'great green room' from *Goodnight Moon.* Or how many of you, if I say 'the barn where Charlotte made her web,' immediately see that web, sparkling with dew, and Charlotte creating a word in the center to save Wilbur's life? How many of you, when I say 'Hogwarts,' see soaring towers, bright flags blowing in the wind, a rocky outcrop, and perhaps students whizzing by on brooms?

"Those images sometimes stay with us long after we have forgotten the title of a book or the main character's name or even the author. It will be the picture that stays, and when we think of that picture, it will bring back all the rest."

Name your teaching point. Specifically, teach your students that readers unleash their imaginations as they read in order to create vivid images from their stories.

"Readers, today I want to teach you that the kinds of books you are reading now demand imaginative readers, readers who will pause and create those vivid images. One way we construct those images is to work hard at releasing our imaginations as we read, paying attention to details in the story and filling in with more imagined sights, sounds, and atmosphere until it's as if we can envision the moment as a scene in a film."

Teaching

Demonstrate how readers often imagine and picture scenes when the action is slower, where the author seems to encourage them to pause and slow down.

"Sometimes, friends, if we're not careful, we can expect the author to do all the work as we read, as if all the information will be right there, on the page, and all we have to do is keep moving our eyes over the print. But the truth is, books aren't like that—especially the kinds of more complicated books you're reading now. These books demand imaginative readers. The author will give you the *opportunity* to linger, to create scenes in *collaboration* with him or her. One way our reading work is becoming so much more complicated, in fact, is that *we* are responsible, in so many ways, for the text coming alive. The more we bring to the book and the harder we work as readers, the more it will give to us.

"Right now, let's think about what releasing our imaginations as we read means. For me, when I think about doing this work, I look for parts of the story where the action seems to slow down for a minute, and we get a lot of details about the setting, about the place. I linger over these details. I imagine what the place looks like. I also imagine what the place *feels* like. I allow myself to be entranced, something that perhaps we don't do enough of in school. I consciously release my imagination, knowing that it will call to mind images from my memories—small moments I've experienced, movies I've seen, other stories I've read—that might help me bring this scene in the story I'm reading into vivid detail.

"Let's give this a try. I'll get us started. In Chapter 4 of *Edward's Eyes*, there is this one moment when the children open a box of books, and they all know it's summer because they are so eager to choose particular books to read for the summer. That seems like a really pretty scene, and I slowed down on that one. Then there's the next scene, which is Maeve setting the table. I can often tell that it's going to be worth it to slow down and linger because there will be a pause in the dialogue. When lots of people are talking, you tend to think about the implications of what they're saying. But when the author pauses and gives you instead some description, that's probably going to be a place you can fill in with your imagination and perhaps create an unforgettable scene.

"I'll read this part aloud to get us started at releasing our imaginations:"

> In the summer Maeve tossed a flowered tablecloth over the television set, serving teas in the afternoons with little cucumber and watercress sandwiches with the crusts cut off, bowls of chocolates and jelly beans, mostly red, and cookies. There were black and green olives, and salads with strange names like endive and radicchio with raspberry and walnut dressing, and for all of us, cakes that were Maeve's trademark. She was not a good cook, Maeve, but she made tea cakes with chocolate and marshmallow and almond cream icing topped with candied decoration. I don't think they were baked. Wren once said that they had to harden out of boredom, standing around in the summer heat.

I put down the book. "Readers, can't you just picture this? There's something so sweet about this picture—a television set, all covered with a flowered tablecloth. I'm picturing that it's probably faded white with pink roses on it. And on top of it are a lot of small delicate dishes; that's what I picture at an afternoon tea, not plastic, but china. On the dishes are delicate sandwiches, and in the bowls are small treats such as chocolates, cookies, and jelly beans. The room will be warm from the summer heat, but not stifling. There are curtains blowing in a breeze. Outside, you can hear the waves crashing as the tide comes in, and the air smells like salt. (I remember they live by the sea!) Sweetest of all are Maeve's cakes: pink and white and gooey inside but rock hard outside—crystallized in sugar icing. While everyone reads or plays baseball, Maeve is in the kitchen, getting all of this ready, to pull the family together to this spot. I love this—it feels like one of those moments that capture this whole family—how Jake loves to describe his family, how Maeve loves them all, how they cling to each other in this house by the sea.

"Friends, to do this work, I thought about dishes I've seen in restaurants and movies, and I let my mind roam over them until I had an image I adored. I drifted into the room in my imagination, and because it felt hot, I imagined an open window, with a sea breeze blowing through it. I remembered from earlier in the book that the house is right by the sea—remember how the dog comes back and shakes on them? I imagined, too, that this is a peaceful, happy moment for Jake's family—a moment when they gather around these special items on this warm summer afternoon. I didn't let any bugs in to mar the picture, just the warm breezes, the salt air, the hard tea cakes, and Maeve's love."

■ *Teachers, play it up—really use your imagination to fill your scene with the physical details from this part and from earlier parts of the book. Fill in, as well, the emotional atmosphere. Your enthusiasm for this work will inspire your students.*

ACTIVE INVOLVEMENT

Read another scene, one that is easy for kids to envision. Ask readers to turn and talk afterwards.

"It is really cool to do this, readers. It's like being a director or a filmmaker yourself—someone hands you a script, and you set the scene. You create the mood. First, you gather up all the details. Then you let your mind drift until it recaptures sights, sounds, scents, details that you want to include. Trust that your imagination, of its own accord, will—if you let it—roam back and collect parts of the image for you from other stories and films you may barely be able to remember as well as from earlier in this story. You saw how I filled in the small missing details until I had a vivid picture and a *mood.* Let's give you a chance to try this. Remember to really work at releasing your imagination—you are collaborating with the author here. I'll read aloud the next part of this scene, and you close your eyes. Really try to picture it. When I stop, pause a moment to let the image sink in, and then turn and describe it to your partner. Partners, you can fill in the details together. I'm going to start just after they eat the cakes. Ready?"

I turned to my storytelling voice, which is lower and slower than the one I use other times:

> [We] were so energized by sugar that we went outside to run around violently in the heat, sometimes playing soccer. Before the sun went down Maeve would come out to hit us baseballs with the fungo bat. We chased baseballs until by dusk we lay in exhausted heaps.

Out over the water there was an orange full moon above, a watery one below. Edward put his head on my shoulder, and the air was still. Then, one by one, the lightning bugs came out.

"Are you asleep, Edward?" I whispered.

"Yes, I am," said Edward, making me laugh.

Sometimes Maeve and Jack would lead us off to bed. But most times, if there wasn't rain coming, they would toss blankets over us and we'd sleep outside, Edward's head on my shoulder, his sweet-smelling breath soft on my neck.

I looked up for a moment, saying, "Wait, picture it, wait. Okay, turn and tell your partner—take turns saying a little and listening, okay?" The students turned to each other. Some recalled times when they had slept outside, on scout and camping trips, and how the bugs would sometimes bite or how they'd hear noises—but here, they said, the kids felt safe, and probably the sea breeze kept the bugs off.

■ *Children will often mimic some of the same imaginative work that you do, feeding off your beginning.*

"Readers, I love how you really worked at releasing your imaginations so that you honored this story and almost created this scene with the author. I heard you describing the whine of mosquitoes, the cool night air on your face, the way Edward's hair would tickle your neck. You made this scene magical, one we'll never forget. That is the way Jake feels about it, too, you can tell—he wants us to remember what it felt like to sleep by the sea with Edward by our side and our brothers and sisters around us."

LINK

Send kids off to read, first inspiring them with notions of how using their imaginations in any endeavor is one way to elevate their work and then leaving them with another vivid image from the book.

"It's beautiful reading work, right? Sometimes it can feel as if we end up putting aside our imaginations as we become adults. But the truth is that it will be your imagination that is one of your greatest gifts as a scientist, a dancer, or anything, really, including being a powerful reader. The same imaginative skills you used to fill in this scene are the ones the doctor uses to imagine how a cancer is spreading from the information she accumulates as she reads the X-rays and MRIs. It is the same imagination that lets the air traffic controller imagine the planes filling the sky as he looks at his radar.

"If you learn to release your imagination, you'll always see more, feel more, and have richer, denser experiences. And this will be especially true with your books. You'll linger in parts such as these where there is little dialogue, and you'll construct an indelible image. You'll close a book, and those images will stay with you.

"I'll remember Edward always, not for how the book ends but for this picture of him sleeping by the sea in his brother's arms, the fireflies blinking and the rain holding off. I know you'll always do this work now, too, readers. Be extra alert to those parts of your book where it would clearly be worth it to linger. Perhaps you'd like to mark some of those parts and describe them in your reader's notebooks or tell your partners about them—or tell me. I love to watch an imagination at work. Off you go."

SESSION VIII

Imagining the Moments in Between the Scenes

> **GETTING READY**
> - Read *Edward's Eyes* through the end of Chapter 4.
> - You'll read the beginning of Chapter 5 in the lesson.

CONNECTION

Recall your recent work imagining scenes, and tell students that readers also imagine the moments in between scenes.

"Readers, we've been working hard at our reading, really concentrating on strategies and habits that will make our reading practices more powerful. I see you, now, thinking about what method you'll use to retell your stories. You are much more alert to the nuances of the stories you are reading. You are developing agency as readers; you are becoming more powerful almost every day, and it's because you are working at it.

"Recently, we worked on using our imaginations to create vivid images as we read, particularly in those parts where the story seems to *want* us to linger—there is a pause in the dialogue or action and some description to help us get started. Friends, I want to share a secret about something you may already be doing as a reader, and it is that imaginative readers also work fast and furiously at imagining the scenes that *aren't* written in their books. One chapter may end with the kids falling asleep on a grassy slope, and the next chapter may open with them playing baseball behind the barn. A powerful reader quickly imagines that the children awoke, had some breakfast, perhaps did some chores, and then gathered together to play. I'm going to call these the 'in-between' scenes—they happen in between the scenes that are written down.

"The author counts on you to do this. She doesn't want to recount the mundane details of breakfast. When the author shifts, on the other hand, to a new setting or time, she hopes that your imagination, from reading hundreds of stories, knows how to fill in the parts that are untold. If last time we said that readers were like a director who takes a script and creates a full scene, this time I want to show you how readers can act like screenwriters, writing the moments in between scenes.

"Readers, as your books get longer and more complicated, there will often be longer gaps between chapters. Sometimes years may pass, or you'll be in a different land! Sometimes these shifts happen even inside a chapter, so you have to work at writing these moments in between scenes."

Name your teaching point. Specifically, teach your students that readers are alert to when the time or place changes in the story they are reading and that they imagine the moments in between the scenes that literally appear in the book.

"So what's important is that today I want to teach you that strong readers are alert to shifts in time and place, and we imagine the moments in between the scenes that are written in the stories we are reading. Readers often find it helpful to turn to setting clues to see if time has passed or the setting has changed—then we know that we have imaginative work to do if we want the story to keep making sense."

TEACHING

Read aloud a section of the text that transitions from one time and place to another, with a gap between.

"Readers, let's go back to *Edward's Eyes*. I'll show you what I mean about how time passes and the setting changes sometimes as you go from chapter to chapter. Watch me, an experienced reader, as I move from one chapter to the next; be extra alert for any reading work I do that is creating transitions between the chapters by imagining scenes that are missing. I'm going to go back to the very end of Chapter 4."

I read:

> We chased baseballs until by dusk we lay in exhausted heaps.
>
> Out over the water there was an orange full moon above, a watery one below. Edward put his head on my shoulder, and the air was still. Then, one by one, the lightning bugs came out.
>
> "Are you asleep, Edward?" I whispered.
>
> "Yes, I am," said Edward, making me laugh.
>
> Sometimes Maeve and Jack would lead us off to bed. But most times, if there wasn't rain coming, they would toss blankets over us and we'd sleep outside, Edward's head on my shoulder, his sweet-smelling breath soft on my neck.

I put down the book and said, "Oh, I see by the white space here that the chapter has ended. So before I go on, I'll just make a mental note to myself—this chapter ended with the kids all asleep by the sea. It was late, late at night, and the moon was up. It was so dark that you could see lightning bugs."

I picked up the book again and said, "Now Chapter 5 starts." I read:

> "What are you doing?" I asked.
>
> Wren, Will and Edward were behind the barn, Wren hunkered down behind a home plate bag, Will sitting to the side reading aloud, Edward pitching.
>
> Will looked at me for a moment as he read.
>
> "The ball should be held as shown…clenching the ball between your bent fingers…."

I put down the book. "Whoa! They are definitely no longer sleeping by the sea. It sounds as if the kids are now playing baseball back behind the barn, and it's hard to believe that it's the middle of the night and they just woke up to play baseball! Let me glance ahead— that's what I do when I want to quickly check what's happening next. Let's see. It's definitely the next day. Hmm, so the kids fell asleep at the end of Chapter 4, asleep by the sea, and Chapter 5 starts with them playing baseball behind the barn.

"So in between, let's see what may have happened. Watch me now, readers, as I fill in the moments between these scenes. I'll have to use my imagination and what I know about the story. Let's see. It was night, dark and cold enough for blankets, and they were by the sea. Now it's daytime, and they're behind the barn. Well, I guess they probably woke up, and perhaps it was a little chilly. I know they're by the sea, and it seems to often be breezy, with crashing waves, so perhaps it was chilly when they woke up, and the children all huddled under the blankets. Maybe Jake could feel how warm Edward was, and he was reluctant to get up because I know he likes to just be near Edward. Maybe some bugs had been biting their faces. There's still more that probably happened before this baseball game—they wouldn't go from just waking up under blankets to playing behind the barn."

Active Involvement

Reread another familiar section of the read-aloud where the setting or time has clearly changed in between sections. Ask students to imagine and then retell the missing scene to a partner.

"I want you to have a chance to do this work as well. Did you see how I paid close attention to how one chapter ended and the next began? Then I began to imagine what happened in between, using my imagination and what I know about the place and the people from the book to fill in. Why don't you give this a try and fill in more of these moments in between scenes? Let me read you the last part of Chapter 4 again, and you get ready to do this work. Close your eyes and picture the scene."

I read:

> Out over the water there was an orange full moon above, a watery one below. Edward put his head on my shoulder, and the air was still. Then, one by one, the lightning bugs came out… we'd sleep outside, Edward's head on my shoulder, his sweet-smelling breath soft on my neck.

"Can you picture it, readers?"

They nodded their heads, with their eyes still closed. I went on: "Now I'm going to read the first few lines of Chapter 5 again. When you've imagined what may have happened in between these scenes and you're ready to compare your in-between scenes with your partner, pull close together and tell each other what you imagined, okay? Here are the first lines of Chapter 5:"

> "What are you doing?" I asked.

> Wren, Will and Edward were behind the barn, Wren hunkered down behind a home plate bag, Will sitting to the side reading aloud, Edward pitching.

"I see you imagining. I bet you're using what you know from the book, and perhaps what you know about baseball, and filling in the rest. When you're ready, tell your partner what you imagine."

Students turned and talked, telling each other that they pictured the family eating breakfast in the kitchen. Many said that Maeve was probably singing and dancing, the way she always did, and that she'd either make them waffles or just push them out with toast. Some pictured the kids folding up their blankets and leaving them on the porch. All of them said the kids would be picking up their bats and gloves and rushing out into the sunshine. Most importantly, students filled in the time changes and setting changes that would happen in between these two scenes—and without really realizing it, they also articulated the shift in mood.

"Readers, I like how much detail you used as you retold these missing scenes. You were filling in the parts that happened in between, which the author counts on you to do. You used what you know about the characters and the places they inhabit, and sometimes you filled in from your imagination, until you had a sense of what had happened since last we read.

"Nicely done, readers. We don't always take so much time to do this work, of course. It becomes almost automatic. Sometimes you pause and take a moment and really picture the missing scenes; other times your mind is doing this work even as your eyes begin to make sense of the next words. Reading is amazing that way."

LINK

Remind your students that they are developing a repertoire of strategies, that this strategy of adding in needed scenes to a text is one of them, and that they will need to make choices about what reading work they pursue each day.

"Readers, let's add this skill to your reading practices. As you go off to read today, I hope you'll remain alert to those moments in your books when the things have changed and the author is counting on you to use your imagination to fill in the in-between parts. You're getting a feeling for how strong readers work hard to almost coauthor the story. I can't promise you that these kinds of shifts will always be marked by chapter changes; sometimes they happen inside of chapters as well. You can keep your eyes open for anything like rows of stars, or extra spaces, or any particular words that seem to indicate these kinds of changes and missing parts, and perhaps we should share those with each other. Then we'll all have more shared expertise and be more alert as we read. Off you go. I'll be admiring how you continue to work hard to improve and share your reading practices."

SESSION IX

Understanding References and Connecting the Parts of Our Stories

GETTING READY

- Read up through Chapter 11 in *Edward's Eyes*.

- You'll use part of Chapter 11, on page 71, in the lesson. If you have already read this far, then you'll return to this part of the story. Otherwise, finish your read-aloud in a prior session right at the bottom of page 70, where there is a natural break in the story—it is still summer. At the top of page 71, it is winter—it's one of those places where readers need to fill in the moments between scenes.

- If you made a chart of the characters in *Edward's Eyes* and/or any timelines of events, have those out during your read-aloud. Also have available any Post-its or jottings you've done as you've been reading aloud.

CONNECTION

Tell a story about a misunderstanding or miscomprehension of a book that arose from not realizing that readers need to synthesize across parts of stories.

"Friends, gather around. I want to tell you about a fiery interaction I had recently with a friend around a book. I have this friend named Dave, whom I really respect as a reader. We pass books back and forth all the time. Well, recently I heard—not from Dave, but from a friend of Dave's—that he was dissing the *Harry Potter* books, saying that they're not that well written. Apparently he had heard from this friend that I thought they were well written, and he had been saying he disagreed. But he didn't say it to me; he said it to our mutual friend. It was like hearing gossip. You know how you hear that someone said something, and you disagree, or you want to defend yourself, but that person isn't there to talk with, so you feel frustrated?

"Well, I had to find Dave and have it out with him. "The *Harry Potter* books are well written!" I spluttered. It turns out, readers, that Dave had been reading Book 6 of *Harry Potter, Harry Potter and the Half-Blood Prince*. The movie was coming out, and he was reading it before he saw the movie. Dave said that the book didn't make that much sense and wandered all over the place. But he had never read the earlier books in the series! Can you believe it? No wonder he felt that way!

"I told him, 'You can't properly judge this story when you don't understand anything that is happening! You don't get the references! You don't even know what happened to Harry's parents five books ago! You're reading as if you have no memory when the author expects you to read with almost total recall. That's how *Harry Potter* fans read. With total recall! They remember every detail. It's not the book that doesn't make sense. It's that you haven't accumulated the history, the references you need to care about the book and understand it properly!'

"To give Dave his due, he agreed immediately. 'Oh,' he said. 'Okay, I'll go start Book 1.' I quietly handed him all the movies too, just in case.

"Well, friends, that's what happened. You can't expect to read a hard book and not have to carry with you the earlier parts of the book, and you don't start a series at the end of one of the books and expect to understand it. Later that night, I had dinner with some *Harry Potter* fans, including my friend Torrin, who is fourteen and knows every detail of every book. He had just reread Books 6 and 7 for the umpteenth time, before and after seeing the movie, to compare interpretations. Torrin recalled for me all the significant references, in the movie and in Book 6, to things that happened in earlier books or that would arise again and be important in Book 7. I left wanting to ensure that all of you become the kind of passionate, informed, expert reader that Torrin is, a reader who can work hard at reading and who has expertise to bring to reading harder, more complicated books."

Name your teaching point. Specifically, teach your readers that one way stories get harder is that moments are connected across many pages, so the reader needs to work more to understand references.

"Readers, today I want to teach you that one way the stories you are reading will get more complicated is that there will be references to other parts of the book or to an earlier book in the series, and readers need to work harder to understand the references and see the meaningful connections between parts of a story. Things that are said or that happen in one part of the story may refer to earlier events, earlier parts—and these events or parts may be separated by many pages. They may even refer to something in another book in the series."

Teaching

Explain that there are several ways that complicated stories refer to earlier parts.

"This is hard and fascinating reading work, friends, so I want to help you by showing you some of the most common ways that more complicated stories will make references. A reference is when something happens or is said, and it doesn't make any sense until the reader understands that this part connects to a different part of the book or even refers to another book.

"Here's how we'll do this. I'm going to tell you about a few of the most common ways that these books make references, and then you can watch me use this knowledge, this reading expertise, to try to understand a part of *Edward's Eyes* that could be confusing. Then I'll read another part of *Edward's Eyes,* and you can give it a try. You may want your reading notebook with you, as some of the jottings you've made as we've been reading the book may be helpful. I know that I often look back over earlier Post-its or notes to see if any of those help me.

"Ready? I'm going to share some reading expertise with you and show you how I use this expertise, and then you'll have a chance to use it, too.

"As someone who is a fairly expert reader, I've learned that more complicated stories often make references that at first seem very confusing. The first thing I know is that sometimes these references are explicit, or obvious. For instance, when Ron doesn't remember what Polyjuice Potion is in Book 6 of *Harry Potter,* Hermione explains it by reminding him how they used Polyjuice Potion to change their appearances in Book 2. It's a really explicit reference to an earlier part. It's almost as if the author doesn't expect you to remember that part, so she reminds you by having Hermione remind Ron.

"On the other hand, sometimes the author *does* expect you to make these connections on your own—in fact, she may want you to make a connection the character doesn't even make. For instance, in Book 6 of *Harry Potter,* there's a moment when Dumbledore thinks back to how Voldemort put his mark on everything he made into a horcrux, or a container for his soul. He stares at Harry's forehead as he thinks this. As a reader, you remember how, in Book 1, the author told you Voldemort had 'marked' Harry. But Harry has no idea that he might be a horcrux. It's an idea that you make as a reader, by connecting across thousands of pages of text. It's fascinating to read this way, making these complicated connections. It lets you read much harder stories."

■ *Teachers, this is one way that books at levels U/V and above build tension—often the reader understands some of the issues in the story before the main character does.*

And so we begin to understand before Percy does in The Lightning Thief *that his father is probably Poseidon, we expect the teenagers to turn on Stargirl, we worry for Bella as she goes off to meet the vengeful vampire in* Twilight, *we understand that Harry Potter has to die in the last book of the series, and that kind of tension becomes almost unbearable—but it's great writing craft. That tension comes because the reader is putting together a lot of small references that begin to achieve meaning as the story progresses.*

"Okay, so the first thing that is part of my reading expertise is that sometimes the reference will be obvious; for example, the author will give me a clue, probably by having one character explain it. Sometimes it's much more subtle, and I have to work hard to build connections and explain the reference.

"What else do I know? Well, I also know that one common kind of reference will be to something that was said or that happened recently in the story. Then the reader only needs to look back or remember across a few pages. On the other hand, sometimes the reference will be to something that happened far back in the book or even in the series. I know that usually that kind of reference helps me understand why characters do the things they do or why certain things happen. It's almost like understanding cause and effect, only the cause may be pages and pages back or even in an earlier book in the series! In that case, you have to read with extra alertness. It's one reason I love reading fantasy series: the authors demand readers who will do this hard work. There's no way to make sense of the later *Harry Potter* books, or the *Percy Jackson* books, without first fully understanding all the parts of the earlier books—and you need to be able to recall those parts, too, which can be a bit of a struggle for me sometimes.

"All right, I think that's all my current reading expertise on this. I know that sometimes the references will be obvious, or explicit, and the author will explain them, and sometimes they will be subtle, or implicit, and it's up to me to figure them out. I also know that sometimes the parts I need to connect are separated by only a few pages, and sometimes the parts are separated by many, many pages."

Demonstrate in the read-aloud text how you first pause and recognize that there is some kind of reference, usually visible, that you don't get at first; then demonstrate how you go back and figure out what the reference refers to.

I picked up the book. "Watch me use this expertise to try to figure out a reference in *Edward's Eyes.* I'm going back to page 34, that part where the kids are playing baseball behind the barn and Edward is learning his knuckleball pitch. Here's what it says:"

It rained for a week, so there were no baseball games. But that didn't stop Edward. He practiced his new pitch every day, no umbrella. He begged Will, Wren, and me to practice with him. And we did. Sola refused. He threw Wiffle balls at first, and then he went to a tennis ball. Finally, in the drizzle of late June, Wren's hair all curly from the humidity, we stood behind the barn, and Edward threw his first baseball knuckleball to Wren.

I stand behind the plate and watch. It is almost as if it happens in slow motion, this ball coming so slowly that we seem to wait forever for it. I can even see the stitching on the ball. And then it darts past Wren. Past me.

Will didn't say anything. Wren didn't say anything. I just looked at Edward and smiled. He smiled back.

"Right behind you, Annabelle Lefty Lee," he said.

"Readers, here's what I'm thinking: 'Wait, what was that? What does he mean, *Annabelle Lefty Lee? Who is Annabelle Lefty Lee?*' I have no idea whom Edward is referring to."

I paused for dramatic effect and then added, "And now, friends, I have a choice. I can be one of those readers who doesn't want to work at reading, who is satisfied to skim the surfaces of stories, or I can be a reader with agency, who works hard to become a more expert reader, which means using my expertise to figure out all the parts of the story and how they connect. So here I am, with a part I don't understand."

I went back into the book, poring over it. "Hmm, the first thing I'm going to do is look right around these words, in case someone here, in this scene, explains who Annabelle Lefty Lee is. Let's see, does Edward or another character explain who Annabelle Lefty Lee is? No, not right here. In fact, everyone seems to understand who she is, which really makes me think this is a reference I'm supposed to understand."

I flipped back to earlier pages and looked up, explaining: "Friends, if it doesn't explain it right away in this part, then what I do is think back to earlier parts. Sometimes I do that in my mind, and sometimes I flip the pages. I'm thinking back over the story. It started with baby Edward coming home, and then he goes to kindergarten and starts to play baseball. Then they sleep outside by the sea, and now they're playing baseball again. I don't remember anything about someone called Annabelle."

I opened up my reader's notebook, where I would have put my old Post-its from earlier in the book—actually, for the class, I had them on a chart, so I turned to these Post-its, saying, "Maybe if I glance over my Post-its—no, no mention of Annabelle Lefty Lee. But I could look at other parts of the story where they played baseball, since this is a baseball scene. I have some Post-its and a timeline I can use. Hmm, it looks like there are a few baseball parts, so I'm going to start with the one closest to this scene. Okay, so I'm going to flip back a few pages and see if I missed something. Hmm, it's not on the page before, where he throws the pitch, and not two pages before, where Edward practices the pitch."

I flipped even farther back, and then I looked up and said triumphantly, "But wait, way back at the beginning of the chapter, on page 31, here it is. It says:"

> Wren, Will and Edward were behind the barn, Wren hunkered down behind a home plate bag, Will sitting to the side reading aloud, Edward pitching.
>
> Will looked at me for a moment as he read.
>
> "The ball should be held as shown…clenching the ball with your bent fingers…"
>
> He got up and went over, showing a picture to Edward.
>
> Edward nodded.
>
> "I'm learning a new pitch," said Edward. "I'm going to surprise Albert Groom on his birthday."

I looked up at the students and said, "So this is the part where he was learning about the knuckleball, and the part where I'm confused is where he has just figured out the knuckleball, so I'm thinking there is going to be something here. I'm looking for anything that explains why Edward says that he is 'right behind Annabelle Lefty Lee.' What does he mean by that? Let's see what's next:"

> …Edward threw a slow-looking, loopy pitch.
>
> Wren caught it and stood.
>
> "That's very odd, Edward," she said.
>
> "What do you mean?"
>
> "No spin," she said. "No spin at all. And it dipped."
>
> Edward smiled.
>
> "It says here in this book," said Will, "that Annabelle Lefty Lee once threw a perfect game when she played in the women's league. She threw a knuckleball. It says here that if it works batters can't hit it. If it doesn't even the pitcher doesn't know where it's going."
>
> "Risky," said Edward. "I like that."

"Oh, now this makes sense. Annabelle Lefty Lee was a pitcher who mastered the knuckleball. We find that out here."

I flipped forward in the book. "Then in this later part, where I was confused, Edward throws a perfect knuckleball. Then he says: 'Right behind you, Annabelle Lefty Lee.'"

I looked up. "I guess Edward is saying that he's coming right behind this famous knuckleball pitcher named Annabelle Lefty Lee, so this is a reference to something that was said a few pages back. I didn't remember it, probably because I didn't expect her name to matter and didn't try to remember it. Also, I happened to have stopped reading in between these two parts because I had to do other stuff, and then when I picked the story up again, I had no idea what Edward was referring to!"

Debrief, naming what you've done that readers can do whenever they come across a seemingly important reference they don't understand.

I put the book back down and summarized: "Readers, do you see how I used my reading expertise to figure out this reference? I assumed that I was, in fact, supposed to understand, so I wasn't willing to just let it go. Then I looked to see if the character explained the reference in that scene. When that didn't work, I thought back over the story, even flipping back through pages and through my Post-its, especially paying attention to any moment in the story that seemed like it could be related to baseball."

ACTIVE INVOLVEMENT

Set the students up to do the same work you've just done. In this case, read another part of the read-aloud text where a reference made is explicable only when the reader connects it to something that happened earlier in the story.

■ *We had been reading* Edward's Eyes *together for read-aloud. I knew that there were a lot of references near the end of the book, including the crucial last chapter that refers all the way back to the prologue. I wanted students to be ready for these references by practicing with ones earlier on in the book; also I wanted to practice this skill before the emotional content of the story got too intense. So I turned to one that I was sure the students would be successful with, starting on page 71. We had finished our last read-aloud session at the bottom of page 70.*

I picked up the book, saying, "Let's give you a chance to try this. You can use your new expertise. You know that a reference might be obvious and that one character might explain it, or it might be subtle. You know that it might refer to a part of the book that just happened or to something way, way back!

"Ready, readers? Let's recall where we were when we read last. It was summer, and the kids have been playing baseball all summer. I'll just reread the last part, where we finished:"

And then it got too cold for baseball, though Edward would have played through northeasters and snow.

Edward and I took Sabine for walks in her stroller, with her snowsuit and knitted hat, down the sidewalks of the town, stopping every so often as people called, "Sabine! Sabine!" from doorways and from across the street, running over to see her.

"Remember that night?" I asked Edward.

"Edward knew what night I meant. It had been a month and a half ago.

"Yes," said Edward. "That's the night we met, Sabine. Do you remember that night?"

His voice rose and Sabine turned her head to find his face.

"And Angela Garden," I said, and Edward and I both laughed and couldn't stop.

Edward tried to teach Sabine how to throw a ball, but she was too young to care. Thanksgiving had gone, then Christmas.

I looked up from the book. "First, readers, this is definitely one of those places in the story where you have to fill in the moments in between scenes, right? We finished yesterday, at the bottom of page 70, and it was summer, and we start now at the top of page 71, and it's winter! Then at the end of the scene, in one sentence, we go through Thanksgiving and Christmas. Let me just pause for a moment. I know you're picturing the fields turning brown and then white, the kids storing their baseball gear in the barn, the sea getting cold, snow falling, the windows closed now in their house by the sea, Maeve dancing in the kitchen, and now Edward and Jake taking Sabine out in her stroller.

"Now, friends, I know you were looking for references. I've written this section of the story up here on chart paper." I pointed to it. "Turn and tell your partner any references that you've spotted."

They did.

"Readers, I heard your conversations, and you're thinking what I am: who is Angela Garden? What night are they talking about? We're really going to need our notes to make sense of this!

Think for a moment, do any jotting, and look over your notes if you want; then turn and tell your partner what reading work you are doing to really understand the references in this section."

Some students began to talk right away. They had been on the edge of their seats while I was reading. Others looked back over their notebooks or thought quietly for a moment. Gradually the meeting area filled with conversations. I heard some kids say they remembered that Angela Garden was the nurse who had helped deliver Sabine and all the children. We had a character list up on chart paper, which helped. Some had notes on her name, which they had noted for its small references to angels and gardens. They began to reconstruct "that night," when the boys had ridden in a police car, lights flashing, through the snow, to meet Sabine, and they started laughing, just as Edward and Jake had, as they recalled the joyous intensity of that earlier moment.

■ *So much of reading work is intuitive! This part of the story is only joyous for a reader who recalls the wild joy of that earlier part of the narrative.*

"Readers, I've been listening to you recall that earlier night, when Edward and Jake walked through the snow, got taken up in a police car, and dashed through the night with lights flashing to meet first Angela Garden and then Sabine."

■ *You could decide to read this part of the story again, from page 61 to 63.*

"As I listen to you laugh and retell that earlier excitement, it reinforces for me how important it is to really make sense of these references, to run your mind back over the earlier parts of the story so that you recapture what happened and what it felt like. Doing so affects your understanding of this part. I heard a lot of you say, too, that this was a reference to something that happened quite a while ago in the story, so you had to run your mind back, and even look at your notes, to recall who Angela Garden was and what night Edward and Jake are talking about in order to understand why they were laughing."

LINK

Remind your students of the repertoire they have at hand, and encourage them to make a plan for the reading work they want to pursue, as well as what they want to talk to their partners about.

"As we go off to read, let's recall some of the ways that we're working on having more agency and becoming more expert readers. You might look over the charts in the room or your Post-its, and remember some of what you are doing to work harder at your reading, including reading between the lines, using your imagination as you read, planning different methods for retelling stories, and now connecting parts of the story. Take a moment to tell your partner what particular reading work might help you lift the level of your reading work today. Then when you have a chance later to talk with your partner, you'll already have some expectations for that conversation. Some of you may change your mind once you begin reading—the book may lead you in a different direction. But it's still smart to have made a plan for the intellectual work you want to do as a reader."

SESSION X

Working Harder When the Book Gets Hard

> **GETTING READY**
>
> - Think of any activity that you've worked hard at when it got hard—something that your students will connect to.
>
> - You will want a piece of chart paper up so that you can record students' strategies for when books get challenging. You may also want chart paper for recording your work as you read a challenging excerpt from the read-aloud text.
>
> - Choose a part of your read-aloud text that rewards rereading and working hard to comprehend.

CONNECTION

Share a story of a moment when the going got tough and you got tougher. Ask students to share with their partners a time when they too got tougher in the face of a challenge. Ask students to think of this in the light of reading work.

"Readers, will you take a moment to share with a partner any time that something has gotten very hard for you, and you dug in your heels and kept working at it? For instance, this past summer I rode my bike in the country on this road that has three large hills right in a row. At the start of the summer, I had to walk my bike up all three of those steep hills. They were just so hard that I couldn't get up them! Also, I was too afraid to go really fast down them, so I lost my speed going downhill, and that slowed me down for the next uphill. But I vowed that by the end of the summer I would ride up all three hills. Every time I rode, I tried to get farther up each hill without getting off to walk. And it was really hard! My legs would hurt, I felt as if I couldn't breathe, and sweat would run down my back—those hills were making me work!

"It's incredibly important that we learn how to work hard like that at academic endeavors like reading. Books can make us sweat, too—they can get hard at times. So we need to be the kind of people who work harder when things get hard! Before we jump into what that looks like in reading, let's call up our 'hardworking selves'—sort of like superheroes who summon their inner powers when things get tough. To do that, remember a time when something you wanted to do got really hard, and you found ways to work even harder. When you have a memory like that, signal to your partner, and tell him or her what you did to work even harder when things got tough."

Kids leaned in and began to talk, telling stories of moving to twenty-speed bikes, jumping rope double Dutch, moving from T-ball to baseball, learning Hebrew, etc.

"Friends, I love hearing how you dig in your heels when something makes you sweat! I know now that each of you has inside of you that superhero who, when something makes you sweat, just works harder. You don't run away, you don't give up, you get tough. Let's think now what this means in reading.

"As I said a minute ago, books can make you sweat, too. And sometimes it's worth it to work harder. Remember that book *Anathem* on my reading log that was giving me so much trouble? I was slipping as a reader because I wasn't reading enough. Sometimes that means the book is too hard, and we need to find a different book. But other times we have to work harder when the book gets hard. It turns out that this book, after Chapter 6, began to make sense. There were no more new characters. Things that were mysterious in the beginning became clear. I started reading lots and lots of pages. By the end, I adored the book. I only slowed down again near the end because I didn't want to finish it! But that book made me sweat, for sure. I had to dig deep down and recall a lot of reading expertise that I hadn't used in a long time to turn me into a tougher reader—sort of a superhero reader! I dug into my reading tool kit for a lot of reading strategies I hadn't needed for a while."

Name your teaching point. Specifically, teach your readers that they already have on hand the strategies they need when a book gets hard.

"Today I want to teach you that when a book gets hard, readers work even harder. One way we do this is to use the repertoire of crucial strategies we already know that help us work through difficulty."

TEACHING

Set your students up to recall the strategies they know that will help them when a book gets hard.

"The trick of this work, readers, is to recognize when your book is making you sweat and then to figure out which of the tools in your tool kit will help you as a reader. Make sure you keep this tool kit well stocked with helpful reading tools, because you may have to use more than one at a time. It's kind of like being on a tricky biking trail, where you have to figure out whether to use your high gears or your low gears and whether to stand up and pedal or get low and coast.

"I'm sure that you already know quite a few strategies for when books get tough—you already have some tools. Turn and tell a partner a few things you do when books get hard. We'll generate a list from these strategies."

Gather your readers back, and list the strategies they named. You might add one or two important familiar strategies that students didn't mention.

I listened in and heard the predictable strategies that readers use—reread, go back to the beginning, figure out tricky words, read a part aloud, talk to a partner. I jotted these on chart paper under a heading that said: "Strategies for Dealing with Difficulty." I gave students just a minute to recall these familiar tools. Then I said, "Okay, readers, let's gather together again. You clearly have some familiar strategies that you're very comfortable with. You know to reread. That's really smart because rereading often clarifies our understanding. Sometimes I even reread a few times. You know to go back to the beginning—also smart. You can go back to the beginning of the paragraph, or the chapter, or the book! And you have lots of strategies for figuring out tricky words, and so forth."

I turned back. "These are great strategies, very helpful tools for your tool kit. We probably have more strategies, and we can add those as well in a moment. Let's do some work, then, to help us with *when* we might use these particular strategies. The next step in becoming more powerful is to realize that you do dig in when it gets hard, and you make choices among these strategies, trying to match a strategy to what you're doing as a reader. Sometimes you have to invent, or find, another strategy."

Set students up to watch you demonstrate using and inventing strategies to read challenging text powerfully. In this case, ask them to research the strategies you use so that they will get ideas for strategies they can use in similar instances.

"Here's how we'll do this. I'm going to bring us to a part of the story that was really, really hard for me. Will you take up your role as reading researchers and research some of the steps strong readers follow, and the decisions they make, when the book gets hard? You may, as researchers, find that you have some of your own expertise that you want to add to mine. So take notes on what unfolds, and add, in the margins, any of your own thinking. That's how researchers act—we make quick judgments and develop theories as we observe. You'll also notice that I may use strategies that aren't on our list, so be ready to add to the list once you've done this research."

I picked up *Edward's Eyes,* saying, "Do you have your reading research lenses on and notebooks ready? Remember, you're looking for tips to learn for what to do when a book gets hard.

"The first part of the book that was really hard for me was the first page!" I read the first part:

> Prologue
>
> The day was crisp and bright. It was fall on the cape. Maeve had packed us a lunch. She kissed us all, Trick and Albert and me.
>
> "You sure you don't want to come with us?" I asked.
>
> "No, Jake. This is for you," said Maeve with a little smile.
>
> Sabine was in her arms. I kissed her cheek.
>
> The ballpark had painted green walls. The grass was green, too. The seats were not yet filled because we were here early. Trick and Albert Groom and I had come for batting practice.
>
> Some baseball players were out on the field, throwing baseballs and stretching. Some were doing sprints across the field. We had seats next to the field, by the dugout.
>
> A ball hit the wall in front of us. Albert leaned over and picked it up. He rolled it around in his hands.
>
> "Do you know what is inside a baseball?" he asked me.
>
> I shook my head.
>
> "Charcoal yarn, wrapped up tightly. Yards of it," he said.

I paused and looked up. "This is really hard. There are so many characters coming so fast. I don't even know who some of them are yet. So for now, I'm just going to make a Post-it with the characters' names on it. I know that helps when there are lots of characters."

I jotted quickly and then went on: "Then, well it's just weird. It starts out with this woman, Maeve, kissing everyone. I do find out the narrator is Jake; I'll star him on my Post-it. Then all of a sudden we're in this park, watching a baseball game. I don't even know how much time has passed. And then for some reason we're talking about baseballs.

"Okay, I've read this twice now, so I've tried rereading. Another good move is to go on, to read forward. Let me see how that pays off."

I read forward:

> He threw the ball back to a baseball player.
>
> It was a good throw. I had never before seen Albert throw a baseball.
>
> "I love the smell of ball parks," said Trick. "Every single one smells the same."
>
> "They do," said Albert.
>
> Some players came close.
>
> Albert Groom touched my arm.
>
> One of the players had protective glasses on. His hair was brown, cut short. He was tall. When he faced the outfield I could read the name on the back of his shirt.
>
> I stood up.
>
> "Willie?" I called.
>
> He turned and smiled. He waved and turned to go away.
>
> "Do you see the stitches on a knuckleball when it's thrown?" I called.
>
> He stopped. Very slowly he turned and stared at me.
>
> "Can you see the ball leave the pitcher's hand and come down the path to you, like a train coming down the track?"
>
> "Willie?" a player called to him.
>
> Willie waved him away. He walked over to me.
>
> "Yes," he said softly.
>
> "Do you hit better now than you ever did before?"
>
> "Yes."
>
> It was a whisper.
>
> "My brother Edward learned how to throw a knuckleball. And he never once struck out," I said.
>
> "Edward," he said. "So that's his name."

I looked up again, and then I looked at our list of strategies. "Okay, so I've read this more than once. And I tried reading forward. But it doesn't explain who Edward is or why these characters are at this ball game. I do have a list of characters at least, and I know who the narrator is, that his name is Jake. And I can draw a line between him and Edward because I know they're brothers. So I'm using my character list, and I've started a time-line. I'll just put on it now 'Maeve kisses them' and 'They talk to Willie at baseball game.' That's two events so far.

"I'm going to use a strategy I should have used before I even started this book. I know that when I tackle a more complicated book, it pays off to research the main characters, the setting, and the problem from the covers. I should have read the covers and even jotted those things down—then maybe now I would know who Jake is and what's going on. Let me see."

I turned to the cover and read the blurb aloud:

> Jake is part of an extraordinary family. He has a life filled with art, music, and long summer nights on the Cape. He has hours and days and months of baseball. But, more than anything in this world, Jake knows he has Edward. From the moment he was born, Jake knew Edward was destined for something. Edward could make anyone laugh and everyone think. During one special year, he became the only one in the neighborhood who could throw a perfect knuckleball. It was a pitch you could not hit. That same year, Jake learned there are also some things you cannot hold.

I jotted quickly: Jake and Edward—brothers. Edward—amazing baseball player. The Cape. Big Problem—Jake can't hold on to some things.

After jotting, I looked back up, saying slowly, "That was really helpful. Now I know that all these characters are probably part of Jake's extraordinary family. And clearly this family cares about baseball. And Edward is Jake's favorite brother. Good. And I guess, too, that Jake is going to lose something—that's the big problem, so I can be alert for that. There's still stuff I don't know. I don't know who this Willie character is. I think I'll jot what I *don't* know, too."

I jotted: "Willie? Seeing the ball as it is pitched?"

Then I looked up again. "Okay, I don't understand every bit, but I know enough now that I can keep reading. Also, another strategy I know when the book gets hard is to keep track of what you don't know and keep going because maybe it's explained later. "

I turned back to the book. "So Chapter 1 begins with Edward being born, and we find out who Jack and Maeve are, and all the rest of the family, too. I think I'll add all those details to my timeline and character list because I'm realizing that this book moves around like crazy. So I've used some strategies so far, and I've even decided on some that I'll keep going with."

Ask children to turn and talk about the tips they discovered in your demonstration that they can try for themselves when a book gets hard.

"Readers, I can see that you've been jotting notes furiously. Turn and tell your fellow researcher what you discovered. Share the tips you gleaned for what to do when a book gets hard. I'll add to our list, based on what you say to each other."

They talked. I added to our list of strategies so that we had a chart that looked like this:

Strategies for Dealing with Difficulty: What to Do When the Book Gets Hard

- Reread the part, or reread even farther back
- Talk to a partner
- Read a part aloud
- Go back to the covers and blurb to research the story
- If it's a series, make sure you have read the first one!
- Go on
- Use lists to keep track of characters
- Use timelines to keep track of events
- Jot questions

Gather the students back and recap. Let them make some decisions about their own reading work.

"Friends, you gathered a lot of helpful tips during your research. Some of you also added some ideas based on your own experience with hard books. I jotted down the results of your research here. Before we finish, would you look over this collective list and tell your partner which of these strategies you feel like you use a lot and which ones maybe you want to add to your tool kit and consider using?"

They talked.

"All right, friends, this is good. I think that you'll be able to make smart choices about what to do when a book makes you sweat. It used to be that when a book was hard, I would encourage you to put it down. There may still be times when that makes sense. But I also want to be sure that you feel confident enough that you can tackle the hard parts of books. When a book makes us sweat, it's not just that we have to be willing to work hard. I expect that of you. It's that we also have to be willing to think hard about *how* to work hard. Nicely done."

LINK

Send your students off to their reading, reminding them that the ability to work hard will help them in any endeavor, not just reading.

"Readers, that ability to analyze, reflect, and then return to your books with agency, expertise, and determination is going to make a tremendous difference to your ability to work through hard parts of the books we'll read. It's also going to help you tackle any kind of difficulty. I'm not surprised that you've solved your difficulties and worked hard in other endeavors when I see you being this imaginative and disciplined at working at your reading. Off you go. Exceed yourself!"

Teachers, please turn to the Resources CD-ROM for Part Three of this unit, "The Art of Literary Conversation."

BRINGING CHARACTERS TO LIFE AND DEVELOPING ESSENTIAL READING SKILLS

By Julia Mooney

PART ONE

When Readers Connect to Characters, We Empathize, Envision, and Predict

Dear Teachers,

Those of us who teach reading know that there is little we can do from the front of the room that will matter as much to kids as will the repeated opportunities to read with deep engagement. The best thing we can do is to put books in the hands of children—and to let those books teach. With that in mind, first and foremost, we teach children to read with an eye on characters, coming to know them as people and to care about them as friends. Children's engagement with characters powers the inferences, envisionments, and predictions that are all part of successful reading.

This unit of study revolves around Kate DiCamillo's powerful chapter book, Because of Winn-Dixie. Two sessions spotlight the simpler but equally moving picture book, Those Shoes by Maribeth Boelts. You could easily substitute other books. Whatever you decide, the unit assumes that you are reading the book(s) you select outside the reading workshop as well as within it.

Assume that your children will be reading books at a very different pace than you are reading Because of Winn-Dixie. Children reading in the level K/M band will read at least four or five books a week. Children in the level N/O band will read at least two or three books a week. Readers reading in the band beyond that will progress more slowly but will still read at least four or five books in the month.

On the following page is a read-aloud pacing chart that shows how you might progress through Because of Winn-Dixie and Those Shoes if you select these as your read-aloud books, and which parts of these books you will reference or read during the sessions themselves.

Unit Pacing Chart

Session	Book	Chapter/Page
I	*Because of Winn-Dixie*	This session assumes you have read the first two chapters.
II	*Because of Winn-Dixie*	In this session, you will reread part of Chapter 2.
III	*Because of Winn-Dixie* *Those Shoes*	This session refers to the first two pages of Chapter 2. In this session, you will also read aloud a short excerpt from *Those Shoes*.
IV	*Because of Winn-Dixie*	This session assumes you have read through Chapter 8. In the session, you will read aloud the beginning of Chapter 9.
V	*Because of Winn-Dixie*	This session assumes you have read through Chapter 9. In the session, you will read aloud the start of Chapter 10.
VI	*Because of Winn-Dixie*	This session assumes you have read through, but not beyond, p. 93 (Chapter 14). In this session, you'll read on in Chapter 14.
VII	*Because of Winn-Dixie*	The link refers to Opal's attempts to connect with people. To pace yourself so that you make it through the book by the unit's end, make sure you have read through Chapter 16 by today.
VIII	*Those Shoes*	This session relies on the first half of the book.
IX	*Because of Winn-Dixie*	The active involvement asks children to consider surprising ways in which a character, perhaps the preacher, has acted. Be sure that by today you have read a few more chapters of the book.
X	*Because of Winn-Dixie*	This session assumes you have read up until, but not past, Chapter 21, p. 147. During the session, you will read a tiny passage halfway down the page.
XI	*Because of Winn-Dixie*	This session assumes you have read through, but not past, Chapter 22. In this session, you will read aloud all of Chapter 23 to the class.
XII	*Because of Winn-Dixie*	In this session, you will read aloud the start of Chapter 24. It is important that you not read it to your students in advance of this session, so you may wish to plan to read another book during the day's read-aloud.
XIII	*Because of Winn-Dixie*	This session does not refer to *Because of Winn-Dixie*, but plan to finish reading the book aloud in preparation for the next day.
XIV	*Because of Winn-Dixie*	In this session, you will reference the last chapter of *Because of Winn-Dixie*. You should have finished the book the day before.

SESSION I

Getting to Know Characters Like We Get to Know a New Friend

CONNECTION

Compare getting to know a new class of children to getting to know characters in a book.

"Readers, I want to let you in on a secret. Come close. Closer, even. I'm going to whisper this. Every year, before the school year starts, teachers all over the world wonder the same thing: 'What will my new students be like?' As we set up the classroom, we think, 'Will these kids be like the ones I had last year? Will they be afraid of the mouse that sometimes scurries across the floor, or will they name it? Will they play together at recess or split up into little groups? Will they feel comfortable enough to laugh aloud or cry softly during our read-alouds?' We are full of questions about you."

"Then you walk in on the first day of class, and very quickly we begin our work to get to know you. We notice whom you like to sit next to and what books you pick. We listen to what you say first to the person who picks you up. We notice what you keep in your desk, what excites you, and what makes you worry. All of this watching and listening and noticing give us an idea of who you are."

"Now that we've been together for a month, I can tell who you are just by your handwriting or by the sound of your voice. I know who likes baseball, who likes making art projects, and who is shy about singing. I can guess who must have dropped puzzle pieces on the floor, and who keeps borrowing books about mummies. I even know whose book bag I tripped over just by looking at all the key chains dangling from the zipper. I pay attention to what you say, do, hold close, because all this helps me get to know you."

"And you know what? This teacher's secret for getting to know our students is also a reader's secret for getting to know characters."

Name your teaching point. Specifically, teach children that readers read characters, noticing actions and choices that reveal what each character is like.

"Just like teachers read students, readers read characters. Readers notice the little things, like how a character talks and acts, because these are telltale signs that let readers know the sort of person this is. Above all, readers notice the choices a character makes."

Teaching

Demonstrate how a reader notices things about a character by showing how you notice things about the main character in the read-aloud book.

"Yesterday, as I read aloud the first few pages of *Because of Winn-Dixie,* didn't it feel like we were all meeting a new girl? We already have a sense of the sort of person she is, don't we? This is the kind of girl who refers to her dad as 'the preacher.' This is a girl who goes to the store to buy two tomatoes and a box of macaroni and comes back with— a dog! Those details say something. We not only read words; we also read people."

"I'm going to reread some passages that we read yesterday, and I want you to notice how I read Opal. You'll see that I figure this person out by watching her actions:"

"Please," said the manager. "Somebody call the pound."

"Wait a minute!" I hollered. "That's my dog. Don't call the pound."

"Huh? She says, 'That's my dog' even when it isn't? That's surprising. I think it shows that India Opal Buloni has guts! It takes courage to holler something that isn't true in the midst of upset grown-ups who are strangers, all to save a stray dog!"

Active Involvement

Read a bit more of the read-aloud book, and then recruit children's help noticing other things about the main character.

"Let's keep reading to see what else we notice. In this next part I'm going to read, Opal has taken the dog outside the store and is checking his mangy fur and skinny body:"

"You're a mess," I told him. "I bet you don't belong to anybody."

He smiled at me. He did that thing again, where he pulled back his lips and showed me his teeth. He smiled so big that it made him sneeze. It was like he was saying, "I know I'm a mess. Isn't it funny?"

"Let me stop. What have we seen Opal doing and saying? Hmm, what is this kid like as a person?" I left a little pool of silence and used that time to show that I was thinking this through. "Turn and talk to your partner about the ideas you are growing about Opal."

As children talked, I voiced over little coaching tips. "Put what you are noticing *now* together with earlier stuff we noticed about Opal, just as you would put pieces of a jig-saw puzzle together to make a picture."

"Thumbs up if you and your partner have thoughts about the kind of person Opal is."

I gestured for one child to share his thought. Mohammed said, "Well, she is the kind of girl who is brave and also has a soft spot for animals 'cause she said she fell in love with a dog who was running all over the grocery store."

I nodded. "Wise observation. It says something about Opal that she has not only rescued a dirty stray dog from being taken to the pound but also fallen in love with that dog! Do you see that as we notice what a character does and says, we piece our observations together into an image of the kind of person the character is?"

LINK

Reiterate how smart it is to read people and to read characters. Nudge children to let their observations spark ideas about their characters.

"I thought we'd be working for a week to learn how to read people, but you are all so good at it already! I'm starting to wonder if maybe you've *already* been doing this. When I said earlier that I've been watching your actions and piecing together an idea of what each of you is like, you haven't, by any chance, done the same with *me*, have you?

"Hmmm… you've been spying on me, and you've noticed some of my little quirks! You haven't by chance noticed that I misplace my reading glasses about five times a day? You haven't been thinking, 'She's the kind of teacher who is absentminded,' have you?'

"Readers, it is smart work to read people. It is important to pay attention to how people act and how they talk and to realize that people's actions are windows into what they are like. That's true in life, and it's true as we read. So today, as you read, pay attention to the things your characters do and say, and let your observations spark ideas about who your characters are as people. You'll want to capture your observations on Post-its."

SESSION II

As We Read On, We Make and Revise Theories

Dear Teachers,

In this session you'll again teach children that skilled readers read people. This time you'll encourage children to notice a character's words, thoughts, and actions, knowing they may need to revise their initial impression. You'll ask children to think, too, about what these observations tell them about who a character is.

You'll be teaching kids to infer. By thinking about what a character's speech and traits say about him or her, children will be moving one step beyond their observations to say, "This character keeps going on scary rides. Oh! That makes me think this character seeks out thrills." When children say, "This character is the kind of person who. . . ," this is also a precursor to prediction work, which we will ask children to do later in this part. Soon children will be able to imagine what a character will do next in one situation or another, how he or she will respond to particular people and experiences.

There are many passages in Because of Winn-Dixie *in which Opal speaks and acts in her precise, special ways. Your goal, however, will be to help readers grow theories about their characters in whatever book they are reading.*

CONNECTION

Tell children a story that demonstrates that astute observers notice as the things around us and the characters in books we read take shape.

"Readers, this past weekend I took Aidan, my four-year-old nephew, to the zoo. As soon as we arrived, we heard a buzzing noise and noticed a small crowd gathered around a huge block of ice. It was a boxy shape, about the size of a refrigerator, and an ice sculptor was working on one edge, sanding it so it was curved. We watched for a moment, and I asked Aidan, 'What do you think it will be?' He guessed a truck, mostly because he's really into trucks, and I guessed a giraffe, mostly because we were at a zoo."

"After watching for a few minutes, we left to go the monkey area and the aviary, where the birds are, and then we passed the ice sculptor again. This time, the block had more of a shape. It looked less like a fridge and more like…it wasn't clear. Aidan still thought it would be a truck, but I noticed a rounded shape toward the top with a skinny part underneath. I changed my idea about it. Now I guessed it would be some kind of bird—one with a small roundish head and a skinny neck—maybe a turkey or a swan or an ostrich."

"Aidan and I left to get some lunch, and when we passed by the sculptor the third time, after we had eaten, we were amazed. The sculptor had done so much! I said to Aidan, 'Now what do you think it is?' Guess what he said? Yup, you're right. He said 'It's a truck!' But it wasn't. There was more of a curved body with arm-like parts sticking out. I watched as the sculptor carved a curved edge on one of the arm-like things. 'Wait,' I thought. It looked like a fin or a flipper more than an arm. I looked again at the top of the sculpture, and what I had thought might be a bird's head looked more like a snout. 'He's making a sea lion!' I realized. It was incredible how the sculptor turned a rectangular block of ice into a playful sea lion. This reminded me so much of getting to know our characters. At first, they're like this undefined blob of words, and then the more we look at them, the more we read on, the more defined they become. They take shape, and we can really see who they are.

"This story is an example of how when we first look at something, whether it's a block of ice or a character in a book, we are likely to have initial ideas about it, but then the more we get to know it, the more we observe and notice, it's likely that our ideas will grow and change. This happens so often when we read. At first, the character is undefined, like a block of ice, but as we turn the pages, it's like the author is sculpting the character into a clearer shape so she becomes more defined."

Name your teaching point. Specifically, tell children that readers pay attention to what characters say and do and think over time, and we continue to grow ideas and impressions about the characters, often revising our initial idea.

"Today I want to remind you that as we read, we pay close attention to what characters say and do, because doing so helps us to more clearly see who each character is. I want to teach you that we need to be willing to revise our first ideas as we read on and accumulate information about characters by continuing to notice how they speak and what they do. We use all this as we read to help us figure out characters' traits, knowing that our first impressions might change. We pay attention to each character's words, actions, thoughts, and decisions throughout the story, because they can reveal so much about that character's personality, desires, and relationships."

TEACHING

Demonstrate how you read, paying attention to grow theories about a character.

"Yesterday we spent some time reading not just this book, but Opal, too. We watched her act in surprising ways in that grocery store, and we didn't just say, 'Wow, that's different!' Instead, we took a second to say, 'What a minute. What does this show about the sort of person Opal might be?'

"Later, as we read on, we learned that Opal is new in town and lonely. We know that she misses her mama, who left her and her father, the preacher, to live on their own.

"What we find when we read is that we start off making general ideas about a character, and then as we read on, those ideas become more detailed, more specific. We do the same thing when we're getting to know people in our lives; as we observe a person's actions, we refine our theories. Listen while I read on in our book, and you'll see that I notice how she speaks, and this helps me refine my first ideas about her."

I picked up *Because of Winn-Dixie* and began rereading a section of Chapter 2:

> Anyway, while me and Winn-Dixie walked home, I told him how I got my name and I told him how I had just moved to Naomi. I also told him about the preacher and how he was a good man, even if he was too distracted with sermons and prayers and suffering people to go grocery shopping.

> "But you know what?" I told Winn-Dixie, "You are a suffering dog, so maybe he will take to you right away. Maybe he'll let me keep you."

"The first thing I notice in this passage is the way Opal tells Winn-Dixie everything about herself right away. It's almost as if she has been keeping stuff pent up inside of her, maybe because she's new in town and has no one to talk to. Now, even though she knows a dog can't respond, she is finally able to say all the things she has been needing to say."

Then I said, "I could just stop, but I'll try to push myself to say more, to see more. So what else? Well, she's telling Winn-Dixie about her dad being too distracted by his work to go grocery shopping. It's like she's saying that her dad is too distracted to take care of her. But she doesn't seem upset with her father for ignoring her, so that makes me think she is nice. Oh—let me say that more exactly. She is, umm, forgiving.

"Readers, did you notice that even though I only read a short passage, I found a ton of clues in it to help us develop ideas about Opal's character traits, about the kind of person she is? To find those clues, we couldn't just breeze through our reading, though. We had to take time to observe her closely and to think about what her behavior might mean."

ACTIVE INVOLVEMENT

Set children up to work in partnerships, noticing what a particular passage conveys about the character.

"Readers, it's your turn to try this out. I'm going to read on in the chapter. I'll stop after a few paragraphs to give you time to jot your thinking down, and then you can discuss your thoughts with your partner. Remember to pay attention to the details. Read with alertness, closely observing what Opal says and does so that you can develop your ideas about her:"

> "But you know what?" I told Winn-Dixie, "You are a suffering dog, so maybe he will take to you right away. Maybe he'll let me keep you."
>
> Winn-Dixie looked up at me and wagged his tail. He was kind of limping like something was wrong with one of his legs. And I have to admit, he stunk. Bad. He was an ugly dog, but already, I loved him with all my heart.
>
> When we got to the Friendly Corners Trailer Park, I told Winn-Dixie that he had to behave right and be quiet, because this was an all adult trailer park and the only reason I got to live in it was because the preacher was a preacher and I was a good, quiet kid. I was what the Friendly Corners Trailer Park manager, Mr. Alfred, called "an exception." And I told Winn-Dixie he had to act like an exception, too; specifically, I told him not to pick any fights with Mr. Alfred's cats or Mrs. Detweller's little yappie Yorkie dog, Samuel. Winn-Dixie looked up at me while I was telling him everything, and I swear he understood.

"Readers, take a few moments to jot down your thoughts. What do Opal's actions and words tell you about her? And remember, usually a person can't be shoehorned into just a word—nice, mean. Usually it takes a sentence or two, at least, to capture precisely what you notice about a character."

After the children jotted for a minute or so, I spoke again. "Use what you have written to springboard into a conversation with your partner. What are we learning about the kind of person Opal is? Partner 2, start off the conversation. Partner 1, listen and respond."

After a few minutes, I called out, "Eyes up here, readers."

Share some of the children's responses.

"I heard some really insightful things just now. Some of you said that the part in which Opal says she loves Winn-Dixie with all her heart shows that Opal is the kind of person who looks beyond appearances and appreciates what's inside a person. On the other hand, I heard another partnership say that Opal loves Winn-Dixie even though he's smelly and ugly because she is desperate for someone, anyone, to spend time with. We're okay with disagreeing in this class because we know that readers often take slightly different meanings from the same text. As we read on, the text will help us know Opal better. Congratulations on paying close attention to what Opal says and does to develop ideas about the kind of person she is."

LINK

Encourage children to dig deeply as they read any book, noticing particulars about a character and asking themselves what those say about who the character is.

"Readers, we've spent a lot of time talking about Opal the past few days, and she's an especially compelling character. But I want you to remember that this work we're doing—stepping into a character's shoes and her world and noticing things about her—you can do with any book, any character. Today, as you read on your own, see if you can dig deeply. Really see what makes your character special. Hear how she talks. See how she acts and what choices she makes. Ask yourself, 'What does this tell me about who my character is?' Collect jotted notes capturing your thoughts as you read."

SESSION III

There's a Thin Line Between Reading and Empathy

Dear Teachers,

In this session, you'll demonstrate for children how to step into the shoes and the world of the main character, seeing things through that character's eyes, living like she does, and above all, wanting what she wants.

At first glance, identifying Opal's wants may seem simple. After all, she names these to herself and to other characters time and again throughout the book. However, as is the case with any well-crafted work of fiction, Opal has lessons to learn, and as she learns these, the things she wants change. The character work you do with children, then, will be rich and will grow in complexity as the book progresses.

You'll notice that in this session we reread excerpts from Chapter 2 of Because of Winn-Dixie. *Whereas your reading of the book can't jump here and there, your* rereading *can. This session's teaching and active involvement work fit nicely with the selected passages from earlier in the book. Of course, the precise passages you select for demonstration teaching aren't crucial. What* is *crucial is that you convey to readers the importance of identifying so closely with the main character that you feel her fears, hopes, longings. This work is essential to successful lost-in-the-story reading, and it lays the groundwork for the prediction and interpretation work children will soon do.*

As you steer children to step into Opal's shoes and world, you'll probably find that some children identify only her most basic wants; one child might say, "Opal wants a dog." Meanwhile, other children will understand the deeper want: "Opal is lonely. She wants a friend." Don't worry about the variation in children's levels of comprehension. Just as Opal comes to understand her deeper wants bit by bit, so, too, your children's understandings will grow over the course of this unit.

Connection

Tell children the story of a time you took on the persona, habits, and desires of a person unlike yourself.

"Readers, give me a thumbs up if you love Halloween!" Lots of eager thumbs went up. "Me too! I love dressing up as someone else. As soon as I step into a costume, it's almost like I become that character. 'Yo ho, ho! Argh, matey,' I'll say as a deep-voiced pirate, limping a bit on my peg leg (I acted this out as I spoke) and looking out over the horizon with my unpatched eye. 'Argh, land ahoy!' Or I'll put on a witch's hat, clutch a broom in my hand, crook my finger, and say, 'I'll get you, my pretty, and your little dog, too!' I cackled and leered, looking like I was ready to pounce on Dorothy just before she makes it to Oz.

"I've been watching all of you as you read and have noticed you gesturing now and then, making facial expressions. Some of you are covering your eyes, and I can see that you're imagining what it's like to be one of the Littles, hiding from a cat. Others of you are reading with your hands on your hips; you look saucy, and I know you're Junie B. Jones mouthing off again! You're doing what all of us do when we dress up for Halloween or take on the persona of someone else. You're entering other people's heads and worlds."

Name your teaching point. Specifically, teach children that readers step into the character's shoes and world, taking on the character's experiences, feelings, wants.

"Today I want to teach you that we do this also as we read. When we enter the world of a story, when we meet the main character, we take on that character's persona. We walk in the main character's shoes. We live in the character's world, seeing, learning, and feeling as if we are the character. Above all, we want what the character wants."

Teaching

Read a passage from your read-aloud text that captures the main character's wants. Demonstrate how you step into the character's shoes, seeing, feeling, and wanting as she does. Assume the character's voice as you read.

"Listen while I reread a bit we've already heard from *Because of Winn-Dixie,* and you are going to see that for me, reading is a tiny bit like acting. I step into the shoes of our main character, Opal, and suddenly she's not the only one who wants to keep this dog. *I* do, too. Remember, she stands up to an angry store manager just to claim this stray dog. I'm thinking she must want that dog pretty badly to go out on a limb for him. Now she's brought the dog home and she's desperate to convince her dad, the preacher, to let her keep him. George (I gestured to a child in the class), will you sit on my chair and pretend to be Opal's dad?" George nodded, and I passed him a copy of the text, his lines marked.

Picking up the book, I walked a few steps away from my seat (now occupied by George) in front of the children. I swallowed, breathed deeply and audibly, and fidgeted with my hands so that the children could tell I was nervous. Then I made a determined face, walked toward George, put my hands on my hips, and said in an eager, bold voice:

> "I found a dog," (I told him.) "And I want to keep him."

George read:

> "No dogs," (the preacher said.) "We've talked about this before. You don't need a dog."

In a loud pleading voice, but still showing signs of being nervous, I read:

> "I know it," (I said.) "I know I don't need a dog. But this dog needs me. Look," (I said. I went to the trailer door and I hollered,) "Winn-Dixie!" (I raised my voice and looked off toward the far side of the classroom. Then I stepped back, as if making way for the large dog as he galloped into the trailer home.)

Switching to the role of the narrator, I read:

> Winn-Dixie's ears shot up in the air and he grinned and sneezed, and then he came limping up the steps and into the trailer and put his head right into the preacher's lap, right on top of a pile of papers.

Putting the book aside and looking up, I said, "I love Winn-Dixie. Look at his hopeful, funny face. I don't see how the preacher won't love him, too. I hope he says yes."

Deconstruct what you've done for children, and show them how readers can infer about the character's wants when we are in that person's shoes. Then read on, continuing to assume the role of the character.

"Readers, did you see how I took on the role of Opal just now? Reading this bit, imagining I was Opal, it really did feel like I wanted Winn-Dixie to be mine for keeps. I wonder if you noticed something else. Opal tells her father that she doesn't need a dog, that it is just that *the dog needs her.* I'm wondering if that's true 'cause I feel like I (as Opal) *do* need this dog. As Opal, I'm in love with him. And we know Opal's new to this town. I bet she could use a friend. Listen as George and I read on:"

> The preacher looked at Winn-Dixie. He looked at his ribs and his matted-up fur and the places where he was bald. The preacher's nose wrinkled up. Like I said, the dog smelled pretty bad.

Winn-Dixie looked up at the preacher. He pulled back his lips and showed the preacher all of his crooked yellow teeth and wagged his tail and knocked some of the preacher's papers off the table. Then he sneezed and some more papers fluttered to the floor.

"What did you call this dog?" the preacher asked.

I paused and then read in a quiet, hopeful voice:

"Winn-Dixie," I whispered. I was afraid to say anything too loud.

"Readers, it seems to me that Opal wants that dog pretty badly. More than anything, I'd guess. Reading this, I feel a little nervous. It seems like a lot is resting on her father's decision. I don't know about you, but I think I'll be pretty disappointed—heartbroken, even—if Opal doesn't get to keep Winn-Dixie."

Name what you've done in a way that is transferable to other passages and texts.

"Any time I begin a book, when I first meet a character, I step right into that person's shoes. I can almost feel myself tying those shoes and then walking around in them, living as that character. It's almost as if I become that person. I really do feel the character's feelings, and above all, I want what he or she wants."

ACTIVE INVOLVEMENT

Read aloud a passage from a picture book you and your children have read aloud together. Then channel children to work in partnerships, imagining themselves into the role of the character—wanting, feeling, and learning as he or she does.

"Now it's your turn. I'm going to read the short opening passage in *Those Shoes,* which we read together recently. Remember that reading gives us a chance to walk in a character's shoes, to live in the character's world, seeing, feeling, wanting with the character. Listen now as if you are Jeremy. That's what readers do; we become the characters in our books. Later you'll have a chance to talk with your partner about this."

I have dreams about those shoes.

Black high-tops. Two white stripes.

"Grandma, I want them."

"There's no room for 'want' around here—just 'need,'" Grandma says. "And what you *need* are new boots for winter."

"Readers, we could talk about this whole book, but let's focus on what Jeremy sees, feels and wants in this part. I've made copies of the section." I distributed them. "Before we talk, take a second to reread this, remembering that you're in Jeremy's shoes, in his world. You feel and want as he does. What's going on here? Underline key parts." I gave them time to do this, then called out, "Okay, partners, turn and talk!"

As children talked, I listened in. After a few minutes, I reconvened the group.

"Readers, I loved listening to you all imagine yourself as Jeremy just now. You really got into that role. Theo said he knows what it's like to want something your parents can't afford—it almost hurts, you want it so badly, but there's nothing you can do. And Francesca, who recalled that a lot of kids in Jeremy's school start to get the shoes, said she thinks it's not just the *shoes* Jeremy wants, but to be like everyone else, to fit in. Francesca, you just grew a theory! Nice job carrying over yesterday's work to today."

LINK

Encourage children to step into the shoes of any character in their books, assuming that person's wants and feelings.

"Readers, all of us learned today that when we step into a character's shoes, living in his world, wanting what he wants, we read more closely. It's as if by stepping into a character's shoes, we step also into that person's head and heart. As you read your independent books, try to do the same thing—step into your character's shoes and wants as if you're that person."

Empathizing and Predicting Go Hand in Hand

> *Dear Teachers,*
>
> *In this session, you will help your children make predictions, reading one step ahead of their eyes, forecasting what's bound to happen, as any engaged reader does. As we help children predict, we'll teach them that predictions, like theories, are tentative. A reader may think, "Perhaps this will happen, but maybe this or that. And then XYZ will. . . because. . . . Furthermore. . . ."*
>
> *Then, too, as we read on, learning more about the world of the book, often we revise our predictions. We think, "I used to think. . . , but now I bet. . . ." In this unit, we invite children to draw on their understanding of characters to imagine their next steps, all the while knowing that these predictions may change alongside the characters themselves.*

CONNECTION

Draw on a familiar, predictable fairytale to illustrate how knowing characters well makes it possible to predict what they will do next.

"Readers, do you recall the story of the three little pigs? I bet you heard it when you were younger. Remember how those three pigs each built a house, one made of straw, one of wood, and one of bricks? And remember how the big bad wolf's mission was to eat those pigs for dinner? So what did he do? He went to the first house and called out, 'Little pig, little pig, let me in, let me in!' And when the first little pig refused (naturally!), saying, 'Not by the hair of my chinny chin chin!' the wolf responded, 'Then I'll huff and I'll puff and I'll blow your house in!' And he did just that. Well, the first little pig scrambled to his brother's house and—what happened next? That hungry, relentless wolf followed him and called out again, 'Little pig, little pig, let me in, let me in!' And just like his brother before him, the second little pig called out, 'Not by the hair of my chinny chin chin!' Again, the wolf said his line and blew the house down. And then what?

"Well, I don't know about you, but I knew what was going to happen next. Even though those pigs were little, they were quick on their feet—or rather hooves! Those pigs were very determined, and I knew that they were going to work together. Those are some smart pigs! So I thought to myself, 'They're going to use those strengths of theirs to trick that wolf, to defeat him.' And I was right! They got him to come down the chimney of that third house, and then they cooked *him* for dinner. I predicted correctly.

"That got me thinking. Aren't we always trying to predict what's going to happen next if we're truly in a character's shoes? It's almost like we can't help it, because as we've said before, what happens to our character is not only happening to that person but also to us!"

Name your teaching point. Specifically, tell readers that when we are in a character's shoes, we can guess his or her next steps.

"Today I want to teach you that when we're in a character's shoes, we can guess what the character will do next. We anticipate his or her next words, next steps. Then we read on, seeing if we were right."

Teaching

Demonstrate for children how readers step into the shoes of a character, pretending to be that person to predict his or her next steps.

"Let me show you how I do this, and then I'll give you a chance to practice it yourself with your own books. Since we are reading *Because of Winn-Dixie* in Opal's shoes, we know that she's gutsy and outspoken, right? She can be a little feisty, our Opal! But we also noticed that she has a soft spot for animals, and certainly for Winn-Dixie. So as I guess her next steps, I'll want to keep those things in mind. Okay, listen while I read a bit of Chapter 9. Remember that when we left off reading, Winn-Dixie had run off from Opal:"

Winn-Dixie started to race way ahead of me.

"You better watch out," Dunlap hollered. "That dog is headed right for the witch's house."

"Winn-Dixie," I called. But he kept on going faster and hopped a gate and went into the most overgrown jungle of a yard that I had ever seen.

"You better go get your dog out of there," Dunlap said.

"The witch will eat that dog," Stevie said.

"Shut up," I told them.

I got off my bike and went up to the gate and hollered, "Winn-Dixie, you better come on out of there."

But he didn't.

"She's probably eating him right now," Stevie said. He and Dunlap were standing behind me. "She eats dogs all the time."

I put the book down and scratched my head as if in thought. "Hmm, I wonder what I would do next as Opal. We know that Opal is feisty. She's telling those boys off! We also know that she's got guts. I'm thinking that as Opal the Gutsy, I'd tell those boys to bug off and I'd march myself right up to that house, witch or no witch!

"What else do we know about Opal? Well, we know that she loves Winn-Dixie. She'd do anything to protect and keep that dog. She's not going to let him get harmed or lost, right? Again, I think she'd brave the house, and the witch, for that animal."

Show children how taking on the character's traits helped you predict what she would do next in the story. Tuck in a tip on when and in what ways readers predict.

"Readers, do you see how I imagined what Opal might do, based on some things we know about her? I stepped into Opal's shoes, taking on her traits and wants to imagine her next steps. This is one thing readers can do to make predictions. Let's begin a chart that tells what we do when we predict:"

Readers Predict By. . .

- Stepping into the character's shoes, imagining his or her traits and wants, and then thinking, "What will the character do next?"

ACTIVE INVOLVEMENT

Ask children to find and share times when their identification with a character has allowed them to predict that person's next steps.

"Readers, right now, take a moment to glance back over your jottings in your independent reading books. See if you can find evidence of a time when you were so acutely aware of your character as a person—his wants and quirks—that you guessed what he would do next. If you don't find a jotting like that, see if you can make a prediction like that right now by thinking what your character might do next."

I gave children a few minutes to do this work, and then I intervened. "Readers, turn and share your predictions. Partner 1, share not only your prediction but also your process of making it. When you're done sharing, walk your partner through your process. How and why did you predict in that particular spot in your book? What about your character led you to make that prediction? Was your prediction a turn-the-next-page kind of prediction, or was it a see-over-the-horizon prediction? Turn and talk!"

LINK

Reiterate that readers make predictions and then sometimes revise these as we read on. Encourage children to use their predictions to grow ideas about characters.

"Readers, as you read your own book today and any day, pay attention to the predictions you make. If you are really walking in a character's shoes, you'll find yourself thinking, 'He's going to. . .' or 'I bet she'll. . . ,' and you'll make guesses about what will happen next. As you read on, you may find that you were right—or almost right—or it may be that you were off the mark. That's okay. Readers revise our predictions as we go. That's part of the fun of reading. And be sure to continue growing ideas about the sort of person your character is. Remember to not only observe but also grow ideas about your character, saying, 'I think maybe this suggests that my character. . . .'"

SESSION V

We Draw On All We Know to Predict in Graphic Detail

Dear Teachers,

In this session, you will aim to deepen children's prediction work a notch. You'll ask them to think about not only what might happen but also how that event might go.

As children predict, you'll encourage them to draw upon everything they know about a character, about how stories usually go, and about their own lives. The beauty of skilled prediction work is that it draws upon other skills, too: envisionment, synthesis, empathy. The richest predictions are ones that include both reflection and projection.

CONNECTION

Share a story that illustrates how readers can learn to see in deep ways.

"Readers, you have gym class later today, and I know that you've been doing basketball drills like dribbling between your hands and shooting layups. I have a feeling some days this is fun and other days, when you're a little chatty and silly and then you get 'a little talking-to,' it's not so fun. Does that sound about right?"

The kids giggled because yes, indeed, they'd been getting "a little talking-to" more often lately during physical education class.

"Right now, predict what will happen at the start of gym today. Predict what Mr. Van Deusen will say, what he'll ask you to do first, and then predict what you'll do." I gave them a minute to think, hoping they'd use the time to make a prediction.

"Let me ask you something. Are you predicting only *wha*t Mr. Van Deusen will say or ask you to do? 'Okay, kids, today we're going to do some basketball drills.' Or are you predicting also *how* he'll ask it, what tone of voice he'll use, how the class will feel on this day, how everyone's mood will be? Because if you only predict the facts and not the feelings, the tone, and the details, then you'll miss an important part of the way your gym class will probably play out."

"I'm telling you this because readers, too, need to predict not only the facts or events that lie ahead in our book but also the mood, the feelings, and the tone of events we anticipate in a later part of our book."

Name your teaching point. Specifically, teach children that readers predict not only what will happen but how.

"Today I want to teach you that as we make predictions, it helps to predict not only what will happen but also how it will happen."

TEACHING

Demonstrate how to read the text, seeing the characters so well that you can predict not only what they will do next but how they will do one thing or another.

"You are all becoming such naturals at prediction. You tell me what you think will happen next in your books almost instinctually, and often you are right. It's like you've gotten the rhythm of reading and predicting. You'll read one bit and say, 'She's going to get to perform in the recital,' and then boom, on the very next page that very thing happens. You're mastering the art of making a simple prediction.

"I've been thinking that predicting is a bit like riding your bike. You are riding in one place, but you can meanwhile see all the way to the horizon. You see big stuff long before it is actually here. That kind of seeing is at the heart of a strong prediction, a skilled one. If you see the character and the shape of the story, then you see the path and you can see what lies ahead. You see not only the facts but also the feelings, the mood. A strong prediction covers not only *what* will happen but also *how* it will happen.

"Let me show you what I mean. In the last chapter we read from *Because of Winn-Dixie*, Opal met Gloria Dump on a dare. It turns out Gloria Dump's not a witch, right? She's a touch eccentric, maybe, but harmless. And she's just offered her ear to Opal. Remember she said, 'Why don't you go on and tell me everything about yourself, so I can see you with my heart.' She can't see that much with her eyes anymore, but she can see by listening so well that she forms a picture of Opal in her mind. Listen now while I read aloud the beginning of Chapter 10. You'll see that it's possible to predict not only what will happen next but also how it might happen if we, as readers, listen and see just the way that Gloria sees:"

Chapter 10

I told Gloria Dump everything. I told her how me and the preacher had just moved to Naomi and how I had to leave all my friends behind. I told her about my mama leaving, and I listed out the ten things that I knew about her; and I explained that here, in Naomi, I missed Mama more than I ever had in Watley. I told her about the preacher being like a turtle, hiding all the time inside his shell. I told her about finding Winn-Dixie in the produce department and how, because of him, I became friends with Miss Franny Block and got a job working for a man named Otis at Gertrude's Pets and got invited to Sweetie Pie Thomas's birthday party. I even told Gloria Dump how Dunlap and Stevie Dewberry called her a witch. But I told her they were stupid, mean, bald-headed boys and I didn't believe them, not for long anyhow.

And the whole time I was talking, Gloria Dump was listening. She was nodding her head and smiling and frowning and saying, "Hmmm," and "Is that right?"

I could feel her listening with all her heart, and it felt good.

"Okay, I'm going to pause. What do you think will happen next—and how will it happen? Take a moment to think of answers."

As children thought, I said, "I want to remind you that you can only answer these questions if you really pay attention to the characters, noticing what they seem to want deep down. Try to see what's been happening not only on the surface but also inside people. So what's happening here? Opal just told Gloria Dump, the 'witch,' a half-blind stranger, her life story. Does that seem really big to all of you? Imagine telling someone you barely know all those things about yourself." I left a brief pool of silence and then continued. "And Gloria really listened, didn't she? I don't know about all of you, but to me, there's nothing better than a good listener. People who really, truly, actively listen with not only their ears but their eyes and their hearts—those people are rare.

"We all agree that Opal is lonely in Naomi—that she wants a friend. So what do we think is going to happen and how?" I paused, then said, "Here's my prediction. I'm willing to bet that this visit will be the first of many. I think Gloria Dump is going to be like a parent to Opal, maybe teach her a lesson or two. She seems very wise."

Deconstruct how you landed on the prediction you just made, and point out that readers do several things to make deep predictions—we step into our character's shoes, sharing that person's wants, and we look closely at the character and the story, thinking how something might unfold.

"Readers, do you see that I thought about what Opal wants deep down to make this prediction? I stepped into Opal's shoes and thought about what she longs for, what she needs. Based on this, I imagined not only what would happen further along—that Opal would visit Gloria again—but also *how* this might happen—that Gloria would become sort of like a parent to Opal and that she might guide her, teaching her some lessons."

ACTIVE INVOLVEMENT

Set children up to practice making deep predictions with their partners.

"Now it's your turn. I'm going to read on a bit in our book, and as I do so, see if you can make your own prediction. You may find that you add to the one I made or that an entirely new prediction comes to mind. Listen:"

"You know what?" she [Gloria Dump] said when I was done.

"What?"

"Could be that you got more of your mama in you than just red hair and freckles and running fast."

"Really?" I said. "Like what?"

"Like maybe you got her green thumb. The two of us could plant something and see how it grows; test your thumb out."

"Okay," I said.

What Gloria Dump picked for me to grow was a tree. Or she said it was a tree. To me, it looked more like a plant. She had me dig a hole for it and put it in the ground and pat the dirt around it tight, like it was a baby and I was tucking it into bed.

"What kind of tree is it?" I asked Gloria Dump.

"It's a wait-and-see tree," she said.

"What's that mean?"

"It means you got to wait for it to grow up before you know what it is."

"Can I come back and see it tomorrow?" I asked.

"Child," she said, "as long as this is my garden, you're welcome in it. But that tree ain't going to have changed much by tomorrow."

"But I want to see you, too," I said.

"Hmmmph," said Gloria Dump. "I ain't going nowhere. I be right here."

"Turn and talk to your partner about the prediction you've made."

Share some of the children's responses.

"Wow! I thought my prediction was big, but you took prediction to a new level. Franny and Harry said they thought Gloria Dump and Opal would become friends in the *same* way that the wait-and-see tree would grow—slowly. They thought Kate DiCamillo was showing that Opal and Gloria were planting not just a tree but roots for their friendship. The two of you didn't just make a skilled prediction, guessing how something would happen. You also noticed how that tree was almost like a symbol for their friendship."

LINK

Nudge children to jot their predictions and to push themselves to make their predictions even deeper.

"Readers, as you return to your independent reading books, remember that you can make predictions at any point, and as you do so, your reading will be much richer if you think about not just *what* may happen but *how* it might happen. As you read on, you may find that you almost had it right, or you may find you were *way* off the mark. Either is okay! Off you go!"

SESSION VI

We React as We Read and Return to Passages that Evoke Reactions

Dear Teachers,

In this session, you'll encourage children to pay attention to the parts in their reading that evoke strong emotions. Often these are moments when a character learns something important or perhaps begins to face something that is essential to his or her evolution.

When Lucy discovers Aslan, dead on the stone table, we weep with her, and we know that she is learning the extraordinary power of sacrifice that comes from love. We know, too, that she has grown up in this moment, faced with the need to acknowledge and draw upon her inner strength. Likewise, when Charlotte tells Wilbur that she is about to die, leaving the care of her offspring to him, Wilbur is forced to face his fear not only of dying but of living, too. These are powerful moments with powerful lessons.

Of course, you won't have to teach children to have strong emotions as they read. They'll have those naturally. Rather, you'll teach them to pause during those moments and to think as well as to feel.

CONNECTION

Share a moment in a film that stirs up a strong emotion in you, and tell children that parts in books also have this effect on us.

"Readers, the other night I watched *Shrek,* the movie, again. I don't even have to ask if you know it. You all grew up with *Shrek.* Even before the movie came out, I bet you met him on paper. You know that ornery ogre turned big softie from Steig's absurd language and those equally fun, silly pictures."

"I have a confession." I leaned in conspiratorially. "I loved Shrek before he turned soft. Maybe I could tell that under that crabby green grouch was a guy with a really big heart."

"So the other night, this is what happened. I got to the part toward the end of the movie where Fiona turns into her ogress self. As her guests pull back in horror, Fiona flinching too, we see Shrek lean in, his eyes wide, not with disgust but with love. It's as if he sees her for the first time. And when Fiona says, 'This wasn't supposed to happen. I was supposed to be beautiful,' Shrek says, 'But you *are* beautiful.'"

"Readers, that part always gets me. It's as if Shrek is saying, 'I love you *even though* you're an ogress,' or maybe even, 'I love you *more* now that you're an ogress.' Her true self is revealed, her imperfections, and he loves that self. That's when it happens. I lean into the screen, crying, because there is something beautiful about times a person really sees someone, imperfections and all, and feels love."

"I've seen all of you experiencing moments of strong feeling as you read. Someone once said that laughter and tears are the best comprehension meters there are. Do you know what that means? If someone is laughing and crying while reading, that means the person is so lost inside the world of the book that he or she is swept away with emotion, which means the person really *comprehends* the book."

Name your teaching point. Specifically, teach children that readers notice and mark powerful parts in our books.

"Today I want to teach you that readers pay attention to the parts of our books that make us feel strong emotions. Sometimes we put Post-its on those parts, and we return to them later not only to feel but also to think."

TEACHING

Demonstrate for children how you read a passage that is powerful, one that moves you, and then mark it. Show readers, too, that you reflect on your strong response, noting what it might mean about the characters.

"I'm going to read a bit to you from *Because of Winn-Dixie,* and I'll show you what I mean. When we left Opal, she was back at Gloria Dump's place for a visit. Gloria was about to show Opal something in her yard. Listen." I opened *Because of Winn-Dixie* to p. 94 of Chapter 14 and began reading:

"Look at this tree," Gloria said.

I looked up. There were bottles hanging from just about every branch. There were whiskey bottles and beer bottles and wine bottles all tied on with string, and some of them were clanking against each other and making a spooky kind of noise. Me and Winn-Dixie stood and stared at the tree, and the hair on top of his head rose up a little bit and he growled deep in his throat.

Gloria Dump pointed her cane at the tree.

"What do you think about this tree?"

I said, "I don't know. Why are all those bottles on it?"

"To keep the ghosts away," Gloria said.

"What ghosts?"

"The ghosts of all the things I done wrong."

I looked at all the bottles on the tree. "You did that many things wrong?" I asked her.

"Mmmm-hmmm," said Gloria. "More than that."

"But you're the nicest person I know," I told her.

"Don't mean I haven't done bad things," she said.

"There's whiskey bottles on there," I told her.

"And beer bottles."

"Child," said Gloria Dump, "I know that. I'm the one who put 'em there. I'm the one who drank what was in 'em."

"My mama drank," I whispered.

"Oh my." I put down the book and paused, looking at the children. "This part gets me every time I read it. I feel like I'm right there next to Opal and Gloria, looking at that tree. I can feel something big is happening for both of them."

"Do you see this worn Post-it in my book?" I held up my copy of *Because of Winn-Dixie*, with an old Post-it sticking out. "This little green Post-it has gotten a bit battered over the years because I've left it in my book all this time to remind myself to pause here. Each time I do so, it's as if I'm experiencing that big feeling for the first time."

"It's a little like my response to that part in *Shrek* when he sees Fiona the ogress. Here's Gloria looking so closely at herself, those whiskey bottles almost a mirror reflection, saying to Opal, 'I have regrets. I've messed up.' And Opal, too, is seeing, really seeing, that the very mother whom she misses so desperately also drank—like Gloria. That's got to hurt." I paused to let this bit of information sink in.

"Opal says, 'But you're the nicest person I know,' and what does Gloria respond? 'Don't mean I haven't done bad things.'" I paused and then repeated, "'Don't mean I haven't done bad things.' What do you think about that? Turn and talk to your partner."

I gave them a minute to talk. Then I called on one child, who said, "I think Gloria is teaching Opal a big lesson. Everyone make mistakes."

I nodded and then asked, "And why does she hang her mistakes on a tree, I wonder?"

Another child called out, "So she looks at her mistakes?"

I nodded and added, "And looking at your mistakes, hanging them from the tree in front of your house, is one way to be sure you learn from them."

"Readers, every time I read this passage, I have strong feelings for both Opal and Gloria. And that reaction makes me think a lot, too. I do that when I read. I notice the parts that give me strong feelings, and I go back and reread those parts to grow big ideas about them."

ACTIVE INVOLVEMENT

Ask children to find parts in their books that evoke strong emotions and to mark those spots.

"Readers, take a few minutes to thumb through your independent reading books and see if you can find a part where your character (and you) felt something. It may be a part that makes you a little misty-eyed or a part where you jumped up and down with excitement. Go to that part and reread it, getting the feeling again. This time, please also think specifically, 'Is the character in the midst of something big here or changing in big ways?'"

Have children reflect on their feelings, and the passage they selected, with a partner.

After a couple minutes, I said, "Partner 1s, share the moment you marked with Partner 2s. Then show how you were feeling as you read that part, and tell what you are thinking now about the character. You might have to explain a little about what's happened that has led up to this part, especially if your partner hasn't read the book."

"Partner 2s, listen. Be the kind of listeners who take in everything. Don't just hear the words your partner says; notice *how* your partner speaks, what your partner's face looks like. Hear the emotion in your partner's voice. Turn and talk."

As children talked excitedly, I crouched alongside one partnership and then another. When children struggled, I coached into their conversations.

LINK

Reiterate that readers can note the parts of books that make us feel strong emotions and return to them later to think about whether the character may be learning a lesson.

"Readers, this is the kind of thing we can do for the rest of our lives. We can mark parts of our books that stir up strong feelings in us. Sometimes those will be little parts that we connect with in some way (maybe they trigger something for us in our own life), and other times we'll react to parts that are big moments for a character—moments of self-discovery, of change. Even when we can't put our finger on what's happening or about to happen, we should mark those spots that make us gasp or cry or swell up with joy, and later we can return to them to think as well as feel.

"Do that sort of marking and thinking today. Of course, you'll be marking other spots in your books too—places where you find yourself predicting, for example, or where you realize that the parts of your character are fitting together like pieces in a puzzle and you are seeing your character in a new way."

PART TWO

As Readers Come to Know a Character Well,
We Grow Ideas About What Makes that
Person Tick

Dear Teachers,

Some units of study are designed so that there are a few very distinct parts, and this particular unit has less clear divisions than most. You began the unit by encouraging children to read characters and then showed them that by reading characters, they can predict what will happen next in a story.

The next part of this unit returns to the idea that readers read characters. In this session, however, you'll teach children that readers don't just read to predict or to get lost in the story, but also to grow ideas about the characters and the story itself. You'll teach readers to notice patterns of behavior, letting those observations inform their idea of who this person, this character, is. The challenge will be for children to look at the larger picture of a character and synthesize what they've learned earlier in the text with what they discover as they read on—to grow a theory about the character that holds weight.

SESSION VII

We Question Why Characters Act as They Do

CONNECTION

Tell children the story of a time when someone you know well did something that made you think, "There she goes again!"

"Readers, you know that tendency we all have when we know someone really well to say, 'There she goes again!'? For example, the other day my friend Sophie called me to announce her new business idea; she'd seen an ad on the Internet describing how to make and sell soap and decided to try her hand at it. I giggled to myself when I heard this announcement, not because I think it's particularly funny but because this sort of project is so like her. Sophie is very entrepreneurial. She's constantly coming up with—and trying her hand at—new business ventures. Last year it was greeting cards and the year before that it was perfumes. Sophie is artsy, and she is full of ideas for how to strike it rich. I love her can-do attitude and optimism. But it's also funny to me that she keeps convincing herself (and trying to convince her friends) that this time she's onto something big. I know Sophie's patterns, her thinking; I know what makes her tick.

"By now you know what I'm going to say next." I leaned in and gave children a knowing nod.

Name your teaching point. Specifically, tell children that we can also come to recognize patterns of behavior in characters, learning what makes them tick.

"Today I want to teach you that as we come to know our character, we notice that the character often acts in similar ways. We think, 'There she goes again!' or 'There he goes again!' When we see patterns in how a character acts, we try to understand why the character acts that way, and doing this helps us understand what makes this character tick."

Teaching

Pick a child in the class, and then demonstrate how you read a person by noticing things about that child that illustrate who she is as a person—the things that make her tick.

"Let me show you what I mean about noticing what a character does a lot in order to form bigger ideas about what makes the character tick, about the reasons behind all those actions.

"I'm going to think about one of you—say, Greta—and I'm going to think about what gives me the feeling of 'There she goes again!' or 'Yup, that's Greta for you!' Hmm, well, one thing is that when I find bright, colorful beads and string strewn around our room, I definitely think, 'There she goes again!' Right? Both depositing stuff here and there and the things themselves—the bright beads and string—make me think of her.

"It's not just the beads, though. When I see that someone has brought in a jewelry-making book or craft supplies from home, you know who I assume did that? Greta!

"So I'm going to put those things together in my mind, like pieces of a puzzle, and try to say some bigger umbrella idea about what makes Greta tick. How about this? 'Greta is passionate about crafts, especially making pretty necklaces, so much so that she wants to share these projects with her friends. That makes me think that Greta is passionate both about creating beautiful things and about sharing her art with other people.'" I paused to give Greta a conspiratorial wink. "I'm not sure I've entirely figured out what makes you tick, Greta, but at least this is a rough-draft idea. You could help me revise it later, okay?"

Active Involvement

Invite children to continue the work you did during the teaching by taking part in a symphony share of "There he or she goes again" in which they name things in this passage that illustrate something about the character.

"Let's try this together on ourselves. After all, each of us is the main character in a story—the story of our own life. So for a minute, will you think about the things you do often enough that people think, 'There he or she goes again!'? Think of more than one thing, and try to reach for patterns that actually matter—not trivial ones." I gave children a moment of silence. "Now think, 'Do those patterns go together in bigger ways, like pieces of a puzzle? Does this action that I do often reflect something bigger about me?'" Again I was silent. "Think, 'What are the reasons I act this way? What makes me tick?'"

Then I said, "Turn and tell your partner the things you do that make people think, 'There he or she goes again!' and share also the bigger idea you grew from this about what makes you tick."

Link

Tuck in a reference to your read-aloud character to reiterate for children how you think, "There she goes again" and then come up with a big idea about that person.

"Readers, I know you're realizing already that we can think in the same ways about things Opal does over and over that make us say, 'There she goes again!' Like we could say, 'There she goes again, telling people stories,' or 'There she goes again, trying to help her friends,' or 'There she goes again, making friends with odd sorts.' If we want to understand what's behind all these tendencies, we would continue to think about these patterns, asking, 'So what's the big idea we can make about Opal, about what makes her tick?' We have said that Opal is apt to spend time with friends, to help friends. So maybe our big idea could be that Opal was lonely, and now she's trying to connect with people. That's a little theory, and it can certainly grow as we read on."

Remind children that they can do this work always as they read, coming up with and adjusting theories as they read on.

"So, readers, as you read today and always, notice when you get the feeling that your character is at it again, when you think, 'There he or she goes again!' and see if you can pause at that moment to grow a theory about what makes your character tick. As you read on, you will probably find that you have to adjust your theory a bit or that you'll add to it. Keep reading and keep thinking."

Flexibility Matters in Reading: We Expect to Revise Our Ideas

Dear Teachers,

In this session, you will help children read with tentative theories in mind, guided by the knowledge that as readers move forward in books, learning more, often we revise our theories. You'll want to convey the message that generating ideas is an ongoing process. We don't just come up with a single idea, hold fast to it, and then plough through our book, intractable. Instead, we keep the idea in mind, and then as we gather new information about the characters and the story, we refine our thinking. Sometimes we add to it or alter it; other times we abandon it altogether for new thinking. And always, always, we think of new ideas.

CONNECTION

Tell the story of a time when you had to adjust your theory about something.

"Have I ever told you the story about Lucky? I'd just graduated from college and moved into a little studio apartment—my first place of my own! It felt a little bare and lonely, so I decided to liven it up a bit with something green. At the plant store, I selected a bold, striking plant called Lucky Bamboo. Believe it or not, this was my first plant, too!

"I brought Lucky home, put her in a pretty pot with water and rocks, and placed the pot on a table near the window. Over the next few days, I took good care of Lucky, and sure enough, she brightened up the place beautifully.

"But then something went wrong. Lucky Bamboo didn't look quite so tall and perky. She wasn't that bright shade of green she'd been when I first brought her home. She was withering! I panicked. Then I had a thought, 'Lucky needs more sunlight. Plants do well with light.' So I moved her to the windowsill and raised the shade all the way. And do you know what happened? Lucky got worse! I couldn't believe it.

"Well, I did a little Internet research, and do you know what I discovered? Lucky Bamboo does better with *indirect* sunlight! So my theory, while correct for some plants, was not the right one for *my* plant.

"Sometimes, readers, we have a theory, but then when we collect more information, we realize we need to revise it."

Name your teaching point. Specifically, teach children that readers sometimes need to revise our theories as we read on.

"Today I want to teach you that when we have a theory about a character, we read with an eye on the way that character acts to say, 'I was right,' or 'Oops—I was wrong!' and then we revise our first impression."

TEACHING

Revisit a familiar picture book to show that when readers come across something in the text that causes us to revise a theory about a character, we rethink our idea, landing on one that feels truer.

"Let's return to *Those Shoes* for a minute. Do you remember when we started this book together, how we decided that Jeremy's grandmother was a practical person? Jeremy wants those shoes *so* badly; he even dreams about them! But all his grandmother can say is, 'There's no room for "want" around here—just need. . . . And what you *need* are new boots for winter.' She's practical, practical, practical—and maybe a bit rigid, too.

"But *then* (I leaned in for emphasis) remember when his grandma tells Jeremy she's set aside a little money and suggests they check out the shoes? We thought to ourselves, 'Hmm, maybe Jeremy's grandmother isn't so practical after all!' We didn't come out and say it, right? But it was as if we knew our theory might need a little revising. And then Jeremy and his grandmother go to the store and discover how much money those shoes cost! Our hearts broke because we knew Jeremy's grandma didn't have the money. We decided, she's practical, yes, but because she has to be, not because she's rigid. And when they find those shoes at a thrift store—but in a size too small—when Grandma says she can't spend good money on shoes that don't fit, we knew it's not that she wants to *deny* Jeremy luxuries. It's that she can't *afford* luxuries.

"When we read on, we realized that we didn't quite have our theory right. We had it partly right, yes, but not entirely, so we revised it. We decided that our theory, not Grandma, was too rigid! That happens often to readers as we uncover more of the text."

ACTIVE INVOLVEMENT

Set children up to think about a time in their own lives when they revised their idea about something and to then share it with their partner.

"Let's try this for a minute, drawing on our own life stories. Take a couple minutes and think back over your lives. See if you can come up with a time when you had an idea about something. Maybe it was an idea about a person, or a place, or about something at school. It could be anything. Be sure to pick a situation when you first thought one way and then later, after collecting more information, realized you had to revise your idea. In a few minutes, you'll share with your partner how you came to revise your thinking."

LINK

Remind readers that theories, like predictions, are tentative.

"Readers, we're learning that theories, like predictions, are rough draft ideas. As we read on in a book, we sometimes pause to say, 'That doesn't seem quite right.' Then we revise our thinking, our theory, based on new information. Other times we may find that, in fact, our theory still holds for us. Maybe we add to it or refine it. As you read, keep your theories in mind and watch for new information that may lead you to change your mind."

SESSION IX

When Characters Act Out of Character, We Take Notice

Dear Teachers,

As children come to regard the characters in their books as friends, there will be times when a character surprises them. Just when children think they have a character figured out, when they are snug in that character's shoes, the character will do something entirely out of character. Perhaps she rises to the occasion in a remarkable way, finding courage she didn't know she had to set right a wrong or to test herself—to grow. This session is designed to help children take note of those moments, knowing that they are there for a reason. When they happen, wise readers sit up and ask ourselves, "Why? Why is she doing this?" Then we look for answers in that part of our book and as we move forward in the story.

The challenge will be for children to look at the larger picture of a character—at both his reliable nature and his moments of uncharacteristic behavior—to synthesize what they've learned from earlier parts of the text with what they discover as they read on, to grow a theory about the character that holds weight. This is sophisticated work. Be prepared for your students to challenge you as much as you challenge them!

CONNECTION

Set children up to recap what they have learned so far.

"We've learned a lot about reading fiction books and growing ideas about characters. Turn and list three things you have learned. List them across your fingers to your partner," I said.

Name your teaching point. Specifically, tell children that a character can sometimes act in a surprising way, and when this happens, readers ask ourselves, "Why?"

"Today I want to teach you that, just like people can surprise us, sometimes a character surprises us. We think the character will act one way, but he or she acts another way. When this happens, we ask ourselves, 'Why did the character do that?'"

TEACHING

Tell an anecdote about one time when people acted in surprising ways and you asked, "Why?"

"The other day I was on one of those hot subway cars at rush hour. All around me, people were frowning. I thought to myself, 'These people are stressed out and crabby.'

"Then the door connecting our car to the one in front of it opened, and a group of boys came prancing down the aisle. 'Let's get this party started,' one of them called out—he was about ten. The oldest in the group flipped on his radio, and loud music started blasting. 'Go, Jason! Go, Jason!' all of the boys chanted as one of them started dancing down the aisle, doing flips and chin-ups and elaborate dance moves on the speeding train. 'Go, Michael! Go, Michael!' the boys chanted as the next boy began making his way down the aisle.

"This was surprising, of course—having kids doing dance moves down the aisle of the subway—but the really surprising thing is that when I turned to see how the cranky people were taking in this act, they weren't rolling their eyes like I expected. The people had begun to smile. Some were tapping their feet. Others were laughing as Michael, the youngest boy, made his way down the aisle.

"I couldn't believe what had happened! Before my eyes, those boys had turned the rest of us into a happy crowd. When the show ended, people were digging in their bags for change for those boys.

"When things like that happen—when people react in ways that surprise me, that don't go with my theory of them—I push myself to ask, 'Why?' and to see if I need to change my ideas about them.

"When the people acted so appreciative of the boys, I realized that maybe they had never been cranky at all. Maybe they'd just been tired, and sometimes the best medicine for being tired is to do something, to participate in something. Those people had been only too willing to be drawn in to participate in something on that subway. That changed my whole theory of them."

ACTIVE INVOLVEMENT

Channel children to retell times in their books when a character acted out of character.

"Right now, think of a time in your independent reading book when your character acted in ways that surprised you, or if you can't think of a time in your independent book, think of a time in *Because of Winn-Dixie*. When did the preacher, for example, act in ways that surprised you?" I gave the children a moment to think and then channeled them to talk about whatever they'd thought about.

LINK

Channel children to share resolutions for the day's reading work.

"We've talked about so many things that readers do to grow powerful ideas. Right now, tell your partner the reading work you expect to be doing today. Turn and talk."

SESSION X

Readers Anticipate that Characters Will Struggle and Grow

Dear Teachers,

In this session, you'll teach children to recognize when and how a character changes. Being able to think, talk, and write meaningfully about a character's internal journey is central to children's ability to comprehend character complexity. Of course, many of your children will be reading books whose characters change in rather straightforward ways, perhaps overcoming a big, obvious obstacle. The more subtle, gradual progression toward growth is more characteristic of higher-level books. Still, you will guide children to spot changes in their characters and to see how those changes fit into the story arc.

Connection

Draw on the image of classes of children you have known to demonstrate that people change over time.

"Readers, you know how sometimes you go through growth spurts over the summer, how in June you're, say, four feet tall and then in August you've shot up two inches? I see it all the time. I'll wave good-bye to a class of kids on the last day of school, and then the next fall, I'll see those same kids lope by me on long gazelle-like legs, and I almost don't recognize them! It's as if they've shot up overnight.

"I bet you notice the same thing when you look at pictures of yourself that span several years. As you're growing, you don't notice the changes because they're gradual—they occur over time—but when you look at photos of yourself in kindergarten, first grade, second grade, for example, you see how much you've changed!

"It's not all physical, either. For some of us, shyness fades, and we realize one day that we're more confident now, more willing to say hello to someone we don't know. People are like that. We don't stay the same. We change."

Name your teaching point. Specifically, tell children that characters change and that readers take note of this.

"Today I want to let you in on something: characters, like people in our lives, don't stay the same. Readers notice when a character changes, and we think about those changes."

Teaching

Demonstrate how you consider what a character is like at the start of the book to notice how he or she has changed.

"Let's think about out friend Opal. By now, she really is a friend, isn't she? And because we've come to know her so well, I know we're all beginning to notice some change in her. Let me show you how I go about spotting that change and thinking about it, and then I'll give you a chance to do the same thing with your partners.

"The first thing I usually do when I'm actively noticing change in a character is I think about what that person is like at the start of the book, because *change* implies that something is different. So let's see, what did we begin this unit noticing about Opal? Hmm…."I flipped through my copy of *Because of Winn-Dixie,* reading over the Post-its. "Oh, I remember. We said that she was lonely, right? She missed her mother and could use a friend. We noticed that she has a soft spot for animals. Early on in the book, we saw her make friends with grown-ups.

"When we left off reading, Opal had gathered a group of guests at her party, and most of them had arrived. Listen while I read on for just a short while, and I'll show you how I notice our character changing:"

> Amanda Wilkinson came and she had her blond hair all curled up and she looked shy and not as mean as usual, and I stood real close to her and introduced her to Gloria Dump. I was surprised at how glad I was to see Amanda. And I wanted to tell her I knew about Carson. I wanted to tell her I understood about losing people, but I didn't say anything. I was just extra nice.

"Hmm, is this the same Opal who couldn't stand pinch-faced Amanda Wilkinson just a few chapters ago? Is this the same girl who's been befriending adults right and left but hasn't yet found a friend her own age?

"Yesterday we talked about characters acting in surprising ways, and I've got to tell you, Opal is throwing me for a bit of a loop here. In fact, it seems like she's surprised herself, too. She seems genuinely pleased to have Amanda at her party, doesn't she? And she's being nice to her!"

ACTIVE INVOLVEMENT

Recruit children to join you in thinking about the change in the character from the read-aloud book.

"I wonder what's changed in Opal to bring about this reaction in her…" I let my voice trail off. Then I said, "Turn and tell your partner how you think Opal is changing."

After a few minutes, I said, "A few of you just pointed out that Opal seems to be opening herself to a kid her own age. Some of you realized that Amanda is actually a bit like Opal. She loves books and stories, and she knows something about loss 'cause her little brother died, so these two have something in common. I heard one partnership say they think Opal might be learning how to give people second chances."

LINK

Remind readers to draw on the full repertoire of what you have taught them, including the idea that characters change.

"Readers, I know you are growing theories about your characters and predicting what they will do next. As you do all this thinking, you should also be on the lookout for change in your characters—and especially notice whether the character changes toward the end of the book, and how."

PART THREE

Readers Grow Alongside Characters

Dear Teachers,

In this third and final part, you'll nudge children to consider the challenges characters face along their journey and the lessons they learn as a result. You'll do this with the read-aloud book, letting children arrive at their own interpretations while also remaining open to their classmates' thoughts and discoveries. These final sessions encourage children to move beyond the realm of the story and into the realm of their lives, thinking about how the challenges a character has faced and the lessons he or she has learned resonate in real life. The hope is that children will come to recognize that there is universality on the page and in the world.

In this first session of Part Three, you'll tell readers that characters are often tested in some way and required to draw on strengths they may not even know they had. The use of a previously untapped strength often represents a turning point for a character, a moment of growth. The character may or may not register this, but the wise reader, who understands the character both as friend and researcher, will recognize that something big has occurred. This is an important step in a reader's journey toward growing rich theories about characters in books, and about themselves, too.

Tension in Stories Often Produces a Turning Point

CONNECTION

Tell children a story that illustrates a time when your heart raced because you were about to be put to a test.

"Today I want to talk to you about a particular kind of change. It's the change that comes when you are put to a test.

"Have I ever told you the story of when I broke the basement light?" The children shook their heads no. "I was about your age, in fact. My friend and I were playing ball in the community room in her building's basement. We weren't supposed to be tossing a ball down there, but it was a rainy day and we were stuck inside. So there we were, throwing this ball back and forth, back and forth. All of a sudden, there was a big crash and then the sound of glass shattering, and it was pitch black. We gasped. The light, one of those long fluorescent kinds, was lying in pieces at our feet. Suddenly we heard footsteps coming down the hallway. 'Hide!' my friend whispered, and we dashed for the nearest large objects and threw ourselves behind them.

"As the footsteps drew nearer, I could feel my heart racing. 'What if the security guard finds us?' I thought. 'What if he doesn't? What do I do? Should I confess? That light will cost so much to replace. My parents will be furious.'

"When our hearts race like mine did in that basement years ago, often it's because something big has happened or is about to happen that will put us to the test. We must step up to the plate or make a choice that will have consequences.

"Remember how our hearts pounded and pounded when we read those two chapters in *Fantastic Mr. Fox*, 'The Terrible Shovels' and 'The Terrible Tractors'? As Mr. Fox dug furiously to keep his family alive, out of the reach and aim of those nasty, mean farmers, we practically dug by the Fox family's side, praying they'd make it! And lo and behold, he found that intricate underground pathway to each farmer's storage room, but not without a whole lot of hard work and thinking—and not without a whole lot of heart racing!"

Name your teaching point. Specifically, tell children that the parts of our books that make readers' hearts race are often moments when the character is facing a test.

"Today I want to teach you that when readers come to a part of the story that makes our hearts race, we know these are apt to be turning points, and we expect that our character will face a test."

TEACHING

Read aloud a heart-racing part of the shared class book during which the main character is put to a big test. Show children how you consider possible challenges the character is facing.

"When we left off reading *Because of Winn-Dixie,* it had just started to rain on Opal's party, remember? I'm going to read a bit more than usual today because you need to hear all of this next chapter to really understand that whole heart-racing reaction that makes you stop and pay attention, expecting a turning point. Listen."

I read aloud Chapter 23 and then put down the book. "Are your hearts racing as much as mine is?" I clutched my chest. "I said earlier that when our hearts race like this, often we know a character is about to face a test. Turn and tell your partner what that test might be for Opal."

After a minute, I said, "Who thinks Opal is facing the possibility of losing Winn-Dixie? Give me a thumbs up if you said something to that effect just now." A lot of thumbs shot up.

"I agree. Winn-Dixie was the first of all those new friends Opal made in Naomi. And he's sort of helped her meet everyone else, hasn't he? I wonder what Opal will do if she can't find Winn-Dixie. If she loses him, like she lost her mama, what is her life going to be like? Tell your partner what you think."

After another minute, I convened the children. "I'm wondering if Opal's changed in ways that might prepare her more for this loss. I wonder if there are other tests she's facing in this moment. Could it be that she's looking at something bigger than the possibility of losing her dog?"

ACTIVE INVOLVEMENT

Have children think about a heart-racing moment in their independent reading books—and consider how the character was tested in that moment.

"Now think about a character in your own book. Was there a time when something happened to your character that made your heart race? Think about that moment, and then ask yourself, 'Is there a way in which my character was being tested at that time?'

"If you can't figure out whether your character was being tested, think about whether your character learned from that time. Think, 'How might this moment be a turning point for my character?'"

LINK

Reiterate the day's teaching point in a way that it is transferable to any text.

"Readers, it isn't just your characters who've faced tests. Each of you has faced tests in this reading workshop. I've taught you stuff that is usually for middle school kids, and each time I look to see if the teaching is flying over your heads, you seem to respond, 'Bring it on!'

"As you read today or any day, remember that authors often test characters. Whenever your heart races, your character is probably about to face something. Read closely, knowing that the author is asking something big of the character and that it is likely that the test will bring the character to a new place. Off you go!"

SESSION XII

Characters Dig Deep to Find What It Takes to Persevere

Dear Teachers,

In this second session of Part Three, you'll invite children to once again step into the character's shoes, imagining how to tackle the problems that person faces. Authors are known to get their characters into pickles—and then to help them find their way out. The goal is simply for children to think, "How might this character overcome his or her problem? What does he or she have to draw upon—or what might he or she attempt—to stand up to an enemy? Or conquer his or her fear? Or find his or her way home?" The hope, of course, is that children think simultaneously, "What might I do to solve my own problems?" We hope that children will begin to think about characters and stories as little mirrors of their lives.

Connection

Draw on a familiar story to suggest that often characters' journeys toward change mean recognizing the strengths they have had all along.

"You all know the story *The Wizard of Oz,* right?" The children nodded. "You know what I love best about that story? It's not the whimsical world Dorothy stumbles into or those wacky characters she meets. It's that all the main characters are in search of something from the wizard, and all of them discover they already have exactly what they were searching for. All along, the Scarecrow has a shrewd brain, the Tin Man has a huge heart, the Cowardly Lion is remarkably brave, and Dorothy has a way home. But they need to go on this long journey to discover their strengths. It's often this way for characters in stories.

"I know, I know, we've been talking about characters' problems and how they go about changing and growing, and yes, all of this is still the case. But often a character has what he needs with himself all along. It's just a matter of discovering this."

Name your teaching point. Specifically, teach readers that characters often can look inside, not outside, for solutions to their problems.

"Today I want to teach you that as we think about and discuss ways that a character might solve the problems of his life, often we discover that the character already has what it takes to solve these himself."

Teaching

Recruit children to help determine and then solve the read-aloud character's problem.

"Readers, what's Opal's problem?" The children raised their eyebrows, puzzled.

"Think about what we know about Opal. What did we learn about her at the very beginning of the book, and what do we know now? What was missing in her life? What has her struggle been? Take a minute to think about this, because then we're going to help her solve it."

I held still as children thought.

"I think you all could easily tell me Opal's problem; you've named it already. Give me a thumbs up if you have an idea." A number of thumbs went up. I called on several children. "She's lonely." "Her mom's gone." "She's lost her dog."

Read a passage from the read-aloud book that illustrates or suggests a solution to the main character's problems. Then get children started solving the problems.

"I'm going to read this next bit aloud, and then I'm going to get us started helping Opal solve her problems. As I read, think, 'How might she solve these problems? What does Opal have in her that she can draw upon to resolve her loneliness or the fact that she misses her mom?'"

Chapter 24

Me and the preacher started walking and calling Winn-Dixie's name. I was glad it was raining so hard, because it made it easy to cry. I cried and cried and cried, and the whole time I was calling for Winn-Dixie.

"Winn-Dixie!" I screamed.

"Winn-Dixie!" the preacher shouted. And then he whistled loud and long. But Winn-Dixie didn't show up.

We walked all through downtown. We walked past the Dewberrys' house and the Herman W. Block Memorial Library and Sweetie Pie's yellow house and Gertrude's Pets. We walked out to the Friendly Corners Trailer Park and looked underneath our trailer. We walked all the way out to the Open Arms Baptist Church of Naomi. We walked past the railroad tracks and right on down Highway 50. Cars were rushing past us and their taillights glowed red, like mean eyes staring at us.

"Daddy," I said. "Daddy, what if he got run over?"

"Opal," the preacher said. "We can't worry about what might have happened. All we can do is keep looking."

"I'm going to stop here for a minute. Our goal is to imagine how to help Opal. What's the immediate problem? Winn-Dixie is missing, right? So what can Opal do? Well, she could post some 'Missing Dog' signs and report Winn-Dixie missing to the local police station, but whether he is found is out of Opal's hands. It's like the preacher says—all she can do is keep looking.

"And what about her mom? She can't post a 'Missing Mother' sign, can she? And there's no way to make a person who's voluntarily left come back, is there?

"So how do you go about filling the hole that person's absence has left in your heart? How do you address the loneliness? *That's* her big problem, right?" I paused. "You know what I noticed just now? All those places Opal and her dad pass looking for Winn-Dixie—they're all places with people Opal has come to know. Sweetie Pie's house, the Dewberrys' house, the library, Gertrude's Pets. That's getting me thinking..." I let my voice trail off, hoping children would pick up on the unspoken thought.

Active Involvement

Have children work in groups of four to come up with possible solutions to the read-aloud character's problem. Nudge them to dig deeply, considering not only what the main problem is and how she might solve it but also what she has within her to help with this effort.

> "Okay, I'm turning this over to you now. See if you can figure out some solutions to Opal's problems, and try to figure out what Opal may have within her that will help her resolve some of these things. You may want to look back over earlier parts of the book or at your jottings. I have a few extra copies of the book on hand that you can borrow. I'm asking a big thing of you, so let's try this. Instead of just talking to your partner, talk in fours."

> I instructed various partnerships to join together so that the children were set up to talk in fours, and handed each foursome a copy of *Because of Winn-Dixie*. Then I said, "As you talk, you may find yourself thinking that Opal is already on her way to solving some of her problems. Turn and talk."

> As children talked, I called out little coaching tips, including suggestions that they draw upon earlier days' work to help them with this task. "You may want to review our ideas about who Opal is as a person—what makes her tick. How might her traits help her?

> "Remember, sometimes we go about trying to solve our problems—or achieve our goals—in one way and then discover there's another way we could go about doing this."

Link

Compliment children on the sophisticated work they've done, and share some of their ideas.

> "Readers, the thinking work you've done today is spectacular. At the start of this unit, I told you that if Opal were real, she would be lucky to have each of you in her life because you have a way of looking, seeing, empathizing, and caring that only a truly good friend demonstrates. Some of you thought that even though losing Winn-Dixie is the worst thing in the world, in some way it is helping Opal grow even closer to the people she still has, to Gloria and Sweetie Pie and even the Dewberrys—and to her father.

> "I'm wondering if letting go of the hope that her mother will return might let her also hold on to the people she has."

The Little Guy in a Story Counts, Too

> *Dear Teachers,*
>
> *Today you'll suggest that main characters don't operate solo. Often secondary characters assume important roles in a story, challenging the main character and teaching him or her—and us—lessons. You'll tell children that wise readers know to keep an eye not only on the main character but on these secondary players.*

CONNECTION

Draw on examples of familiar characters to illustrate for children that secondary characters have important roles in stories.

"Readers, we've spent a lot of time getting to know our main characters in this unit, and we've gotten really good at figuring out what makes those main characters tick. Meanwhile, though, a book is made up of more than one character, right? And those other characters—the secondary characters—are on that page, in that story, for a reason. I mean, Wilbur may have found a way to keep Zuckerman from killing him, but not without a lot of help from Charlotte and not without a lot of lessons from her along the way, either. And I doubt that Mr. Fox, no matter how cunning and quick he is, would have found a way to save the day without the help of his children and Badger or the encouragement of Mrs. Fox!

"The truth is, it's rare that any of us goes on journeys all on our own. We share this earth and our lives with other people, and we learn some of our most valuable lessons not from operating on our own but from interacting with others."

Name your teaching point. Specifically, tell children that readers note the lessons that secondary characters teach the main character.

"Today I want to teach you that readers take note of secondary characters in the story. We think about how a particular secondary character influences or affects the main character, knowing that there are different sorts of roles these characters are apt to play."

Teaching and Active Involvement

Ask children to suggest secondary characters in their lives and in books and to talk about the roles these characters play.

"Let's do something a bit different right now. Jot a list of secondary characters in your life, making sure to roam about through different parts of your life. Think about family, friends, coaches, neighbors, counselors, and jot some names down."

After a minute, I said, "Here is the hard part. Beside each name, jot a few words that capture the role this person mainly plays in your life. I know many people play lots of different roles, but think, 'What is the main role this person plays?'"

After children did that, I said, "So I want you and your partner to list the secondary characters in our read-aloud book and brainstorm the roles each of those characters plays. If you do this well, you will come to realize that these characters don't all play the same role. They have different jobs to do in the story of Opal's journey. Some of the characters in Opal's life will be people who test her, who make things hard for her. Someone who challenges us is an important secondary character, right?"

Link

Channel kids to record thoughtful Post-its, including Post-its about secondary characters.

"Readers, as you read today, I know you have lots of things to think about. Maybe one of them will be the secondary characters in your story. What I'm going to ask you to do is to try to make sure that as you jot your thoughts on Post-its, these are actually thoughts—not just what is right there in the book. And I suspect some of them will be thoughts about your secondary characters."

Readers Learn Vicariously Alongside Our Characters

Dear Teachers,

You'll end the unit by reflecting on the journey the class has taken together and by asking children to consider the lessons they've learned, both as a class and side-by-side with the characters in their books. You'll issue children an invitation to think about how they themselves might live differently in the world because of the characters they've met and befriended. The message you'll convey is that when we step into the world of a story, really living in a character's shoes, we take away more than fleeting memories of a beloved book, a fun adventure. We take away ideas about how we might make our own life stories more meaningful, how we might move along our life paths with greater awareness, dignity, and grace.

CONNECTION

Reflect on the journey the class has taken in this unit, and suggest that children think about the lessons they have learned alongside their characters, imagining how those lessons can help them live differently.

"Readers, today is the last day of this unit on characters. I don't you know about you, but I feel like we've been on quite a journey! We've traveled to Naomi with Opal, meeting all of her new friends, losing and finding Winn-Dixie. And I've also, in a way, traveled with each of you to different places you've encountered in your independent reading books, some magical and some much like our own. It's been so much fun!

"As we wrap up our work, I'd love for us to think for a minute about the lessons we've learned along the way, side-by-side with our characters. I find that book endings make me think quite a bit about my own life, reflecting on how I live in the world now and how I might want to live differently."

Name your teaching point. Specifically, tell children that as a character figures out solutions to his or her problems, readers think about what that person has learned that's applicable also to our own lives.

"Today I want to teach you that as a character resolves a problem, we ask what the character knows now that he or she didn't know at the start of the story. We think of the lesson our character has learned, wondering how this book might change the way we behave in our own lives."

Teaching and Active Involvement

Revisit a passage in the read-aloud book that reveals some lessons the main character has learned. Recruit children's help to uncover these.

"Let's return to *Because of Winn-Dixie* one last time—at least for today. Let's revisit a moment I know you all loved, and together let's try to figure out what Opal has learned and how we might also apply these lessons to our own lives. In a minute, you'll have a chance to do this with your own books:"

> Outside, the rain had stopped and the clouds had gone away and the sky was so clear it seemed like I could see every star ever made. I walked all the way to the back of Gloria Dump's yard. I walked back there and looked at her mistake tree. The bottles were quiet; there wasn't a breeze, so they were just hanging there. I looked at the tree and then I looked up at the sky.
>
> "Mama," I said, just like she was standing right beside me, "I know ten things about you, and that's not enough, that's not near enough. But Daddy is going to tell me more; I know he will, now that he knows you're not coming back. He misses you and I miss you, but my heart doesn't feel empty anymore. It's full all the way up. I'll still think about you, I promise. But probably not as much as I did this summer."

That's what I said that night underneath Gloria Dump's mistake tree. And after I was done saying it, I stood just staring up at the sky, looking at the constellations and planets. And then I remembered my own tree, the one Gloria had helped me plant. I hadn't looked at it for a long time. I went crawling around on my hands and knees, searching for it. And when I found it, I was surprised at how much it had grown. It was still small. It still looked more like a plant than a tree. But the leaves and the branches felt real strong and good and right.

"Goodness! She has grown, hasn't she? Remember when we made predictions about Gloria's role in Opal's life, and we decided that Gloria might end up teaching Opal a lesson or two? This feels huge. It seems like Opal has learned, finally, to begin to let her mother go. What else has she learned, do you think? Take a minute to think over her journey and to review this passage. Push yourself to read between the lines a little. Opal doesn't come out and say, 'I learned. . . ,' does she? But we can find her lessons in her actions, her words, this little speech to her mother."

I left a pool of silence while children thought. Then I said, "Give me a thumbs up when you have some ideas," and called on a few children to share.

"Readers, you see so much now. I love this idea that Opal has learned how to fill her heart with other people, not just memories or lists about her mother. And that notion that she's found peace—so many of us spend a lifetime searching for it—you're right; Opal, it seems, has found it. You also said so wisely that it isn't that Opal no longer misses her mother; it's that she's learned how to cope with that missing. She's found a way to live without her mother, to fill the void of her mother with friends and love.

"It seems to me that we can take some lessons from our friend Opal. Many of us who've lost someone in one way or another—or maybe in the future, when we lose someone— can think to ourselves, 'I will miss this person dearly, but I will draw upon the people who are still present in my life; my heart can still feel full.'"

Set children up to mine their books for lessons characters have learned and then to share these with a partner. Nudge them to think not just "What has my character learned?" but also "What have I learned?"

"Readers, take a few minutes now to talk to your partner about some of the lessons a character in one of the books you've read recently (or not so recently) has learned that you might also apply to your own life. You'll be swapping lessons, and it may be that something you've learned will help your partner, too."

LINK

Tell children that they are now the sort of readers who read alertly, looking for ways in which characters have changed and grown, learning lessons alongside their characters.

"Readers, like Opal and any character, you too have grown so much during this unit. I've watched you turn into these remarkably alert, astute readers—the kind who read not only with your hearts on your sleeve, letting the characters and the story seep into your hearts, but also with your minds buzzing with predictions, connections, ideas, and now lessons.

"Today and every day, as you read, keep searching for those lessons your characters learn and ask yourself, 'What have *I* learned that I can now apply to my own life? How can I live my life differently because of these lessons?'"

LEARNING FROM THE ELVES

A Genre Study of the Complexities and Themes of Fantasy

By Mary Ehrenworth

Dear Teachers,

I have come to love fantasy novels, particularly young adult fantasy. There's no doubt that the Harry Potter *series stirred this love. Who couldn't adore a book that got millions of children to read? The teen fascination with* Twilight *and* The Hunger Games *did the same thing—literally millions of teens are reading and talking about these books. They join blogs, they dress up like the characters, they attend the film releases, they compare the books to the movies. Fantasy has been a force for good in literacy.*

Fantasy books are mostly about the struggle between good and evil. They are about the emergence of something good, even in the darkest times or in the weakest of us. It's probably that theme, of the essential goodness and courage of mankind, that makes these stories so romantic, intense, and ultimately satisfying. The great thing about getting kids hooked on fantasy is that they do get hooked. They'll be drawn to the intense characters, to the romantic and danger-filled narrative, and to the underlying themes. There are so many fantasy series now, which is why this is a great book club unit. From The Secrets of Droon *and* Dragon Slayers' Academy, *through* Narnia *and* Harry Potter, *to* The Hunger Games *and* The Lord of the Rings, *there are gorgeous fantasy titles. One thing that I particularly love about fantasy, for our diverse classrooms, is that the lower-level titles don't look particularly childish—all these books have dragons on the covers—and the higher levels allow your highest-level readers to read complicated narratives without straying into plot developments that are not appropriate for their age.*

Like the historical fiction unit, this unit aims to support your students in developing into more powerful readers of complicated texts. There may, therefore, be favorite fantasy lessons that you have up your sleeve—more on archetypes and quest structures, more on the myths, legends, and allegories—so please, if you adore fantasy,

continued on next page

tuck those in. You may also choose to teach using the structures of book clubs more than I've done in this unit. What I've done here is try to imagine a unit of study that helps students launch into a genre at a knowledgeable level, continue to learn how to study stories and work on their reading, and emerge with an increased sense of power and confidence, better able to tackle more complicated texts.

Whenever you author a new unit of study, you'll want to seize this opportunity to read deeply within the genre and to share your reading with friends and colleagues. I can't emphasize enough the power of reading the same fantasy novels that your students will be reading. You'll also find that when you author a new unit, you have an opportunity to induct your classroom community into intellectual terrain and new literary vocabulary. This unit has been written for readers who have already experienced many previous units, including the one on book clubs, and who are, for the most part, reading texts within or beyond the O/P/Q band of text difficulty. You'll see that students are expected to be able to carry on some aspects of their reading—their logs, for example, and their jotted notes—with increasing independence. You can find Part Three on the Resources *CD-ROM. This final part particularly supports students in thinking about archetypes, quest structures, and thematic understanding, not only in fantasy, but in other genres as well.*

Yours,

Mary Ehrenworth

SESSION I

Building the World of the Story When It's Another World

CONNECTION

Launch the new unit by speaking passionately about the reasons to read fantasy, about the impact the *Harry Potter* series has made on the world, and about the impact you hope this unit has on your readers.

I had around me many gorgeous fantasy novels, their covers adorned with dragons, castles, and symbols. As I spoke, I gestured with these books. "Fantasy readers, today is the day when we start our unit of study in fantasy. Some of you are avid fantasy readers, I know. Others of you are a little unsure about this. You're not quite sure how you feel about dragons, and dwarves, and epic quests where the world is imperiled. Friends, let's begin, then, by thinking about *why* we would read fantasy. Here are some reasons. Reason one: because the stories are extraordinary. These are wild, dangerous, romantic tales, where the fate of mankind may rest on the choices made by the main character. Everything is more important, more intense, more vivid in fantasy stories. Reason two: because when you study fantasy, you are really studying the human condition. The stories are never really about elves and hobbits; they're about the struggle between good and evil, they're about how power corrupts, they're about the quest to be better than we are, they're about how even the smallest of us can affect what happens in this world. Reason three: because if you become a powerful reader of fantasy, you're likely to become a more powerful reader of all texts. Fantasy novels are incredibly complicated. You have to figure out where the story takes place, what kind of world it is, who has power there, what the rules are. You'll enter narratives that stretch over many novels, and you'll read hundreds and even thousands of pages. You'll emerge, like the characters in these stories, changed.

"It's not accidental that the most widely read book of our time is a story of a boy who finds he can do magic and whose life becomes an extraordinary quest to rid the world of evil. There is something transcendent about the essential notion of *Harry Potter*. Who doesn't want to feel that our troubles are of extraordinary significance, to measure ourselves against the heroes and villains of the ages, to forge bonds of friendship that will be tested by torture and by love? With 400 million copies translated into over sixty languages, it's a book that made the whole globe into a book club. If you read all seven novels, you read a story that spreads over four thousand pages. You'll be reading in a club that has no fewer than 400 million members, and you'll read thousands of pages together; this is the epic quality of fantasy."

■ *If you are a reluctant fantasy reader, I urge you, this one time, to keep that reluctance in the closet and to either act as if you are entranced by these stories or, at the least, come to them with a willing spirit. It is true that our intention in teaching this unit*

is bigger than fantasy—it is to lure and support youngsters to become adept at reading complicated stories, ones with multiple plotlines, complex characters, and unfamiliar settings, and (at a more essential level) to lure them toward reading. But at the
start of the unit, we are unabashedly over-the-top focused on one thing: fantasy!
The lure of fantasy is a magical one. Fantasy will be good for your kids. Harry Potter
has been good for kids! Think of your chalk or your smart board marker as a wand,
and swirl some magic into the classroom with your words.

"I want that for you, readers, all of it. I want you to embark, from this classroom with
these friends, on wild adventures that make your head spin. I want you to feel the release
that comes when you escape into other mythic worlds where magic happens. I want you
to find stories that will spread over many books, that will keep you up at night, that will
fill the corners of your life with their secrets. You may or may not emerge from this study
a fanatic—a Dungeons & Dragons player, a follower of *Avatar,* a reader of manga—but
you will, I am sure, know more about this wild and beautiful genre. You will also, I hope,
have more insight into the human condition. And you will, I feel sure, emerge with an
increased confidence that you can tackle truly complicated texts."

**Name your teaching point. Specifically, teach your students that fantasy readers use
multiple resources to research the settings of their stories.**

"Friends, today I want to teach you that fantasy readers understand that our first task is
to ask, 'What kind of place is this?' Fantasy readers look for clues about the time period
and the magical elements, in particular, using the covers, blurbs, and details from the
beginning of the story for their research."

TEACHING

**Overview some of the common settings of fantasy stories, talking about how you use this
knowledge to research the setting of fantasy texts.**

"Experienced fantasy readers expect certain kinds of places. Often, fantasy stories are
set in a medieval world full of swords, horses, castles, dragons, and so forth—like The
Lord of the Rings books, for instance, or the Narnia books. A second common setting is
a futuristic world full of spacecraft, intergalactic travel, advanced technology—such as
Star Wars. And the third common setting is the ordinary world, where it seems at first
as if everything is normal, but then gradually you'll notice that there is an infiltration of
magic—so there is this kind of blending of the world we know with magical elements.
Harry Potter is like this.

"So knowledgeable fantasy readers know to gather up clues, right away, about what kind of place they are in. Sometimes it's a little tricky because the story might or might not begin right away in the magical world. *The Hobbit,* for instance, starts right off in a place full of creatures who only grow to be three feet tall, and they use carts and horses to farm, and there are wizards, so the reader knows that this place is magical. But other times, the story starts off in an ordinary place, in the here and now, and you think it's going to all happen here, and then the characters are transported. That's what happens in Narnia—Peter, Edmund, Lucy, and Susan all walk through an enchanted wardrobe into the magical kingdom of Narnia. In *Harry Potter,* Harry starts off also in the ordinary world, but that actual world becomes magical. He doesn't go to another kingdom; he still lives in London, in the modern world, but magic enters that world and transforms it."

- *Teachers, if you have access to a smart board, a DVD player, or an LCD projector that attaches to your laptop, it's extremely engaging to show some short clips from the first minute or two of fantasy films, either in the lesson or in a prior read-aloud session. A few seconds of a scene from* The Fellowship of the Ring, *with Gandalf in his wizard robes and Aragorn wielding his sword from horseback, or the scene of the wardrobe opening into Narnia can illuminate this teaching. Other effective films include the Disney stories* Sinbad *and* Treasure Planet *or the death star from* Star Wars. *My colleagues and I in the Teachers College Reading and Writing Project have often launched this unit by showing a few scenes during our read-aloud session and engaging readers by asking, "What kind of place this is?" when referencing just two or three minutes of a film clip. We've encouraged them, as a class, to glean everything they can about that place, including the technology, the magic, the legends, and power holders, all of which can be found in the first two minutes of a film scene. Sometimes we do this with two contrasting stories, two contrasting worlds—this provides readers a way to quickly compare multiple texts. Of course, this also brings all our readers, including those who are less proficient or those who speak languages other than English, into this exciting conversation, accomplishing an introduction that would take several days if it revolved around reading short stories.*

"Okay, readers, I've tried to jump-start your reading a bit here, as you can tell, by giving you a little expertise on how fantasy stories tend to start. That means I expect you, from the very first moment you begin reading, to be alert for details about what kind of place you encounter in the story you are reading. Things unfold rapidly in fantasy, and you have to get oriented quickly, before a dragon arrives or you get swept through a portal to another world."

Set readers up to watch as you demonstrate what it means to orient yourself to a fantasy novel, asking, "What kind of place is this?" and attending to details that help you create the setting.

"Friends, watch how I do this work. I'm going to try to name what I do as a reader while I do it so that you can really see the steps I follow. Then you'll have a chance to practice on the story we read together and, of course, afterward in the stories you'll read with your book clubs."

I picked up *The Paper Bag Princess.* "Okay, so first, *before I even open the pages,* I look carefully at the covers of the book. I know that with the stories being this complicated, I want to get all the information I can from the covers. So I'm looking to see if there's a blurb that might tell me who this story is about and, more important, what kind of world this is. No! There is no blurb on this book cover. That doesn't seem fair, but it's okay. Next, I'll look at the cover art and the title because those can also tell me a lot. The book is called *The Paper Bag Princess,* and there is a girl with a bent crown, a huge castle-like door, and a gigantic smoking dragon on the front cover. On the back cover there is another image of the same dragon breathing cataclysmic fire over the head of the girl. Hmm."

I opened to the inside of the book. "Inside, the story starts:"

> Elizabeth was a beautiful princess. She lived in a castle and had expensive princess clothes. She was going to marry a prince named Ronald.

I looked at the page for a moment, saying, "And there's a picture of a snotty-looking prince, with his nose in the air, and a besotted girl, staring at him with hearts flying around her. The room looks like a castle, with arched windows, stone walls, and old wooden chairs. And their clothes are definitely medieval (that's from the Middle Ages, like you'd see in the time of King Arthur). Okay, so I definitely see from the furniture, the buildings, and the clothes that this story happens in a place that is medieval. On the next page, it says:"

> Unfortunately, a dragon smashed her castle, burned all her clothes with his fiery breath, and carried off Prince Ronald.

"Aha! So there is magic here, too; this is not historical fiction from the actual Middle Ages. A dragon has entered. That is definitely a magical creature. He has even magically managed to smash Elizabeth's castle and burn all of Elizabeth's clothes without harming her at all."

- *You'll notice, teachers, that I repeat what I am doing as a reader, which is paying attention to the clothing, the furniture, the buildings, the forms of transportation, the lighting, and so forth, and that I'm exaggerating how readers do this work right at the start of the book by looking carefully at the covers and first few pages. This setting work is almost exactly the same as readers would do in historical fiction, except that there is an added aspect of being alert for magical elements. This is good training for young readers. Too often, when a child is reading fantasy, historical fiction, or even just contemporary fiction that is set someplace other than a familiar school setting, that young reader moves swiftly through and past the setting details without accumulating them. In more complicated stories, though, the setting is literally setting up the reader—it incorporates the mood or atmosphere, and it often incorporates some of the conflict for the character, so it is definitely worth paying attention to!*

I put the book down. "Okay, readers, I think I know enough. It seems pretty clear that this story begins in a place that is medieval. It has castles, and old-fashioned clothes, and princesses. And it is magical. There are dragons. There are *not* subways or buses, or laser guns, or spacecraft. And the story started right away in this magical kingdom."

Name what you have done that is transferable to other days and other texts.

"And I know all this because I didn't just open to page one and start reading; instead, I took a minute to consider carefully what I could learn from the pictures and text on the covers, the clues about daily life, and the appearance of any magic. Fantasy readers know that it helps to do this and to continue building our sense of the world of the story as we read the first chapter of the book."

ACTIVE INVOLVEMENT

Give your students practice mining the opening of a fantasy novel for clues about the story's setting by asking them to think back to the opening of the novel you recently began reading aloud to them.

"Readers, let's give ourselves a chance to practice this work together. Earlier today we began *The Lightning Thief.* I saw when we were reading it that your jaws were practically hanging open as the story unfolded. Like me, you were entranced and shocked with how much happened and how wild it was. In fact, most of your conversation was simply retelling to each other what you *think* happened. You seemed as unsure as Percy was about what had really occurred on this field trip to the Metropolitan Museum. It didn't help that at the end of the first chapter, after Percy Jackson's teacher has turned out to be a demon and tried to *kill* him in the middle of the museum, his favorite teacher, Mr. Brunner, apparently denies that any of it even happened."

I picked up *The Lightning Thief.* "Friends, we dove right into the story, so everything happened fast and without any warning. When Mrs. Dodds suddenly turned out to be a demon, it was pretty confusing. Let's revisit the start of that book now (which is something fantasy readers often do) and see if we could have gathered more clues a little earlier. This will give us a deeper understanding of the kind of place in which Percy lives."

I held the book up so that everyone could see it. "Readers, I'm going to show you the cover and read you what's on the back blurb—this book has a blurb! This time, follow my example in using the strategy of really researching the time period and the magical elements within the story by paying extra attention to the covers and the start of the story."

"Okay, so on the cover is an image of New York City, seen from the water. Lightning crackles down past the Empire State Building. Emerging from the ocean, apparently dry even though he comes up out of the deep waves, is a dark-haired boy. He holds some kind of sword in one hand."

■ *If you have a document camera, you could show the cover, or you could hold it up. If not, just give a detailed description, as these words alone, which are carefully chosen, should give the students some hints that there is something magical and something real here. Even if you do show the cover, you may decide to support your students by doing a voiceover of what you are seeing as you hold the text up.*

Ask students to turn and talk about what they glean from the front cover alone. Listen in, and then summarize what you heard them say, encouraging them to jot notes another time. Read on, continuing to scaffold their work.

Conscious that this time I'd be channeling students into multiple turns and conversations, I gave them just a minute before intervening. "Readers, I can tell you have a lot to say already, before we have even opened the book, about the clues that help us answer the question 'What kind of place is this?' Turn and tell your partner what you might surmise just from the front cover."

They did. I jotted some notes. Then I spoke over the hubbub, summarizing their conversations before giving those conversations yet more food for thought. "Pause for a moment, friends, and I'll share some of what I heard you say. A lot of you spoke about how this book is clearly set in modern times because you can see New York City landmarks, such as the Empire State Building. Many of you described the kids' clothes as being contemporary—another clue that it's here and now. But then you spoke of the sword that glows and the way the kid emerges from the waves as being magical. It's not like you normally see kids on Fifth Avenue who have glowing swords and who can walk through oceans and not get wet.

"You're really researching thoughtfully. I'm going to show you the back cover next because that will help you with your research. I imagine that you'll want to jot. If you were doing this with your club book or your independent reading book, I'd definitely expect that you'd know to make a Post-it or a quick notebook entry about all you are realizing; as researchers, we record our observations so that we can hold on to them. When you read harder books like this one, you definitely want to use a ton of strategies to jump-start your reading so that right from the start you read the opening of the book with as much power and knowledge as possible."

■ *I had written the blurb from the back cover on chart paper, but you could also use an overhead projector to show the book itself, or duplicate the back cover so that at least a few of your readers can hold it while others look on. Otherwise, just read it, which is fine. They can jot as you read.*

> Percy Jackson is about to be kicked out of boarding school…again. And that's the least of his troubles. Lately, mythological monsters and the gods of Mount Olympus seem to be walking straight out of the pages of Percy's Greek mythology textbook and into his life. And worse, he's angered a few of them. Zeus's master lightning bolt has been stolen, and Percy is the prime suspect.

> Now Percy and his friends have just ten days to find and return Zeus's stolen property and bring peace to a warring Mount Olympus. But to succeed on his quest, Percy will have to do more than catch the true thief; he must come to terms with the father who abandoned him; solve the riddle of the Oracle, which warns him of betrayal by a friend; and unravel a treachery more powerful than the gods themselves.

I put the book down. "Whoa, I can't believe how much better prepared we would have been as readers if we had read this first! I could see you jotting furiously. Turn and tell your partner about the research this blurb helped you do."

They did, and again I jotted what they said; then I again spoke over their conversations, quieting them for a moment. "Readers, I heard you say that the blurb tells us that Percy lives in the modern world, goes to boarding school, reads textbooks, studies Greek mythology. And you also said that you found out that there is magic in this world—it seems that the Greek myths are, in fact, real. Zeus is one of the characters. There is an Oracle and a magic lightning bolt and monsters."

I looked down at the notes I'd taken of all that students had found, and I said, "Our research paid off, didn't it? If we were just starting the book, we'd now open to the first page and get started, reading with this same sort of alertness. But we've already read the first chapter, so let's instead review what we read (and fantasy readers do that a lot, especially with the beginnings of our books) and see if there are any clues about the setting that we might have missed. Why don't you use this timeline we made after reflecting on the first chapter to prompt your recollections, and talk to your partner about clues you can recall about this world that blends the real and the magical."

Channel students to use a chart-size timeline of the first chapter from your class read-aloud to prompt their recollections of clues that chapter contained about the setting, and to share these clues with their partner.

I flipped the chart to our timeline and asked students to turn and talk, using the timeline to prompt recollection of clues they'd gleaned from the first chapter about the nature of the story's setting.

The Lightning Thief—Chapter 1

- Percy introduces himself.
- Nancy Bobofit bullies Grover on the bus.
- Mr. Brunner leads the kids into the Metropolitan Museum.
- They have lunch by the fountain.
- Nancy bullies Grover again.
- Nancy ends up in the fountain—the water grabs her.
- Mrs. Dodds takes Percy into the museum to punish him.
- Mrs. Dodds turns out to be a demon and attacks Percy.
- Mr. Brunner throws Percy a pen, which turns into a sword.
- Percy kills Mrs. Dodds.
- Mr. Brunner and Grover say they've never heard of Mrs. Dodds.

■ *Teachers, we'll be using some of the timelines and charts, such as this one, in a variety of minilessons, so you may want to keep these charts, which will be generated during your read-aloud, handy. This timeline simply records the major events of each chapter. As stories become more complicated at these higher levels, some of the graphic organizers that students may not have needed for a while become useful again. For* The Lightning Thief *(especially if you intend to read the whole series), not only timelines but also maps and lists of characters are useful. I'm imagining that during or after your first read-aloud, you might have worked on a timeline because Percy gives a kind of "backstory" in the first chapter, meaning that he fills you in on events that occur before the story starts. Then events unfold very rapidly.*

In a voiceover, I coached them to synthesize what they'd learned from examining the book's covers with this new information. "Readers, I can hear that you're still retelling the events of the story. Remember that your job here is to use all the details you've gathered from the covers, from the blurb, and from what we learn at the start of the first chapter to figure out what kind of place this is."

They talked. I gathered them back, saying, "Readers, please let me bring you back and share some of what you said. A lot of you stated that this place is magical, or mythological, and that the Greek gods are alive here. The story happens in the here and now, not long ago. We know this from what Percy's clothes look like on the cover, from what it said in the blurb, and from how Percy introduces himself. Some of you mentioned that now you know that this place has real monsters, knowing this makes it easier to suspect Mrs. Dodds, especially after she seems to appear and disappear so quickly. And now some of you are thinking that Percy might have some magical powers; when Nancy was bullying Grover, she ended up in the fountain. Interesting, right? Next time, we'll research a little more carefully before starting to read a fantasy story!"

LINK

Send your students off, reminding them to research the settings as they begin their stories.

I put *The Lightning Thief* down, saying, "Fantasy readers, this work is going to be very important now for you. The books you and your club mates have chosen are complicated. The places will be unusual. You'll want to be alert to details about these places, especially at the start of these stories. So not just today but whenever you pick up a new fantasy book, you'll want to research the place carefully, using the covers, the blurbs, and the details about daily life, technology, and magic that are given you at the beginning of the story to answer the question 'What kind of place is this?' Off you go, readers—go to it. I'll be eager to see you do this work and, after a bit, to listen to conversations in which you share your research with other members of your book club."

- *Teachers, I didn't tell the readers yet that the work I've suggested is important to fantasy reading will actually pay off in other genres as well, though of course, with the exception of the magical element, this work can help students any time they pick up a complicated book. I'm saving this point for a lesson at the end of the unit, where the students will have a chance to reflect on how the strategies they used for reading fantasy might help them in other genres. You, of course, could make a different decision.*

- *I set this lesson up assuming that we had not done a lot of research from the covers of this book before we read the first chapter aloud. I wanted to situate this work in what I see kids doing often, which is grabbing a book and starting to read it. One thing that is really interesting about reading strategies is that they are especially useful when attempting to do some new and challenging work. This means that readers can learn a strategy and use it for a time, but then once readers become comfortable with the genre and text level in which they are reading, the strategies go underground. However, once the reader tackles a new genre or progresses toward significantly more challenging texts, suddenly it is time to brush off the old strategies and reuse them. That's part of what I hope we convey to students in this lesson. It's not that you learn a strategy, master it, and then use it all the time, or that you learn a strategy, use it once, and then never need it again as you learn new strategies. It's more that you turn to your repertoire depending on the kind of reading work you're doing.*

SESSION II

Hey, They Seem as Confused as We Are: Learning Alongside the Main Characters

GETTING READY

- Prior to this session, read through Chapter 3 in *The Lightning Thief.*

- Have *The Paper Bag Princess* on hand. We're assuming you've read this in a prior read-aloud. It takes no more than twenty minutes to read the whole story.

- Across this whole unit, you might find it helpful to make a timeline for events in the read-aloud text. This is an essential tool when reading complicated stories. If you have your timeline displayed visibly, you can add to it during read-alouds and then use it to scaffold partner work during minilessons.

CONNECTION

Tell a story about your reading experience where a main character seems confused by his or her environment.

"Readers, I think you know that I'm in a fantasy book club with some friends. We're reading *The Hobbit,* which has been around, of course, for a long time, but with the new film out and all the recent editions of J.R.R. Tolkien's books, we were excited to reread it. We also read *The Paper Bag Princess* to launch our club, and we've been having some interesting discussions, comparing Bilbo from *The Hobbit* to Elizabeth from *The Paper Bag Princess.* They're both on quests to conquer dragons—big, fiery, fierce dragons—that guard something the main characters both want. Elizabeth wants Ronald. Bilbo wants the dragon's treasure.

"But, readers, there's something that is really different about Elizabeth and Bilbo. Here's what it is: Elizabeth understands her world. Think about it. When a dragon smashes her castle and burns up her dress, she knows to put on a paper bag. She knows how to follow a dragon's trail of burnt forests and bones. She gets it. She might be confused about her personal life, but she understands the world she lives in.

"In my reading club, we've talked about this a lot because in the book we're reading, *The Hobbit,* everything seems more complicated, and the main character, Bilbo, seems as confused as we often are about how things go. He doesn't know about trolls, for instance, so he is almost devoured by them. He doesn't know that dwarves cheat and lie, so he is frightened. He doesn't know anything about elves, so he can't make friends with them. And he doesn't know about the power of the magic ring he finds, so he puts it on his finger, not knowing that is the beginning of a dark history that will haunt him and his family and his whole world. The truth is this: my club is as confused about things as Bilbo is. We're reading slowly, cautiously exploring this strange new world the same way Bilbo is. We don't know who to trust. We're not sure we understand the rules. I'm telling you this because it turns out that a lot of more complicated fantasy stories are like this. They begin with the main character being sort of an outsider, someone who is marginalized or who doesn't have a lot of knowledge about this world. Then, as the main character finds out a lot of stuff, we get to learn alongside the main character. It's sort of a way that these books make the incredibly steep learning curves they contain manageable—the main character and the reader both start out confused, and we learn hand in hand."

■ *Teachers, one thing that happens in harder fantasy and historical fiction is that often the author tries to help the reader by giving information through the mouths of characters. You'll note, for instance, that a character will ask about a legend or a historical incident—and an experienced reader knows to think, "Aha! I'm supposed to pay attention here. This is a tip for me, not just for the character." Any time one character describes some incident, legend, or history, we're supposed to learn about it, too. Tumnus tells Lucy about Narnia. Gandalf tells Frodo about the history of the ring of power. Dumbledore tells Harry about Voldemort's history. Alert readers sit up and take note at these times. Or sometimes the main character has a dramatic learning experience. He or she comes away with new realizations—and we are supposed to forge those new realizations, too. We're on the same learning curve as the main character.*

Name your teaching point. Specifically, teach your students that fantasy readers expect to learn alongside the main characters and are alert to clues that characters are in the midst of important learning experiences.

"Readers, today I want to teach you that in complicated stories such as these fantasy novels, often the main characters begin without a lot of knowledge, and they have a steep learning curve. When the main characters are told important information or have new and unfamiliar experiences, alert readers see those moments in the story as opportunities not only for the characters to learn but for them to learn, hand in hand with the main characters."

TEACHING

Tell students that when reading fantasy stories, you expect to feel a bit confused and to learn alongside the main characters. When they ask questions or are given illuminating experiences, these are opportunities for you to sit up and take note.

"Let me show you what this looks like. I see you reading *Dragon Slayers' Academy,* and *Harry Potter,* and *The Lion, the Witch and the Wardrobe,* for instance, so I know this will help you. In the stories you are reading, indeed in most fantasy stories, often the main characters are a little bit outsiders. Wiglaf doesn't know much about Dragon Slayers' Academy yet, Harry doesn't know much about magic or Hogwarts, and Lucy definitely doesn't know much at the beginning about Narnia. And so, as they go to these new places, these characters ask questions, they look for clues and explanations, they try to learn as much as they can—and the reader gets to learn as well!

"Often, readers, characters in fantasy stories go to new places as they embark on quests or journeys. That means there are a lot of opportunities for the characters to learn about these places. In a way, by making the characters a little ignorant, the author helps us learn alongside those characters. So instead of being frustrated that our main characters aren't more expert, we can try to build our expertise at the same pace that they do. We listen for when characters ask questions, we pay attention to the answers they get, and we try to learn rapidly."

■ *Interestingly, when readers take in the information from the back cover of their story, they often begin the story knowing more than the main character does. In a way, that lets us read with a kind of bird's-eye view, alert to those learning opportunities that will bring the main character along his or her learning curve. At the start of* The Lightning Thief, *for instance, a knowledgeable reader knows more than Percy does about his environment. This helps us recognize those moments when he is being given important clues.*

"Readers, I've read a lot of fantasy. I know how these kinds of books tend to go, so I read fantasy expecting that I will be learning alongside the main characters. I don't get frustrated because I'm a bit confused—but I recognize this confusion, and I know the best response to it is for me to be extra alert to moments when the main characters ask questions. It is as if I have asked those questions, and I listen intently to explanations. I also notice when the main characters are given learning experiences, and I learn alongside those characters. I almost read the moments of illumination (when the lights go on) like a nonfiction reader would, keeping files in my mind (or in my notes) about what I learn. And I know that the more complicated the story is, the steeper the learning curve will be for the main characters—and for me."

Demonstrate by returning to passages you read earlier in the read-aloud book, showing how both you and the main characters learn from these passages.

"Let me show you what this looks like. You'll see that there are certain moments in a story in which you can almost feel the author saying to you, 'Listen up! This matters!' Readers, often those moments are marked by the main characters visibly trying to learn. Sometimes their learning isn't totally successful—in complicated stories it takes a long time to learn everything. But it's like you can see them *trying* to learn.

"For instance, let's go back to Chapter 2 in our read-aloud book. I'll reread a bit. Please watch how alert I am to times when a main character asks a direct question or gets to hear an explanation. Percy has just returned to school with Mr. Brunner, Grover, and the other students after the incident where he was, he thinks, attacked by Mrs. Dodds. He is confused about what's going on, what's real and not real—and we are as well. Notice, readers, that Percy is definitely not an insider yet in this world. Just like Lucy in Narnia, Harry at Hogwarts, and Wiglaf at DSA, Percy has a lot to learn. And then there is this moment when Percy overhears Mr. Brunner asking Grover questions about Percy."

I motioned to our continuing timeline:

Chapter 2

- Percy gets expelled from Yancy—still has to finish term.
- Percy goes to Mr. Brunner for help—overhears conversation about "the Mist" and a "Kindly One".
- Mr. Brunner tells Percy he's "not normal".
- Percy returns to city by bus with Grover.
- He and Grover see three old ladies with yarn, and one cuts a thread.

"Readers, do you recall that experienced fantasy readers are extra alert any time the character asks a question, hears an explanation, or has a new learning experience?" I ticked these off on my fingers. "Then comes this moment when he eavesdrops as Grover explains to Mr. Brunner why he is worried about Percy." I read:

> Mr. Brunner asked a question. A voice that was definitely Grover's said, "...worried about Percy, sir."

I froze.

I repeated that last line, adding: "I am freezing on the spot, too, all ears. Percy expects to learn something important, and so do I. Listen up:"

I'm not usually an eavesdropper, but I dare you to try not listening if you hear your best friend talking about you to an adult.

I inched closer.

"…alone this summer," Grover was saying. "I mean, a Kindly One in the *school!* Now that we know for sure, and *they* know too—"

"We would only make matters worse by rushing him," Mr. Brunner said. "We need the boy to mature more."

"But we may not have time. The summer solstice deadline—"

"Will have to be resolved without him, Grover. Let him enjoy his ignorance while he still can."

"Sir, he *saw* her…"

"His imagination," Mr. Brunner insisted. "The Mist over the students and staff will be enough to convince him of that."

"Sir, I…I can't fail in my duties again." Grover's voice was choked with emotion. "You know what that would mean."

"You haven't failed, Grover," Mr. Brunner said kindly. "I should have seen her for what she was. Now let's just worry about keeping Percy alive until next fall—"

The mythology book dropped out of my hand with a thud.

Mr. Brunner went silent.

I put down the book and paused, visibly thinking. "Readers, you'll remember that Percy was shaken by what he overheard. He went back to his dorm room, where he lay awake, trying to figure out all these things, which he knew he didn't understand. Readers, that was a signal to me to figure things out, too. Just as Percy probably replayed this conversation in his head, I reread it several times. As I did, several things became clear. You'll see. I'll show you my notes."

■ *This work is a little tricky, teachers, because part of it seems intuitive—you have to recognize when the author is seemingly trying to hand over information. I think that if we alert our readers to this possibility, they can also conduct some inquiries in their own books, and they'll begin to see the places where this is happening.*

I put my notebook page on the overhead. On it I had jotted:

"Kindly One" in school—Mrs. Dodds?

Percy in danger—deadline of summer solstice

And he's "ignorant"

"Mist" convinces people they haven't seen things

Grover feels he failed when he did not see Mrs. Dodds for what she was

---

Name what you have done in a way that you hope is transferable to other texts on other days.

"Readers, do you see how I was extra alert as soon as I realized this was an important learning opportunity for the main character, Percy, and therefore for me? I could tell that a conversation like this would probably reveal important new information, so I was ready to learn. What matters is that as soon as I realized that a significant conversation was about to happen, where the main character would probably learn something secret—after all, he was eavesdropping—I was alert and ready."

Active Involvement

Remind students of text markers that reveal that the character is learning—direct questions, explanations, and unfamiliar experiences—and help them use text markers to note more passages in the read-aloud in which they can learn alongside the protagonist.

"Readers, what often happens is that as the story moves along, there are fast parts and slower parts, and there are parts where it's almost all action and parts (like the one I just reread) where it's pretty much all conversations. I hope you see that readers expect to learn something from conversations, especially any conversations the main character overhears or ones in which direct questions are posed. In a fast-moving story like *The Lightning Thief*, there will be important conversations even in the middle of action. But you'll know that when you see the main character asking direct questions, listening to explanations, or having new and unfamiliar experiences, these are clues that you should be alert to learn alongside the character."

I jotted on the chart paper:

Clues that Alert Readers to Listen Up and Learn Alongside Characters

- Direct questions

- Explanations

- Unfamiliar experiences

"Let's give this a try. I'm going to read the next part of the story, which is Chapter 4. So far, we've mostly been talking about the characters and adding to our timeline of events as we read during read-aloud, as we would at the start of any story. This time, though, can you be extra alert to any clues such as the ones on this list and be ready to mine any moments when Percy visibly learns something new? We'll start right where we finished, which was just as Grover appeared at the summer cottage where Percy and his mother were staying. Grover is frantic. And he has hooves."

■ *Teachers, you'll want to choose an excerpt that you've already read aloud so that students can ponder the new information that is given in this excerpt and not just be on the edge of their seats, wanting you to read on for the action. In an intense story like* The Lightning Thief, *it can be almost unbearable to pause in the midst of some scenes.*

I took hold of my pen and notebook, demonstrating that I planned to take notes, and then resumed reading the story where we had left off:

My Mother Teaches Me Bullfighting

We tore through the night along dark country roads. Wind slammed against the Camaro. Rain lashed the windshield. I didn't know how my mom could see anything, but she kept her foot on the gas.

Every time there was a flash of lightning, I looked at Grover sitting next to me in the backseat and I wondered if I'd gone insane, or if he was wearing some kind of shag-carpet pants. But, no, the smell was one I remembered from kindergarten field trips to the petting zoo—lanolin, like from wool. The smell of a wet barnyard animal.

All I could think to say was, "So, you and my mom…know each other?"

Grover's eyes flitted to the rearview mirror, though there were no cars behind us. "Not exactly," he said. "I mean, we've never met in person. But she knew I was watching you."

"Watching me?"

"Keeping tabs on you. Making sure you were okay. But I wasn't faking being your friend," he added hastily. "I *am* your friend."

"Um…what *are* you, exactly?"

"That doesn't matter right now."

"It doesn't matter? From the waist down, my best friend is a donkey—"

Grover let out a sharp, throaty "*Blaa-ha-ha!*"

I'd heard him make that sound before, but I'd always assumed it was a nervous laugh. Now I realized it was more of an irritated bleat.

"Goat!" he cried.

"What?"

"I'm a goat from the waist down."

"You just said it didn't matter."

"*Blaa-ha-ha!* There are satyrs who would trample you underhoof for such an insult!"

"Whoa. Wait. Satyrs. You mean like…Mr. Brunner's myths?"

"Were those old ladies at the fruit stand a *myth*, Percy? Was Mrs. Dodds a myth?"

"So you *admit* there was a Mrs. Dodds!"

"Of course."

"Then why—"

"The less you knew, the fewer monsters you'd attract," Grover said, like that should be perfectly obvious. "We put Mist over the humans' eyes. We hoped you'd think the Kindly One was a hallucination. But it was no good. You started to realize who you are."

Invite your students to turn and talk, sharing what they deduced from this portion of the read-aloud. Then summarize what they learned, pointing out they may have gleaned even more than the character did.

> I looked up. "Wow, readers, I could see you taking lots of notes. Every time Percy asked a question, I saw you pick up your pencils. That's what I mean about being alert to the questions and explanations. Why don't you compare what you and your partner learned—turn and talk."

- *You might find it useful to duplicate the excerpt or to project an enlarged version with an overhead projector because it is such a dense passage. You could make a handful of copies and distribute these so they can be shared, making a point of channeling a copy toward readers who will need extra scaffolding.*

> After the readers talked among themselves, I summarized some of what they said. "Readers, many of you gathered a lot of information about satyrs in this part, and like Percy, you realized that Grover is, in fact, a satyr. Some of you took notes on the Mist as well, thinking that it seems to produce some kind of hallucination. Percy learned all of that in this section, and you were alert, ready to learn at his side. A few of you even noted that Grover said Percy *attracts monsters.* Hmm, that might be useful to know! I wonder if Percy caught that comment. Sometimes there is this odd thing that happens, when we as readers realize that maybe we gleaned even more from a conversation than the character did."

LINK

Give your students a moment to talk about the learning curve of the main character in the book they are reading with their book club. Then encourage your students to take notes as they read, and send them off.

> "Readers, one thing you'll need to decide as you read is the role that writing will play in your reading. It's possible that you'll want to keep a page in your notebook where you jot new information as you learn it—sort of like Jack keeps a notebook in the Magic Tree House books, where he jots down what he learns about the new places he visits. Remember, where the character goes, we go, so it might make sense for us to do a similar sort of note-taking. Or perhaps you will decide to jot on Post-its, sorting and categorizing and talking about the information on them when you meet with your club. Or maybe you just want to note especially productive places in your book as you read them; then before your club meets, you can use writing as a way to nudge yourself to reread and reflect and rehearse for your conversations.

"If you do some of this work today in your books—if you find places where the character's learning curve is visible—take note of that so you can share your observations with other members of your book club when you meet together. Remember that you will often find yourself continuing to learn about a place as you read deeper into a book. And the magical elements in the world of your story may continue to appear as you progress across the pages rather than just being laid out for you all at one time, in one place. I know that in *Dragon Slayers' Academy*, for instance, Wiglaf continues to learn about dragons and their habits right through until the end of the story. Actually he keeps learning in the next book as well. That means that readers of those books keep learning this stuff, too.

"Before we go off to read, please take a moment to talk to others in your book club about the learning curve of your main character. Is your character far along on this learning curve or just getting started? You'll have a chance to do lots of thinking about the character's learning as you read, but you can figure out where your character is on the journey toward figuring out the world, and that'll help you to know where *you* should be on the same journey. It may be that the character has figured out a lot of stuff that has passed you by, so what's needed is for you to reread. Or it could be that both you and the character are supposed to still be utterly in the dark. Turn and talk about your character's learning curve—and your own."

Readers took a few minutes to get started talking about this, and as they talked, I moved among them, signaling that it was time for them to shift from talking to reading. In this way, they dispersed, club by club, from the meeting area.

OPTIONAL MINILESSON YOU MIGHT AUTHOR

Teachers, I can imagine that you might want to author a lesson in which you teach your students that in more complex books, characters have complicated emotional lives. Even though your students are reading within the (new) genre of fantasy, it will be important for them to continue to draw upon all they have been taught from previous units on character and reading historical fiction. They'll need to resist closure when they think about characters because they'll find that characters defy simple labels and often lead tangled emotional lives. There is often a greater cohort of characters in these stories as well, so it's productive to examine a few of the major characters, paying close attention to the pressures they suffer, the forces that are exerted on them and by them, the relationships they make, and all the intricacies that are found in their complicated inner lives. Of course, characters do not exist in isolation—one character's problem may be the other character's problem as well, or the other character may cause the problem.

Sometimes the emotional conflicts of one character affect another character. Sometimes their behaviors are stimulated by multiple and even contradictory forces.

In *The Lightning Thief,* for example, Percy is fascinating, not just because he is the son of Poseidon but also because he has adolescent anxieties about Annabeth, tremendous loyalty to his mother, friendship for Grover, adulation of Luke, surprising skill at sword fighting, and so forth. Annabeth is also complex, with her complicated family history, her long magical history, and her new relationship with Percy. And Grover is interesting, with the mystery in his past, his eagerness for a quest, his guilt over his own history, and his odd stance as part teenager, part mythic creature.

This work will pay off in the books your students are reading, even lower-level fantasies such as *Dragon Slayers' Academy* and *The Spiderwick Chronicles* (levels O/P). Wiglaf is complicated—he has conflicting desires and pressures. The twins in Spiderwick are multifaceted. They have sibling issues, divorce issues, school issues; their emotions flare and affect each other. Jared's inner emotions surface often, as do Mallory's and their mother's. It will be fascinating to consider their emotional lives and how those affect their behaviors.

SESSION III

"Oh, What a Tangled Web:" Plotlines and Problems Begin to Multiply

CONNECTION

Tell a personal story about a time when problems began to multiply.

"Friends, do you ever have a feeling in your life that even as you figure out one problem, another one starts to pop up? And then you figure that one out, or you think you do, and then *another* problem comes up? Or the first problem comes back?

"For instance, when I rescued some abandoned kitties, it was insane how many problems arose. First, they were under my car in the snow, and I didn't know what to do with them. Then I got the parking lot attendants to take care of them for me until I could take them home. Then I got them home and thought one was dying. After super-expensive midnight surgery, I found out the cause was just a hairball. Then I realized I don't know anything about cats. Then I found out I was allergic to cats, but I decided you can't give animals away once you've given them a home, even if they need expensive surgery and even if you're allergic to them. Then the cats used their claws to rip up all the furniture. Then I got a sinus infection because I was allergic to them. Then I had a sort-of fight with my mom because I hadn't asked anyone before bringing the cats home. Then I got the bill for the surgery—snap!"

■ *Teachers, you could decide to give your students an opportunity to tell each other some stories where problems kept arising. Any opportunity to see that the issues that arise in books (such as problems that have many parts and are not easily resolved) also arise in our lives makes reading a more meaningful experience. So if you're not rushed for time, you might give students a moment to think of times in their lives when things began to get worse instead of better—or you could return to this thinking in writing workshop. If your students are reading books at and above level R/S/T, chances are that the stories they are reading have multiple plotlines and unresolved problems, which means that the stories they write might have these, too.*

"*Crazy,* right?! Readers, the stories you are reading become more complicated sometimes, and one of the ways in which they get more complicated is that there is more than one problem and that some of the problems don't get resolved by the end of the book. Especially if you're reading a series, you may find that as you finish each book, some things have been resolved, but others haven't. In fact, new problems may arise even near the end of the book, problems that won't get resolved until later in the series, if at all.

"I'm thinking about the *Harry Potter* series, for instance. At the end of the first book, Harry's big problem was that he wanted to find the sorcerer's stone. And he did. But when he found it, he also found Lord Voldemort, who was released from his years of not having a body and became a sort of evil spirit who would come back in the next book. So Harry solved one problem, only to have another arise—like what happened when I found those rescue kitties and took them home finally, only to learn I was allergic to them. But, readers, the other thing you'll find in your books is that there may be more than one problem. Lord Voldemort is not Harry's only problem. Harry is *also* lonely and *also* bullied by the Dursleys. Part of that gets better in the first book—Harry makes friends with Ron and Hermione. But part stays just as bad—he still has to go home to the Dursleys, who seem to dislike him more than ever. And so on. It's like my cat story. One problem resolves itself, and another arises. And some problems just don't get resolved."

■ *Teachers, one of the great advantages of* Harry Potter *is that with the 400 million copies of the book and the universal release of the movies, the narrative has entered into the realm of cultural literacy. This means that often I'll turn to this familiar story to demonstrate complicated reading ideas. Time and again, I'm surprised and thrilled to see young readers manage complex thinking by linking it to their ideas about Ron, Hermione, and Harry. If you have older readers, you might, in a similar way, take similar advantage of* Twilight.

Name your teaching point. Specifically, teach your students that in complicated stories, there are multiple plotlines and problems. One way to keep track of the characters, problems, and story lines is to use charts, timelines, and other graphic organizers.

"Readers, as you tackle more and more complicated books, the stories will begin to have multiple plotlines. This means that the main characters will have more than one problem and that problems will arise for other characters, and it also means that the problems will not all be resolved by the end of a story. Often readers find it helpful to use charts, timelines, and other graphic organizers to track the problems that arise in a story in order to follow the multiple plotlines."

TEACHING

Share a transcript of a club conversation that demonstrates the many problems that arise and aren't all solved in a complex story.

"Readers, yesterday I was listening to Sam, José, and Michael talk about the end of the first book in the series they're reading together—*Dragon Slayers' Academy.* I got so intrigued by their conversation that I wrote it down. I think that it illustrates some of these issues of more complicated stories—specifically, it illustrates that in complex books like these, there will often be more than one problem. I'm going to put the transcript of their conversation up here. Can you put on your reading researcher lenses and see what this conversation suggests to you about the notion of multiple plotlines and problems? You might want to do some jotting, so I'm glad you've got your notebooks."

■ *Teachers, earlier in the* Units of Study for Teaching Reading, *you were introduced to the idea that transcripts of student work can be used as a teaching tool. This method of teaching accomplishes several things—it demonstrates your teaching point (as long as you choose or edit the transcripts carefully) and it also honors your students, constructing your learning community as one where peer interactions are as important as teacher-student interactions. It takes a few minutes to transcribe student conversations, although with new technology, I see more and more teachers doing on-the-run videos, as well.*

I put the transcript up for students to see:

Michael: I can't believe Wiglaf killed the dragon!

José: I know. That was all he wanted, to kill a dragon so he could get gold for his family.

Sam: But now his gold was taken anyway! So he killed the dragon for nothing.

Michael: I know, and he feels bad about it, too. Now Wiglaf has a new problem—he doesn't like killing dragons.

Sam: But the dragons don't know that. And I notice the next book is called _Revenge of the Dragon Lady_.

Michael: Well, that's a new problem for Wiglaf.

José: So the book ends and Wiglaf is still poor. And now he has a new problem—he's at a school for dragon-slayers, and he's a dragon-liker. And the dragons hate him.

Michael: And what about Wiglaf's friend Eric—when is he going to impress everyone? He's so desperate to kill a dragon, but it was Wiglaf who did it.

Sam: Actually, Eric's problem is that he's a girl. Wiglaf is a secret dragon-liker, and Eric is secretly a girl. I read ahead. Her problem is worse than Wiglaf's. And it stays worse for longer. And Angus has problems, too. He's Mordred's nephew. That stinks. And he can't stay away from sweets.

José: At least Mordred's happy because someone has killed a dragon.

Michael: Nah, Mordred will always want more gold. You can tell. He's greedy, and greedy people are never satisfied.

José: Whoa! These folks have a lot of problems.

Channel your students to mine the transcript you've shared for evidence that the story being discussed presents multiple problems and plotlines.

"Readers, I see you have some notes and ideas. Why don't you turn to your partner and share your research? What did you notice about the issue of multiple plotlines and problems? Turn and talk."

■ _Clearly, teachers, this transcript closely matches the teaching point. A hint—you can set some students up to produce the kind of teaching tool you think might be useful to your class. This means that you might gather a club and do some preteaching beforehand and then transcribe some of their work. They'll be aglow during the lesson._

They talked. I gathered the students back. "Readers, it's kind of amazing, isn't it, how much is happening in _Dragon Slayers' Academy,_ how many plotlines and problems arise. And we definitely saw that by the end of the story, only some problems were resolved. Michael, José, and Sam are having a rich conversation about the different problems in their first book."

Tell students that the members of the book club you've just studied used a graphic organizer to organize all their ideas about the characters, and share their graphic organizer.

"Readers, yesterday when I pulled alongside this book club, I recommended that they invent some kind of chart or other graphic organizer to keep track of the problems that are arising in the book so that they can track how those problems get solved, or how the problems change, or which new ones arise across the book or across the upcoming books in the series. Right now this club is doing a good job remembering the problems in the story, but as they keep reading, it will become even more complicated. Let me show you the simple chart that this club made, for instance, because it might give you ideas for a chart you and your club could make." I flipped over the chart paper spiral to reveal this chart, made by the members of that club.

Character	Problem	Solution/Change	By the End
Wiglaf	Needs gold	Kills a dragon	Mordred takes the gold
Eric	Wants to impress everyone by killing a dragon	Goes with Wiglaf and finds dragon	Can't figure out how to kill dragon, and Wiglaf gets the glory
Mordred	Wants gold	Sends students to kill dragons	Takes everyone's gold
Eric	Is a girl	Dresses as a boy	Still hasn't told anyone
Wiglaf	Is poor	Can't keep gold	Still is poor
All the DSA students	Mordred bullies them	None	Mordred still bullies them and steals from them
Wiglaf	Wants to kill a dragon	Kills a dragon	Finds out he hates killing dragons, and dragons want revenge

■ *Teachers, you can imagine that it might be helpful to do separate charts for separate characters, once readers have this much information.*

"Readers, I could imagine how this quick chart would really launch a long conversation, can't you? I can also imagine that there would be other ways to keep track of the problems. You could make plotlines for each character, for instance, or you could do one plotline for the big problem and then underneath include the smaller problems as they arise. The point is not that there is one kind of graphic organizer you should make but that readers often find these kinds of graphic organizers helpful when books get complicated. My club has finished *The Hobbit,* and now we're into *The Fellowship of the Ring,* and you should see the timelines and charts we have! We have one plotline for the ring of power; we have another for Sauron. We have a chart like this one for all the members of the Fellowship of the Ring who go with Frodo on his quest. These quick charts and timelines are great starting places for our conversations. They don't take long to make—it's not that much writing—but they help us extend our club conversations because we've done so much thinking."

ACTIVE INVOLVEMENT

Channel your students to chart the multiple problems found in the current read-aloud text.

"Readers, we've been keeping a timeline of the big events in *The Lightning Thief* as we read. But I'm not sure that's enough. A lot is going on in this story. We're at Chapter 9 now, and let's consider not just what's happened but how many problems we can name for Percy and/or his friends. Let's try that for a moment—turn to your partner, and jot down all the problems that you can discern so far in this story. I'll try to catch what you're saying and jot it up here."

As the students turned and talked, I went among them, listening in, repeating some of what they were saying to help other readers, coaching, and visibly trying to chart what they were saying on a large sheet of chart paper.

■ *Teachers, I purposely made it clear that it was impossible to catch everything. There was too much; I couldn't capture it logically just by jotting. Thus, I try to use my actions to reiterate the critical need for charts and graphic organizers to track characters and problems in complicated stories.*

"Whoa, readers, I'm going to interrupt you. It's too hard for me to catch everything! I've jotted that Percy doesn't know for sure who his father is. But then one of you said he finds out who his father is—it's Poseidon—but that Percy is still upset but now it's because his father doesn't contact him. Then I heard one of you say that another problem is that Clarisse hates Percy. But someone else said that Clarisse's problem is that her dad, Ares, is a jerk. Then someone said that Percy has a problem because he can't talk to Annabeth, but someone else said that Percy's problem is that his mother has been killed and that he has to rescue her from the underworld.

"Yikes! Readers, this story is so complicated, with so many problems emerging for so many characters, that it will be helpful to organize a little writing to keep track of these problems and how they change, as the *Dragon Slayers' Academy* club did. Please will you start this work now, in your notebooks, and we'll use it to begin our next conversation around the read-aloud? I can imagine that you might start a chart that is just Percy's problems, or you might include Annabeth and Grover in it, or you might envision some other kind of time-line or graphic organizer that would capture this thinking across the book. Why don't you sketch one out to practice this work and to help us prepare for our next read-aloud?" As the students began to create charts and timelines in their notebooks, I circled among the group.

LINK

Reflect on how you'll use these charts and graphic organizers for your own reading and book club conversations, and send your students off to do the same.

"Readers, of course this work will make a lot of sense for some of the club books you are reading, as we saw from the work the *Dragon Slayers' Academy* club did. I'm actually thinking, for my club, of making one chart for Frodo about the problems he has around the ring of power and another chart for Boromir about the problems he has around the ring. Or maybe I should do two timelines, and then I can show how they come together. I just got to this point in the book where Boromir attacks Frodo to get the ring. The wiz-ard, Gandalf, and the elves have been pressuring Frodo to destroy the ring. Frodo's prob-lem, or one of his problems, is how to get the ring to Mordor. But Boromir's father has been pressuring him to bring the ring to him, so Boromir's problem is how to get the ring away from Frodo.

"Yes, readers, I am beginning to imagine some of the work I might do now, and I'm sure you are, as well. As I ponder mine, see if it helps you to imagine your work. I think if I chart some of these problems, I may begin to see how some of them are related. Did you see how I just realized that one of Frodo's problems is related to one of Boromir's? You may find that also, that the solution to some problems makes new problems for other characters. Hmm, all very fascinating. I know you'll have a lot to say when you meet with your clubs. If you create any work that might help the rest of us with our books, be sure to share. Off you go."

■ *Your students will love to hear about and see the work that you are doing for your book club. It gives an authentic tone to the book club work you ask them to do. Any time you can start or end a lesson with "You know, in my book club," you truly speak as a mentor reader.*

SESSION IV

Using Our Pencils as We Read: Preparing for Partner Conversations and Book Clubs

CONNECTION

Celebrate the learning tools, such as character charts, timelines, and maps, that have been supporting your conversations around the read-aloud text. Show that you have learned some of these methods of using your pencils as you read from other fantasy readers.

"Readers, I've been thinking about the work we've been doing with *The Lightning Thief,* and I've been realizing that every time we gather for a discussion or move to do more reading, the first thing we do is look over the timeline we've been making of the big events. And now we have a few charts up that some of you made showing the big (and lesser) problems that the characters struggle with. When Percy received his quest and set out on his journey with his companions, some of you volunteered to start a map of the journey. You even showed me the map that's on the inside cover of the *Deltora Quest* books. It made me realize that a lot of these stories have maps—and probably we should be making our own maps as another way to support our work.

"Readers, there's no doubt that these things we've made really support our reading work and our conversations. I can't even count how many times I've looked back at our time-line. And now I find myself turning to this chart of characters and their struggles to add to it and to reflect on how complicated things are for these characters. For instance, as we've been finding out more about Luke, I've added that he seems to feel he can never please the gods and that his father, Hermes, has betrayed him. Our chart gives me a place to put that information so that I'm better prepared to talk about the idea.

"When some of you suggested that it would be helpful at this point in the story for us to start a map, it made me realize that probably all of us have ideas for thoughtful things we can be making and writing that would support our reading work and our conversations. I imagine that you are already doing really productive work on your own, with your Post-its and reader's notebooks, for the stories you are reading and sharing in your clubs. You're experienced at preparing for conversations, you've been in book clubs before, and a lot of you have read fantasy series before and seem to realize, perhaps more than I did, how complicated these books can become. For instance, I didn't start a list of names at the beginning of *The Lightning Thief* because I thought I'd be able to remember everyone. But those of you who have read a lot of complicated stories, especially ones that spread over series, started one of those lists right away!"

■ *Teachers, I'm assuming by the time you embark on this unit that your students have been keeping Post-its (probably for years), that they have learned to accumulate and extend these Post-its in reader's notebooks, and that they keep a reader's notebook as a place to hold their thoughts about the books they are reading. Of course, as with all our teaching, if we keep notebooks as well, the kids will keep better notebooks. When my Teachers College Reading and Writing Project colleagues and I work in classrooms in which the kids have flourishing reader's notebooks, it is almost always the case that the teacher will have his or her own vibrant example of a reader's note-book, full of jottings, occasional drawings, and more extended entries. This is one of those times when we need to tweak our own personal habits so that we are involved in the work we ask students to do. My laptop may serve as my writer's notebook now, but I still keep a notebook from which I can teach within the writing workshop. In the same way, even though as an adult reader I tend to write in the margins of my books and then on pages in my laptop, for the sake of my students I make deliberate use of a reader's notebook that mirrors that which I am asking them to keep. The charts you make in the room during the read-aloud are also examples of your collective reader's notebook.*

Name your teaching point. Specifically, teach your students that experienced readers use pencils as they read to deepen engagement with books and extend literary conversations.

"Readers, today I want to teach you that experienced readers have a repertoire of writing about reading strategies that we draw upon to support our reading work and our conversations. One way to extend this repertoire is for a learning community to share with each other the different ways that we use our pencils as we read."

TEACHING

Set your students up to display and share ways they have used their pencils as they read. You'll ask each reader to "publish" a favorite notebook page, and you'll channel readers to study each other's techniques, borrowing good ideas.

"There are a few ways to do this work, friends—to share learning practices within a community. One way is for partners or clubs to get together often and use their Post-its and notebooks to support their conversations. You do this often. Another is to read a community text—some story that we all are engaged in through read-aloud—and together we make the things and do the writing that extends our thinking. We're doing this with *The Lightning Thief.* But there's one more method to share work, and that is to have a kind of informal publishing of favorite pages from your notebook. When the *Deltora Quest* readers suggested that we make a map, I realized that it would be helpful if our whole community had access to all our practices. No one of us, by him- or herself, knows enough or has invented all the creative ways that readers use our pencils as we read to deepen our engagement with books.

"Yesterday I told you that we would take some time today to display some favorite pages from our notebooks. I see, as I look at your tables, that some of you have taped Post-its to some pages and that around these Post-its you seem to have other writing. I see that some of you also left your novel nearby, with some pages marked, in case we want to see what you were reading. Thank you, that's very helpful. I wonder, sometimes, what to do with my Post-its when I finish a chapter, so I'll be looking for some helpful methods. And I see that some of you seem to have done a lot of drawing. In fact, I see that this club has been making maps that you've tucked into your books. That's intriguing! And wow, what's this? Some members of this club appear to be collecting ideas by using boxes and bullets like we did in nonfiction. I'm curious about that work, too.

"Friends, as we explore each other's methods, let's remember our purpose. Our aim is to come away from this inquiry with more ideas for how to use our pencils as we read our own stories. You can't carry your notebook with you, as it's now sitting on the table, ready for others to come visit it. But you should definitely carry a clipboard and some paper with you. I imagine that you'll want to take notes on some of the methods you see others using, and you may even want to copy some of the charts and diagrams so that you'll have a model. Put a reference to the source (for instance, say 'Sarah's *Deltora Quest* map') so that you'll know how to find the original author if you want some advice. Some teachers call what we're about to do a 'gallery walk.' In art galleries, you walk around, looking at the work and admiring it. If you're another artist, when you do a gallery walk, you do it thinking, 'What can I learn from this work?' Let's try that now."

■ *Teachers, you could also do what we often do in writing workshop, which is have the kids write comments to each other about things they admire in each other's work.*

ACTIVE INVOLVEMENT

Rally your students to participate in this inquiry with the lens of really honing their own methods for using their pencils as they read. Send them off to take notes and interview readers.

"Okay, readers, let's all walk around and try to chart inventive methods we learn for using our pencils as we read. You're responsible now for coming away from this inquiry with a few ideas and examples to extend your own work. I see that you have your clipboards and pencils ready. Let's move quietly around the tables, desks, and shelves."

They did so.

■ *Teachers, many of our readers do truly inventive work with their pencils as they read. Some make illustrations of favorite parts of the story. Others love to do webs, timelines, flowcharts, and charts. Others like to write long, reflective responses. Some, given the opportunity, will use colored pencils to go back into their notebooks, highlighting important parts, adding headings, writing small comments and drawing illustrations in the margins. One of my colleagues, Jerry Maraia, whose students kept insightful and beautiful reader's notebooks, told his students that when they read, they are like Jack climbing the beanstalk—they are entering a land of the imagination. Like Jack brings back the gifts from the castle, they too need to bring back artifacts from this realm. Jerry's students use their pencils to describe their thinking, to extend their responses, and to deepen their engagement with their books. Their reader's notebooks became something his students, even his most struggling students, were tremendously proud of, and Jerry uses them as a major assessment tool. The trick is to use your pencil quickly, for a few minutes, so you get lots of reading time.*

I walked also, taking notes, audibly praising the work I saw, asking sometimes for explanations of how the work was helping a student as a reader, copying some of it, and starting a chart that we could hang in the classroom.

"Readers, let's come to the meeting area. I see that you have notes and drawings on your clipboards. Why don't you take a moment to tell the other members of your book club about how this has inspired you to outgrow yourself—what did you see that you want to try also, and why? I'll tell you what I learned—I learned that I should have started a glossary of the gods and myths to support my understanding of *The Lightning Thief.* I never thought of turning to nonfiction reading to support my reading of this fiction novel, but a bit of research on the gods could really help me. Thanks for that idea. Let's see what you came away with."

They talked. I gathered more notes for our chart, and after a few minutes, I voiced over to summarize, saying, "Readers, what I most like about what you're doing is that you're really trying to use writing to tackle the hard parts. One reader told me that he was making a chart to display what he knew backwards and forwards for a while, until he realized that he needed his writing to help with the hard parts rather than to be a display case! He was struggling with the time shifts in his book, so he began to keep multiple timelines and to mark places in his book where he thought time had shifted. His writing became more messy, more problematic—but also more useful. Now he has a timeline in his notebook on which he is taping his Post-its to show every important shift in the story. Another thing I like is that a lot of this writing is in the form of quick charts, sketches, and timelines—it wouldn't take many minutes to do.

"Look up at the chart we've begun here. For now, just look up here at this chart. It doesn't have all of your work yet, but it's a start. Please look at it and think about where you are in the story you are reading right now, and then reflect on whether any of these methods and strategies for using your pencils as you read would make a lot of sense for you as a reader. Turn and tell your partner."

Using Our Pencils as We Read

To Hold On to the Story	To Deepen Our Engagement
Character lists, charts, and webs	Writing long about reflections
Charts of problems, solutions, changes	
Timelines of events, emotions	Illustrations of significant moments
Maps	Descriptions of lasting images
Setting descriptions and illustrations	Charts of other titles and characters who can be compared across books
Quick jottings about responses	
Writing about predictions and theories	Writing long about themes and lessons
Glossaries	Quoting and celebrating craft
Facts and information sections	

■ *Teachers, you will undoubtedly create a more vibrant individualized version of this chart, perhaps with student examples tied to it or with specific examples from the read-aloud. This chart just indicates that you would want to gather together the methods your students are using, and perhaps add to them, so that they have a tool in the classroom that helps them use their pencils as they read.*

LINK

Remind students of the need to get a lot of reading done, and give them an opportunity to reflect on their balance of reading and writing time. Then send them off.

"Readers, as we ponder this chart, which is just a preliminary recording of our inquiry, I want to remind you that almost all of this work is fast and done on the run as you read. You pick up your pencils as you read or after you finish a chapter, and you do a few minutes—no more—of quick jotting. It's really important that you make choices about the writing you do as you read that protect your time for reading, reading, reading. Remember that a rule of thumb is you'll probably read at least sixty pages a day, in school and at home (although many of you will get so absorbed that you will read lots more than that)."

PART TWO

It's All About Good and Evil

SESSION V

"Here Be Dragons": Thinking Metaphorically About the Problems Characters Struggle With

GETTING READY

- Have *The Paper Bag Princess* on hand.

- Read through the end of Chapter 12 in *The Lightning Thief.*

- You could bring in an image of the Carta Marina to show your students. There are zillions of images online. It has sea monsters attacking ships in places the mariners considered dangerous. The Lenox Globe, of which there are also zillions of online images, was the first map to include the phrase "Here Be Dragons."

- If, in the previous lesson, you or the students made some charts of the many problems that characters face in *The Lightning Thief,* it would be helpful to have those nearby.

- Select an excerpt from your read-aloud text that gives evidence for the big emotional conflicts, or "dragons," with which characters struggle. We use an excerpt from pages 191–192. You could show this on chart paper or on a screen, or you could duplicate and distribute it.

CONNECTION

Share a story that demonstrates metaphor, such as the "Here Be Dragons" term on the Lenox globe, which symbolized the host of unknown dangers that travelers might encounter.

"Readers, have you ever seen old maps, the ones that reflect what the first mariners who charted the oceans believed about the oceans? I love these charts because they are so gorgeous and mysterious and symbolic. One mapmaker in particular wanted to show that someplace was dangerous, so he wrote 'Here Be Dragons' on that area. The Latin words for that were *Hic Sunt Dracones,* which were written on a famous globe called the Lenox Globe, from 1503.

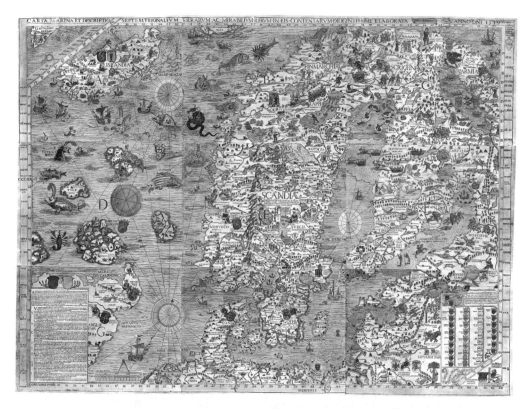

"Or the cartographers, the mapmakers, might show sea monsters lurking along the coast. There is this really beautiful map that I adore, called the Carta Marina. It was created in the sixteenth century, and it shows dragons attacking boats as well as all the other mythical dangers people would encounter if they ever dared to leave the familiar shores of their homeland.

"Readers, what's fascinating about these charts is that the dragons and sea monsters on them are symbolic. Sometime, long ago, mariners probably saw giant squid and then pictured them on their maps as sea monsters. But mapmakers also put dragons on maps to show that the explorer was coming to a place that was unknown and dangerous. They also showed dragons in places where earthquakes happened. They marked the borders of unknown terrain with *Hic Sunt Dracones.* 'Here Be Dragons' has come to be a symbolic expression that means, 'Look out! You're in dangerous territory—don't go there.'"

■ *Teachers, you can decide how far you want to go in explaining and exploring the metaphoric qualities of this saying. You'll notice, in films, stories, and conversations, that people use this expression about dangerous emotional territories, to say, "I'm not sure you really want to explore those emotions." How do I feel about my relationship with my brother? "Here Be Dragons!"*

Name your teaching point. Specifically, teach your students that some of the dragons that characters face are metaphoric dragons. One way readers think about these "dragons" is to consider the inner struggles that characters face.

"Readers, today I want to teach you that in the stories you are reading, the characters face dragons—not just literal dragons, which some fantasy characters do encounter, but also metaphoric dragons, which are the conflicts inside characters' souls that haunt them. Powerful fantasy readers learn to think metaphorically about these 'dragons.'"

TEACHING

Return to the short fantasy text you shared earlier, and suggest that in this text the character faces concrete and also emotional challenges, or dragons. Use this example to suggest that fantasy readers need to think metaphorically. Foster the idea that all characters have dragons.

"Let's go back to a favorite story to illustrate this thinking." I picked up *The Paper Bag Princess.* "Remember *The Paper Bag Princess?* Well, in *The Paper Bag Princess,* Elizabeth literally faces a dragon. When I think about the big problem that Elizabeth has, it's that a dragon has smashed her castle and taken Prince Ronald away. And of course, readers, Elizabeth conquers this dragon. She finds the dragon, tricks him, and exhausts him, and she completes her quest by rescuing Prince Ronald.

"But, readers, *The Paper Bag Princess* is a more complicated story than just this simple quest. If this was just a story of how Elizabeth rescued Prince Ronald, then there would not be any significant character changes in the story, and the story wouldn't be a memorable one. But Elizabeth does change. She has a second important, life-changing moment when she faces up to something hard—something as hard as or harder than the flame-breathing monster she has already conquered. Do you remember what I'm referring to?

"When Elizabeth gets to that cave and rescues Ronald, Elizabeth finds that Ronald is just as much of a monster as the dragon was! At least the dragon was polite, even if he did want to eat her. Ronald turns out to be monstrously cruel. 'Elizabeth,' he says, when she has finally made her way through danger and death, through burnt forests and fields of horses' bones, to this cave, 'You are a mess! You smell like ashes, your hair is all tangled and you are wearing a dirty old paper bag. Come back when you are dressed like a real princess.'

"Readers, I came to this part of the story, and here's what I thought. I thought: 'Aha! *Hic Sunt Dracones!* Here Be Dragons! This is Elizabeth's real dragon! Ronald is her dragon— *he* is the thing that she needs to conquer. He's the problem she has to get past. His cruelty and indifference, his snobbery, his way of ignoring, demeaning, and humiliating her—that's her dragon. If I were a medieval cartographer and I were making a map of this story, I would show Ronald as a dragon to symbolize the role he plays in this story."

■ *Teachers, this is a huge and powerful move to make as a reader, to begin to think metaphorically. It's one reason that I love to start any year, any grade, with* The Paper Bag Princess. *It is such a lovely move, to go from thinking about real dragons to thinking about what other dragons characters face. There is something about the literalness of the dragon imagery, the way it symbolizes danger, that seems to help young readers move into metaphoric thinking gracefully. I've heard third graders talk spontaneously about the dragons in Oliver Button's life, for instance.*

"Do you see how I did this, readers? I thought *metaphorically.* I moved to thinking about dragons not as real animals but as *metaphoric* dragons that characters face. When you do this, readers, you can begin to think deeply about the dragons in all characters' lives and in our own lives as well. Take a moment and ask yourself: 'What are my dragons?'" I paused, as if considering my own dragons. "I have a few, readers. You'll know them from writing workshop. My friend Audra talks often of how, across the many years of our lives, we'll tend to write about the same issues, the same themes—the same dragons. It's a provocative question to ask, isn't it: What are your dragons?"

Link the idea of physical and also metaphorical dragons to your read-aloud text, showing students that you can scan graphic organizers to figure out the deepest struggles that a character—in this case, the protagonist of the read-aloud—encounters.

"Now watch me as I try applying this way of thinking, of thinking metaphorically about the dragons that characters face, to *The Lightning Thief.* I say to myself, 'I bet Percy Jackson has dragons in his life—big issues that haunt him—that he needs to get past.' That's how you think about this, readers. You think about the things that characters need to get past; it's like an internal quest that characters are on. So I don't mean small stuff, like when Percy wants to do well on his mythology final exam. I'm talking about the big emotional conflicts that are Percy's dragons."

I picked up the book, and then I looked at our timeline of events and some of the charts we had produced in earlier lessons about the multiple problems the characters in this story face. Then I said, "Friends, I'm thinking back over all the problems we've been talking about. Just looking at some of our timelines and charts, for instance, I'm reminded of the monsters Percy faces, like the Minotaur who kills his mother. That incident caused another problem in Percy's life: how to get his mother back from the underworld. That leads to all sorts of related problems. Hmm, let me see if I can group some of these problems together or if any of them become emotional conflicts rather than real physical monsters. So I'm letting go of the actual monsters and focusing on the metaphoric ones."

I thought a little longer. "Well, I guess when I think metaphorically, readers, after Percy's mother is killed by the Minotaur, it feels like one of Percy's dragons is the guilt he feels about her death. All he wants is to get her back, to get rid of this feeling. This emotion colors all his actions. It makes him secretive with his friends. It drives his actions. Yes, this guilt feels to me like one of Percy's dragons."

ACTIVE INVOLVEMENT

Give your readers a chance to try thinking metaphorically about characters' dragons either in the read-aloud text or in their own stories.

"Readers, do you see how I pushed myself to think metaphorically, considering what big emotional conflicts the character struggles with? I asked myself, 'What are Percy's dragons? What haunts him? What does he need to get past? What drives him?' To do this work, I considered all the charts and timelines as well as all the notes I've made so far about the multiple problems characters face, and this time I tried to analyze the emotional aspect of these problems.

"Let's give you a chance to try this work, readers. One way to do this thinking is to look back over your notes, reconsidering the many problems that a character faces, and then to see if some of them add up to a big emotional 'dragon'—a place in the character's emotional life where you might say 'Here Be Dragons!' You might be able to do this for Annabeth or for Grover, as well as for Percy, as we've done so much work recently charting the multiple problems that become visible in complicated stories like this. Use all your materials, readers, and when you begin to have some ideas, turn and talk with your partners."

They did.

■ *Teachers, you'll find that any public records you've made, such as charts and time-lines of the multiple plotlines and problems in your read-aloud text, are helpful. There is just so much to think about in complicated stories. Having tools at hand that help us to recall important parts of the story means that students can move more easily from recalling the plot to thinking deeply about characters.*

After partners had been working and talking for a few minutes, I called them back. "Readers, I heard some fascinating conversations. Clearly it's productive to ask the question: what are this character's dragons? Some of you focused on Annabeth, and I heard you say that her relationship with her dad is her dragon; she seems haunted by it every time it comes up. Others of you talked about Grover and how he seems to have some secret dragon that we don't totally understand yet—he often mentions that something terrible happened on his first quest, but we don't know more because every time he mentions it, he says that he can't talk about it! I love the way you're uncovering dragons that are kind of lurking behind corners. And Percy seems to have a few dragons, right? Some of you talked more about his guilt. Others of you talked about his feelings about his father—that he seems to feel abandoned and that it makes him want to prove himself."

■ *Sometimes, when young readers move to having exciting theories, they begin to stop using the text as evidence for those theories. They love the new language they are acquiring; they like the sense of intellectual headiness that comes with this kind of grand thinking work. Next, in this minilesson, therefore, we'll show them how to zoom in on a part of the story to support their thinking. You could, of course, make this a second session, if you feel as if this minilesson has already done enough new work for one day. Sometimes we make our peace with our kids being excited but a little unleashed, and then we rein them in on another day.*

Talk up the need to ground this metaphoric talk in concrete references to passages of text. Demonstrate by rereading a passage from the whole-class read-aloud and excavating it.

I picked up the book again. "Readers, I want to show you one more thing, since you're doing this incredible thinking. Sometimes, when you are thinking metaphorically like this, it's helpful to ground your thinking in specific moments in the text. Readers, look, for instance, for places where the character seems to be struggling with this dragon—places where this big emotional conflict becomes visible. Let me show you one such moment." I opened the book to page 192. "I'm going to show you a specific moment in the story that supports our thinking. It's in that last chapter we read together, after Percy, Grover, and Annabeth have defeated Medusa. Grover asks Percy to explain more about their quest, about why they are seeking Zeus's lightning bolt. I copied parts of it for you. The first part begins with Percy asking Grover a question." I distributed and then read aloud this passage:

"How are we going to get into the Underworld?" I asked him. "I mean, what chance do we have against a god?"

"I don't know," he admitted. "But back at Medusa's, when you were searching her office? Annabeth was telling me—"

"Oh, I forgot. Annabeth will have a plan all figured out."

"Don't be so hard on her, Percy. She's had a tough life, but she's a good person. After all, she forgave me…" His voice faltered.

"What do you mean?" I asked. "Forgave you for what?"

Suddenly, Grover seemed very interested in playing notes on his pipes.

"Wait a minute," I said. "Your first keeper job was five years ago. Annabeth has been at camp five years. She wasn't…I mean, your first assignment that went wrong—"

"I can't talk about it," Grover said, and his quivering lower lip suggested he'd start crying if I pressed him. "But as I was saying, back at Medusa's, Annabeth and I agreed there's something strange going on with this quest. Something isn't what it seems."

…

I thought about what Medusa had said: I was being used by the gods. What lay ahead of me was worse than petrification. "I haven't been straight with you," I told Grover. "I don't care about the master bolt. I agreed to go to the Underworld so I could bring back my mother."

Grover blew a soft note on his pipes. "I know that, Percy. But are you sure that's the only reason?"

"I'm not doing it to help my father. He doesn't care about me. I don't care about him."

Grover gazed down from his tree branch. "Look, Percy, I'm not as smart as Annabeth. I'm not as brave as you are. But I'm pretty good at reading emotions. You're glad your dad is alive. You feel good that he's claimed you, and part of you wants to make him proud. That's why you mailed Medusa's head to Olympus. You wanted him to notice what you'd done."

"Yeah? Well maybe satyr emotions work differently than human emotions. Because you're wrong. I don't care what he thinks."

Grover pulled his feet up onto the branch. "Okay, Percy. Whatever."

"Readers, this moment seems packed with evidence for your theories about these characters' dragons, doesn't it? Take a moment to analyze it, and then go back into your conversations, but this time, really use some specifics from the text to support your theories."

They did.

■ *Teachers, a different way to do the active involvement section of this minilesson would be to ask your readers to open up their own books and consider what dragons their own characters face. The advantage, clearly, is that there is more likelihood of transference into the students' independent work when they actually work in their own stories during the lesson. I think this is a question of timing and scaffolding.*

LINK

Inspire your readers to think about the dragons in their own lives, as well as those in the lives of their characters.

"Readers, this was a lot. Today you learned to think metaphorically about the dragons that characters face. You learned to zoom in on moments in the text where these dragons become visible. You learned some Latin. *Hic Sunt Dracones.* I'm entirely sure that you'll bring this thinking into your writing, as well, thinking hard about your own dragons. That's what is so gorgeous about doing powerful reading work. We illuminate our own lives as we shine a light onto the lives of the characters in our stories.

"I know that many of your book clubs have finished one book and begun another, and I expect that you'll find this way of thinking useful as a means of comparing characters across books. For example, as you get to know the characters in your second book, you can compare the dragons (the metaphoric ones) that various characters face. Let's go off to read, and I'll be looking across your notes and your conversations to see where you are noticing that *Hic Sunt Dracones!*"

SESSION VI

What's This Really About?
Thinking About Themes and Life Lessons

CONNECTION

Tell a story about a fellow reader who speaks of books in terms of their themes and life lessons.

"Readers, one of the members of my book club, Nate, is obsessed with The Lord of the Rings books. We're on Book Three now, *The Return of the King.* We've read *The Hobbit* and *The Fellowship of the Ring* and *The Two Towers.* We've seen the movies. We've followed Frodo and his band of elves, dwarves, and men across Middle Earth, through epic battles and silent moral struggles. And every time we come to a new part of the story, whether we're looking at part of the film or reading the book, Nate says, 'Oh, this part is really important. I love this part.' I realize that Nate has read these books so many times that he has practically memorized them. Finally I had to ask him. 'Nate,' I said, 'why do you keep rereading this story? After all, you know what happens with the hobbits and the elves and so forth. What makes this story so important to you?'

"Nate stared at me. I thought at first that I had hurt his feelings, that he wasn't going to answer. But he was just building up steam. When he did speak, the words came out in a torrent. 'Mary,' he said, 'this story isn't about hobbits and elves. This story is about the struggle between good and evil. This story is about how power slowly eats away and corrupts. This story is about how the physically strong can use their gifts to protect others.

This story is about how even the smallest and physically weakest can find moral strength to defeat evil. This story is about love and how love drives us to be better than we are.' Nate stared at me. 'That's why I keep reading this story,' he finally added. 'It's teaching me how to live. And I'm not an elf.'

"Oh," I said. "Well then, I think I'll get back to these elves and hobbits. Clearly I have a lot to learn from them.

"Friends, you can imagine that this was a humbling moment for me. Here I had been following Frodo across Middle Earth and adoring Aragorn and Legolas. I had been deeply involved in these characters and the problems they faced. But it seemed as if I was missing what these stories were really about. Frankly, readers, I realized that the story was so exciting that I was basically a plot junky. I just wanted more, more. This has happened to me before. When the last Harry Potter book came out, Book Seven, I stayed up the whole night to read it. I just *had* to know how things turned out, how Harry would defeat Voldemort. When the narrative plunged into other areas, such as Hermione and Ron's relationship and even Harry's feelings about Dumbledore, I practically skimmed over those parts, pushing on to discover what happens with Voldemort! I was only interested in *what happened,* not in what the story might be *about.* And those are two different things. What happens is the plot; we all know how to talk about that. But what it's about, well, then we're on to theme and life lessons, and Nate taught me that sometimes I hadn't given that enough thought."

- *Teachers, you'll notice that in these minilessons, you'll have opportunities to talk up books that your readers might love. If you have older readers, you can talk up* The Hunger Games; *if you have younger ones, you might talk up* Gregor the Overlander, *a series by the same author, Suzanne Collins, that has similar themes of survival. Or I might mention* The Supernaturalist, *by Eoin Colfer, author of* Artemis Fowl. *In that book, kids have been kept on another planet solely for the purpose of doing medical experiments on them. It's a fast-paced, exciting plot and is also a commentary on the medical industry, the fate of poor children, and the ability of children to be activists.*

Name your teaching point. Specifically, teach your students that stories are not just about "what happens"; they are also about underlying themes and life lessons.

"Readers, today I want to teach you that often, with great stories, the plot is a vehicle for teaching about ideas. The stories are not just about what happens. Stories are also about themes and life lessons. Insightful readers mine these stories for these themes and life lessons."

Teaching

Recall some familiar fantasy tales, and retell them in terms of themes and life lessons. Then use the read-aloud text to demonstrate how to mine the story for possible themes.

"Readers, fantasy novels are incredibly helpful in teaching us how to read this way—to mine for themes and life lessons. That's because fantasy is almost always about a struggle between good and evil—that's the most common, indeed essentially a universal theme, of fantasy stories. In the plot, there are usually clearly delineated characters who represent good and others who represent evil. As you witness these characters struggle, even though you are not an elf, you too can learn about this theme. Think about *Star Wars*. On the one side are Darth Vader and the forces of darkness; on the other are young Luke Skywalker and his valiant Jedi companions. Readers, you don't have to *be* a Jedi knight to learn from Luke about how hard it is to struggle against evil, to be strong, to trust yourself, to learn from your mistakes, and so on."

■ *Teachers, I reference* Star Wars *because I assume that, like* Harry Potter, *it has entered into cultural literacy. You could substitute Harry and Dumbledore for Voldemort and the Malfoys for this example, or you could do some angled storytelling of any fantasy tale to set up the connection.*

"One way that readers do this work is that we ask ourselves questions at any time in our reading: 'What is this story beginning to be about? Is the main character learning? Is the main character teaching? Am I learning?' Then as we recall the story, instead of focusing on the plot we try to mine the story for big themes and life lessons. It's actually not that hard to do, but it's just really easy to *not* do, especially if you're a plot junkie like I am. Watch me do this work with *The Lightning Thief*. Instead of saying that this story is about satyrs and demigods, I'm going to push myself to ask questions: 'So far, what is this story beginning to be about? What is Percy learning? What is he teaching? What am I learning?'"

I picked up the book and looked at all our charts and timelines. "Well, so far, Percy has been struggling to figure out his powers. He's learning about himself. (In fact, he's rather like Luke Skywalker, I think.) He doesn't really know how strong he can be yet, so he's always testing himself, a little further each time.

"Let me be specific. What evidence do I have for that? Well, in the part we just read, where Percy dives off the St. Louis Arch to save that little child from the Chimera, Percy definitely goes further than he's ever gone before. He really puts his own life on the line to save someone else's. So if I ask myself about the life lessons that Percy is learning, I guess he's learning that little by little he can be a better person than he ever thought possible. And he's learning that inside of himself, he has special powers.

"Now if that's what Percy *learns,* what does he *teach?* (Mostly, in these important action-packed moments in the story, characters teach each other lessons.) Well, I guess Percy taught this boy he saved, and everyone else there, that sometimes strong people defend weaker people, even when it's dangerous. Hmm, that's interesting to me. I've always been preoccupied with the problem of bullies and how to stand up to them. Wow! I could even think of the Chimera not just as a literal monster but as a metaphorical one, as a bully! And Percy shows that we can protect others if we stand between bullies and their prey."

- *Teachers, you don't have to include that bit about thinking metaphorically. It just seemed like an opportunity to recall prior teaching and to show how you can learn to think metaphorically at any point in your reading—you don't have to wait until the story is over or do it only when you are consciously setting out to do that thinking work.*

I looked up from the book, which I had been holding open to this page. Then I continued. "But what about *me?* What if I move to what lessons Percy teaches me? I'm not a demigod, but I guess I'd like to believe that inside all of us is the ability to be strong. I don't want to leap off the St. Louis Arch, but I'd like to be able to stand between bullies and those they pick on. And I'd like to become stronger, as I grow, than I was as a kid—not physically stronger, but more sure of myself, more willing to get into the fray."

I looked up. "Wait, this is working! Now that I'm thinking hard about this theme, that all it takes to stand up to bullies is courage, I'm even realizing that it's not Percy's demigod powers that make him so incredible during that battle on the arch. It's his compassion and his courage that make him incredible. And those are qualities that any of us can learn more about. Aha! I'm starting to be on to something."

Name what you have done in ways that you hope will be transferable to other texts, other readers, other days.

"Readers, do you see how I thought back over the story, thinking first about what's been happening in the story and then asking myself what the story could really be about? And when I did this work, friends, I didn't try to make some huge, grand statement, the kind that might be on a bumper sticker (or a state exam). Instead, I tried to find lots of words for what I was thinking, and I went back to the story to find some moments that made this theme, or lesson, visible. Also, readers, if you're stuck, follow the same process I did: think about what lessons characters learn, and then move to what they teach each other, and that may bring you to lessons they teach us."

ACTIVE INVOLVEMENT

Give your readers a chance to practice this work, preferably on an accessible text.

"Readers, even simple fantasy stories often have powerful themes." I held up *The Paper Bag Princess.* "Why don't you try this work now, using *The Paper Bag Princess?* Talk among the members of your club, trying to name the lessons you can learn from this book. If that feels successful, move on and try mining the story you are reading for themes and life lessons. Ask yourself, 'What is this story beginning to be about?' And remember, stories can be about more than one theme, and they may teach more than one life lesson. So readers keep going in their conversations, saying to themselves: 'What else could this be about?'"

■ *Teachers, I modeled this on* The Lightning Thief *and gave students a chance to try this work on* The Paper Bag Princess *because the latter is a more accessible text, and its themes are more readily apparent. Often, when you move to heady intellectual work, it's easier for all your students to do the work if the text itself is easy. Typical themes that students arrive at for* The Paper Bag Princess *are that girls can be strong and that sometimes we are mistaken in love.*

"Friends, as I listen to your conversations, I want to remind you to support your ideas by saying what in the story makes you think this. Sometimes we have a tendency to start spouting grand themes or popular sayings, like 'Don't judge a book by its cover.' But it's better to play around with your own language, to say your ideas in your own words, and then to return to moments in the story that seem to support those ideas. So go back to your conversations, but this time, try to say to each other, 'What in the story makes you say that?' If you are getting stuck, you can always ask yourself, 'What is the character learning? What is the character teaching?' That might get you to a life lesson you could be learning from the book."

They did.

"Readers, another way to think about the themes and life lessons in the stories we read is to consider which themes and life lessons matter the most to us personally. When I think about *The Lightning Thief,* for instance, there are so many important themes and life lessons: that it's hard to lose people we love; that it takes a long time to really discover who we want to be; that inside us, sometimes, are special powers; that our friends can stand by us; that we can recover from big mistakes. But not all these themes matter equally to me right now in my life, so I may consider the many possible meanings of a story and decide to focus on one or two that seem significant to my own learning. For instance, I am interested in the idea that we can recover from big mistakes. Clearly Grover has gone on since his bad incident on his first quest. He has continued to seek half-bloods and to try to protect them. He hasn't lost faith in himself. That seems really important to me. I tend to be haunted by my mistakes—I relive them in my thoughts, and I wish I could go back and change things. But this book is teaching me that it's also important to go on. Do you see how I took a personal angle on the themes and lessons, thinking about which meaning might be important to me? You can do this, too, in the conversations you are having or in the writing you do in your notebooks."

LINK

Send your readers off, reminding them to consider what their stories may really be about.

"Readers, from now on, when we're talking about our books, let's push ourselves to consider what these stories are really about. You may find, as well, that different stories have some of the same meanings. You'll definitely find that one story suggests many possible meanings.

"Let's take one moment, as well, to consider when doing this work makes sense. It's not going to be the kind of work, readers, that you do in the first chapter of a book. A story has to unfold a bit before we can ask ourselves what the story is beginning to be about. So if you're just starting a new book, it might make more sense to be thinking hard about what kind of place you encounter or to track the many plotlines and problems that arise. Before we go off to read, please take a moment to talk together with the other members of your club about what your plans are as readers today. What work do you hope to accomplish individually and as a club?"

They talked briefly.

"Off you go, readers."

SESSION VII

There's No Such Thing as True Good or Evil

CONNECTION

Tell a story about a reader who describes that characters are never fully evil or fully good.

"Friends, recently I was talking with a couple of young friends. One is a fourth grader, Jackson, who adores *Harry Potter.* We were talking about Professor Snape and about how awful he is to Harry. For a teacher, he really is incredibly cruel. He taunts Harry, he misjudges him, he punishes him, sometimes unfairly. I was saying how much I detested Snape—he's everything I *don't* want to be as a teacher! But Jackson, who also dislikes Snape, nevertheless reminded me that Snape was not all bad. 'Listen,' Jackson said, 'characters are not all bad or all evil—there's no such thing as pure good or pure evil.' Then he reminded me of how Snape sometimes protects Harry and how Snape tries to serve Dumbledore. It's true, I realized, that characters aren't all one way. They may be good but still be flawed, and sometimes it is hard to sort out whether a character is mostly good but flawed or is mostly evil but with some glimmers of good. Snape is a perfect example of that. It won't be until the final chapters of *Harry Potter: The Deathly Hallows,* after the reader has journeyed through almost four thousand pages of the story, that we find out whose side Snape has been on all along."

- *Teachers, one thing you'll notice, if you have extended conversations with your young fanatical fantasy readers, is how insightful they do become. One inspiration for this unit was, indeed, several conversations with Jackson, Torrin, and other young fantasy readers, who showed in their talk that they were doing a lot of high-level reading work, driven by their compulsion to understand all the parts of these stories. Just go talk to one of your kids who really knows* Harry Potter, *and you'll have your own transcript with which to begin this lesson.*

"Friends, I think this is intriguing for us to investigate. I'm sure, for example, that if we paid more attention to how nuanced characters are (that means multifaceted, or with many layers) in the stories we're reading, we'll know more about them, and we may find that we're more sympathetic to the evil characters and more discerning about how the good characters may be flawed. Some of you already think this way as writers. For instance, recently I listened to Jackson tell me about the realistic fiction story he is writing. It's about a kid who stands by and does nothing when he sees a bully tormenting a younger child on the playground. Then later in the story, the main character gets bullied, and he decides, from then on, to try to stand up to bullies. But here's what I found fascinating about Jackson's goals as a writer. Jackson wanted to also give the reader some insight into the bully. He decided that he would show the bully getting yelled at by a parent on the way to school. Jackson thought this might make us more sympathetic toward the bully, which would make his character more complicated and interesting.

"These conversations, friends, have got me thinking about the characters in the stories we are reading. As these stories become more complicated, the characters become more complicated as well. Often they are not simply good or evil. They are good but perhaps are flawed, or maybe they are evil but are still compelling. I'm thinking of the gods in *The Lightning Thief*, for instance. I expected Zeus to be powerful and all good, but he's jealous and insecure and untrusting. He does try to be a good ruler, but he still has flaws."

■ *Teachers, there are more obvious characters, such as Luke, that spring to mind in* The Lightning Thief *as ones who are both heroic and flawed, or not all good or all evil. I've deliberately left the more obvious ones so that the kids can focus on those during their active involvement. It's somewhat tricky to balance during lessons, but it's helpful if the example that we leave for the kids is easier than the example we use in our demonstration. I can imagine demonstrating this lesson with the dragon from* The Paper Bag Princess *as well. He is clearly the "villain" in the tale. He leaves a trail of destruction and death. But he treats Elizabeth honorably. He is courteous and responsive; he is not "all bad." In fact, in the PBS version of the tale, when they made the animated version, Elizabeth goes off in the end with the dragon.*

Name your teaching point. Specifically, teach your students that characters are complicated—they are usually more than one way. Experienced readers are alert for the character flaws in the hero and the admirable traits in the villain.

"Readers, today I want to teach you that as the books we read become more complex, the characters also become more complicated. They are not just all evil or all good—they are nuanced. This means that powerful readers delve deeply into their characters' strengths, flaws, and motivations across the whole arc of the story."

Teaching

Analyze a character from the read-aloud text, looking for signs that he or she is more than one way.

"As the characters in your stories become more complicated, friends, you have to do more complex reading work—you can no longer simply list character traits. Characters will shift. They will be unpredictable. They may be good but have significant character flaws that get in the way of their being good all the time. I'm thinking, for instance, of Poseidon in *The Lightning Thief.* At first, he seems cruel and selfish. He has, after all, abandoned Percy. He left Percy's mother. Here's what Percy says about Poseidon early in the book:"

> I felt angry at my father. Maybe it was stupid, but I resented him for going on that ocean voyage, for not having the guts to marry my mom. He'd left us, and now we were stuck with Smelly Gabe.

"And Poseidon can be rather childish. A bit later in the book, Annabeth, daughter of Athena, says:"

> "One time my mom caught Poseidon with his girlfriend in Athena's temple, which is *hugely* disrespectful. Another time, Athena and Poseidon competed to be the patron god for the city of Athens. Your dad created some stupid saltwater spring for his gift."

"So Poseidon didn't protect Percy from monsters. He didn't even claim Percy as his son. But then, with each encounter with Poseidon, we find out more about him. I found out that Poseidon rules a big kingdom, and he seems a little overwhelmed with the problems of this underwater kingdom. I found out that he worries about justice and whether Zeus will do what is right. Finally, I saw that Poseidon could be funny and affectionate. In fact, he shows Percy several times that he loves him. I even began to feel sorry for Poseidon, to wonder what it must be like to have children who will not live as long as you do. I realized that Poseidon wasn't bad; he was just complicated."

Active Involvement

Set your students up to try analyzing a character. Remind them of a character from the read-aloud text who is complicated.

"Readers, do you see how I thought about a character, and I thought about that character across the whole book? And I tried to think about all the incidents this character is involved in. I thought hard about the character's strengths and flaws, about behaviors and motivation, and I tried to be sympathetic. I also expected that the character would be nuanced, would be more than one way.

"Readers, stories you are reading are full of characters who are like this—good characters who have significant character flaws, bad characters whom you admire in some ways, and even untruthful characters who deceive us! *The Lightning Thief* is full of characters like this who are complicated. Perhaps the most complex and surprising character is Luke, whom we consider a hero at the beginning of the story and who shows himself to be a villain at the end.

"Let's give you a chance to try this work. Open up your notebooks to see what you've been jotting about characters as you've been reading. Recall any specific incidents where you saw that a character you thought of as good was in fact flawed or where a villain acted admirably. You may want to flip through your book to find a specific moment. You could also think about *The Lightning Thief* if you want to practice this work by delving into Luke's character, in which case, really push yourself to remember what you know about Luke and why he behaves the way he does. I'm going to give you a few quiet moments to think."

I did. They looked in their notebooks and books. Then, after a few minutes had passed, they began to turn and talk. After another few minutes, I gathered them back.

■ *Teachers, I promoted Luke as a possible character to analyze because he is so clearly neither all bad nor all good. You could have suggested that some students return to Snape, from* Harry Potter, *as many know him well, or they could consider the dragon from* The Paper Bag Princess. *Many students will be eager to go right to their books, and you could be ready to coach right into those characters.*

Convene the class to share what you overheard students saying to each other, tucking tips into this retelling.

"Friends, I heard some intense conversations. One of you was describing Luke, and I heard you say that you are actually sympathetic toward him, even though he tries to poison Percy. You said that Luke feels like he can never be good enough for the gods and that he has no option but to join with stronger evil forces. Some of you talked about how much even Percy admires Luke's courage and his gifts with his sword. And you said that Luke seems genuinely fond of Annabeth. It's really interesting, isn't it, friends, to realize how nuanced characters can be.

"A few others of you talked about Luke and about some of the villains in the stories you are reading, and I heard one of you say that some of these villains are actually pretty cool—they may be beautiful or handsome, they may be extremely intelligent, and they have pretty interesting characters and complicated motivations, even though they act in evil ways. Some of you talked about Voldemort, for instance, and how, as Tom Riddle, a lot of bad stuff happened in his family, which gives you a little sympathy for why he tries to create a family of Death Eaters in *Harry Potter.* A few of you strayed into the fantasy films you've seen, and I heard you talk about Nero, from the *Star Trek* film. He, too, is a pretty cool character. He's intense and creative and passionate. He has suffered. He's cool-looking. He wears a leather coat and has gorgeous markings. He's almost more cool than Captain Kirk. You're probably supposed to like him a little bit."

LINK

Send your students off to read, first reflecting that people in our lives, like characters in our stories, are often complicated.

"So, friends, remember that as you move to more complicated stories, some of the villains may be compelling characters and some of the heroes may have troublesome aspects. It's something we can think about in our writing, as well—how to make our villains more fascinating and our heroes somewhat flawed.

"There's one other thing I need to say. This work is helpful in our lives as well as in our reading. When we realize that characters are complicated, it makes us more empathetic to people in our lives. We try to really think hard about why people do the things they do. We realize that people can be flawed but can still be good. And they may seem mostly evil but still have some good qualities. This merits some thought. I imagine that you'll want to do some writing, as well as talking, about how people in your lives and characters in your stories are complicated. I know it's making me reconsider some of the friends I judged harshly or some moments when I, too, have made mistakes. You'll see me later with my writer's notebook open!

"Off you go."

■ *Teachers, whenever there is an opportunity to show that the work we do lets us be more insightful about people in our lives, take it! After all, the point of all this is to show that reading teaches us how to live. Books provide escape, they amuse, they delight. They also give us visions of possibility and insight into our own strengths, flaws, and aspirations. This lesson helps me reflect on my own character and on my relationships with others, and I hope it helps me move toward increased empathy and understanding. It can do the same for your readers. You could author a minilesson to help your students think about empathizing more with people in our own lives.*

Teachers, please turn to the *Resources* CD-ROM for Part Three of this unit, "Emerging from Fantasy and Bringing the Magic with Us."

A STUDY OF FAIRYTALES AND MYTHS CAN TEACH ARCHETYPES AND ALLEGORY

By Mary Ehrenworth and Julia Mooney

Introduction

There are compelling reasons for students to become familiar with fairytales, folktales, fables, and myths. Readers who know these genres also know a lot about how stories go, and about literary traditions. If a knowledgeable reader senses that the text he or she is reading is a myth, the reader expects that it will turn out to be a cautionary tale, or that it will explain how something came to be. If it's a fable, readers know that this is not just a cute story about animals, but that they are going to learn a significant lesson. If the text follows a fairytale structure, these same readers will not be surprised at dramatic acts of vengeance, reprisal, and jealousy. Readers who came of age with a dark queen who puts a beautiful child into a long sleep and plots her death, or an old woman who lures children into her gingerbread house and then bakes them alive in an oven, expect that the characters in fairytales (and in novels that are reminiscent of fairytales) may find themselves in high-risk situations.

Moreover, these knowledgeable readers often see more in contemporary novels than readers who are not familiar with literary antecedents first forged in classic fairytales, folktales, or myths. It is not infrequent that a contemporary tale is, in fact, a retelling of a classic tale. Exploring the antecedents of a story often gives a richer understanding of that story. In contemporary novels and nonfiction texts, there are often allusions to famous literary characters. Recognizing these famous characters, knowing their storylines, and understanding the lessons those storylines teach constitutes developing what many refer to as cultural literacy. Readers who have been immersed in a heritage of common stories have a shared cultural literacy.

When she was ten, Mary Ehrenworth found a copy of Andrew Lang's The Blue Fairy Book *on a dusty shelf in a New England store. It brought her into magical realms, where characters died for love, where magic existed, and where justice was sometimes dark and vengeful. Soon after, she discovered Edith Hamilton's* Mythology, *a book full of characters that turn into spiders, snakes that hiss from the heads of beautiful, terrible women, and courageous heroes trying to impress the gods. Julia Mooney, Writer in Residence at the Reading and Writing Project, remembers with great fondness her sixth-grade study of Greek mythology and the report she wrote about Hermes, messenger of the gods. Mary and Julia hope that your students will take as much pleasure in these fairytales, folktales, fables, and myths as they did.*

To see what it means to recognize antecedents and allusions, for a moment, let's take the Greek myth of Icarus and Daedalus. In this ancient tale, Daedalus makes a set of wings out of feathers and wax. When he and his son, Icarus, set out to try them, Daedalus tells Icarus not to fly too high, too close to the sun. But Icarus, being a headstrong youth, flies too close to the sun. The wax begins to melt. Daedalus calls to him, but he cannot stop his son from falling to his death. This story teaches lessons, as so many Greek myths do. It's a cautionary tale—not to be reckless, not to be, as the Greeks called it, *hubristic,* or too proud. It also teaches that young people are often reckless, that they consider themselves immortal, but that they are vulnerable. It's an unbearable storyline for a parent. When readers describe a "Daedalus moment," they describe a moment when a loved one is seen in imminent danger, and his or her fate cannot be prevented. When we describe a character as being an "Icarus character," we mean a character who is young, headstrong, and reckless. And possibly doomed.

Now let's imagine that we're reading *Icarus at the Edge of Time,* a gorgeous picture book, aloud to our class. It's by Brian Greene, a top physicist and expert on black holes. Even as we begin to read the title to the children, as we say that it is a story about a young boy, who lives on a spaceship, in the future, we say… his name is Icarus. If we want to develop our students' sense of cultural literacy, we might pause at that point. "Often," we might say, "the names used in a story mean something. They're not accidental. The name Icarus has a history. In fact, I've put out some short versions of the Icarus story. We're going to take five minutes right now, while you are sitting in this meeting area, to really quickly research the story behind that name and to think what that story might make us think about this book we are about to read." Then we could distribute a few versions of the myth for children to huddle around, and we could meanwhile skim through one version with a group as well. Children would not need to read every word of the myth to grasp the essential storyline—and the allusion. It's a good feeling to recognize an allusion. And it deepens the complexity of our reading comprehension.

We want this cultural literacy for our children. It's not that there is any one single story that matters more than another; it's that we want our children to have a rich, deep, historical understanding of story itself. We want them to know that a common thread of cautionary and explanatory stories crosses cultures, from African folktales to German fairytales to Greek myths. Some stories, like *Cinderella,* appear in many cultures. Something about the notion of remarriage, of stepchildren, of siblings who detest each other, of victimization of the young and the beloved, has written itself into multiple versions across cultures and continents. It's entrancing to follow a story around the world. This is a way to learn not only about stories but also about cultures. This interpretation work brings a community of readers together as well, which is one of the most important reasons to read. It teaches us to read at an allegorical level, understanding that the character depictions are not really about foxes, or princesses, or wolves, but about human characteristics, our strengths and our weaknesses, and universal truths.

Structuring the Unit

The challenge in this unit will be to ensure that children have enough time for wide, extensive reading. If a student's reading for the day is only a picture-book version of *Cinderella*, that is not enough reading. The flip side to this is that many of these texts will be written at levels of text complexity that will be challenging for some readers, again making it important for a teacher to think carefully about a way to structure the unit that allows for time to read these classic stories as well as time to read novels.

We suggest that the minilessons and read-aloud work focus on the fairytales, folktales, and myths, and that children have some time to work in these texts, reading either in partnerships or book clubs. It will be important that the children also continue to read chapter books, either independently or in book clubs. If you have the resources to do so, you might channel them into titles from the accompanying book list on the *Resources* CD-ROM. You will find books on this list that include a lot of clear allusions to classic tales, or that are retellings of classic tales. Some scholars are calling many of these "fractured fairytales," which are retellings with a twist. But the work of this unit doesn't depend on every child reading a chapter book that is a "retold tale," as they'll be able to practice what you are teaching during the read-aloud, and to speculate on possible connections between the classic tales and any novel they might be reading.

You'll choose a few texts to read aloud during the unit. We chose three picture books: *Icarus at the Edge of Time*, by Brian Greene; *The True Story of the 3 Little Pigs!*, by Brian Scieszka; and *Tikki Tikki Tembo*, by Arlene Mosel. These are retold tales. The first is a retelling of a Greek myth, the second of a fairytale, and the third of a folktale. Each picture book anchors one part of the unit. As we read these books aloud, the children will have opportunities to read short versions of these genres from the collections and picture books you make available. See the book list on the CD for some delightful short picture books. If it's hard to secure a variety of books, we recommend drawing on these anthologies: *D'Aulaires' Book of Greek Myths; Tales from the Brothers Grimm*, by Cooper Edens; and *Aesop's Fables*, by Lisbeth Zwerger.

A word about independent reading: remember that children need to be devouring chapter books that they can read with high comprehension and rate. If they do not spend class time reading those chapter books, the chances that they'll read them outside class are not good. We therefore caution against devoting the entire class time to work with short texts. It is also important that children have opportunities to link the fables, folktales, fairytales, and myths to longer contemporary texts, as the goal of the unit is to show readers the added layer of meaning they can derive from such connections. We want children to see how these traditions live in their current reading.

So, for the unit, you'll want to devote a portion of class time to reading novels, and a portion of time to reading from baskets of short texts you'll make available for students to read, being sure that your students can read the texts that you offer them. Of course both kinds of texts will travel between home and school.

Overview of the Unit: Teaching Points

PART ONE:
Pigs, Wolves, and Unhappy Children—Understanding Archetypes

We help readers develop a deeper familiarity with a few common fairytales, reading multiple versions of them. In particular, the focus will be on the notion of archetypes—character roles that appear in more than one story. We will explain that archetypes are nuanced, contextual across cultures, and even changeable. As part of this, we will explain that authors sometimes intentionally mix up archetypes to challenge or poke fun at traditional roles. Our recommended read-aloud text for this part is Jon Scieszka's The True Story of the 3 Little Pigs!

I. ▸ Today I want to teach you that readers often come across *archetypes* in stories—characters such as villains, victims, and heroes who appear in more than one story. Readers who read many fairytales, for instance, begin to recognize that the stepmother is often evil, and that the younger daughter or younger son is often the victim of jealousy and plotting; these are archetypes and you'll find others as well.

II. ▸ Readers, today I want to teach you that sometimes when we read, we begin to notice that even when a character appears again and again, those characters are not completely the same. Even archetypes are nuanced! Alert readers, therefore, ask ourselves, "How is this archetypal character a little different in this version than in the other version?"

III. ▸ Readers, today I want to teach you that as we become familiar with some common characters, we see them appear not only in other fairytales, but in books and movies, too. Attentive readers study how the characters and the storylines are similar and how these are different when they occur in different texts or movies.

IV. ▸ Today I want to give you an important tip. When readers read many fairytales and books that cross cultures, we notice that archetypal characters may be different in one tale in each story in part because the stories reflect different cultures. When we read, alert to what might be cultural differences, we ask ourselves, "Is this archetypal character acting or talking differently because she is from this particular culture?"

V. ▸ Readers, today I want to name what some of you are already discovering. When readers become experts on fairytales, we notice that some authors mix up the archetypes on purpose. The hen may turn out to be not so silly after all when she says the sky is falling. The experienced reader recognizes that the author is playing with one role or another, possibly poking fun at an archetype, because we are familiar with how that common character type usually acts.

PART TWO:
Recognizing Allusions, Antecedents, and Story Structures from Famous Myths

We'll explore the most famous characters and storylines of Greek myths and aim to develop an understanding of common story structures of this genre. Readers learn that myths are both lessons and cautionary tales, and that they often offer explanations of how things in the world came to be. You may want to read aloud a book that references a classic Greek myth (we recommend Icarus at the Edge of Time)*, first introducing children to versions of the myth itself. Readers will thus see that modern books often allude to Greek myths, which act, therefore, as powerful antecedents for later works.*

VI. ▸ Today I want to teach you that readers often come across allusions to mythological characters in the books we read. A book might say that someone "has hair like Medusa's" and you'll understand that reference if you know Medusa. We know that these references are there for a reason; they convey something meaningful. In time you will read lots of myths, coming to know famous characters, but meanwhile readers can also do some research when we come to something that we suspect references a myth or another classical tale.

VII. ▸ Readers, today I want to point out that as readers read myths, we will start noticing kinds of stories that keep occurring. When you read myths, you'll see that many of them are cautionary tales in which a character is punished for a trait or an action that displeases the gods. The moral of those stories is "Be careful" and "Don't do this!"

VIII. ▸ Yesterday, readers, we learned that many myths are cautionary tales. Today I want to teach you that another kind of story is a story that explains how something in the world came to be. We read myths, thinking, "Could this story be explaining how a creature or a natural occurrence, like the seasons, came to be?"

IX. ▸ Readers, listen up. I have something important to teach you today. Because readers come to expect that myths have predictable story structures and purposes—we know, for example, that myths generally teach a lesson or explain how something came to be—this gives us a powerful way to compare myths. We can say, "These two myths are the same in some important ways," and then, of course, we'll also say, "These two myths are different in important ways." We can also compare myths to novels that are based on those myths.

X. ▸ Readers who are familiar with how myths tend to go know that myths reward characters with good traits and punish those with bad ones. The Greeks teach lessons! We can carry this way of thinking to other genres, considering what kinds of characters in chapter books, for example, tend to get rewarded—and therefore what lessons the book implicitly teaches.

PART THREE:
Allegory Means They're Not Just Animal Stories!

In this part, we'll introduce readers to Aesop's fables, and through these, learn that even small characters play an important role in stories that teach clear lessons. The focus will be on the morals these fables teach, and on the related cultural idioms, such as "crying wolf," that people often cite. Readers may also read folktales and discover that the expectations they've come to have about Greek myths also hold true for folktales—that most are cautionary or explanatory tales. We recommend Tikki Tikki Tembo *as a classic favorite. Finally, children learn to draw on an "invisible backpack" of reference texts, to keep using what they know as they read chapter books.*

XI. ▸ Readers, another tip. Readers who expect stories to teach lessons keep in mind that unlikely characters, such as animals, teach lessons. In fables, each animal plays an important role in the overall message. So when readers see an animal playing the role of a character in a story, readers ask ourselves, "What lesson might this animal be teaching us?"

XII. ▸ Today I want to point out to you that as readers become familiar with how fables go, we begin to realize that fables have given us lots of familiar idioms, or expressions. The phrase "sour grapes," for example, comes from a fable—and readers who know fables will find other expressions in books and in life that come from fables and will think, "Wait a minute! I know where that expression comes from!" For example, "country mouse" and "crying wolf," are references to Aesop's fables. When we read fables, we learn not just lessons but also "cultural idioms."

XIII. ▸ Readers, today I want to point out that you already know that it helps to think, "What kind of story might this be?" You already know that stories that act as cautionary tales (saying, "Watch out!") and that punishing bad traits might be based on myths because myths do that. The lessons in fables are sometimes more hidden than the ones in Greek myths, so readers dig deep to find them. But we still see lessons.

XIV. ▶ Readers, today I want to teach you that when you read lots of fables (like lots of myths) then you start to see ways you could categorize these stories. Fables, like myths, can be separated into kinds of stories, and one big pile will be "stories that explain how things came to be." We can compare and contrast different "how things came to be" stories and when we are doing that, one thing to think about is that these stories will sometimes be different because of the culture that is telling or retelling the story.

XV. ▶ Readers, I should not have to teach you that always, we bring all of our knowledge to the books we are reading. Whenever you are reading anything, you can say to yourself, "Whoa! This is reminding me of something," and establish a link to a classical text—a fable, a fairytale, a myth.

SAMPLE MINILESSON

Part Two, Lesson VI

GETTING READY

- Prepare some copies of a very short version of the Icarus myth for children to read (available on the *Resources* CD-ROM). You may choose to have certain readers read it aloud in small groups. Choose those readers ahead of time.

- Bring *Icarus at the Edge of Time*, which you will begin during the lesson and continue during read-aloud.

CONNECTION

Build a sense of excitement for the read-aloud text, and incite curiosity about a mythological reference.

I gathered the children close and held up the book for them to see. "Readers, I have the most gorgeous picture book to read to you today. It's about a boy who lives on a spaceship sometime in the future. The author is a famous scientist named Brian Greene. He's an expert on black holes and the many dimensions of time! So I think we may learn a lot about black holes in this story, which will be very cool. And maybe we'll learn something about time, and space, and what people call 'the fourth dimension.'"

I scanned their faces, building up a sense of intrigue. "I know sometimes in movies or books, characters run into trouble if they go back or forward in time. In *Star Trek*, for instance, Captain Kirk worries about how he and Spock will affect the future, and even the present, if they change what happens in the past! Isn't it wild to think about how if you went back in time, you might change the present? Or to wonder whether, if you traveled into the future, you might ever meet yourself there? I can see from your expressions that you're as fascinated and mystified as I am! Let's see what we find out in this story—if we find anything out about space and time, and how they're related, and maybe other lessons."

"Readers, the book is called, *Icarus at the Edge of Time*…"

I paused. "Hmm, *Icarus*…wait a second…" I paused again, as if thinking hard.

Name your teaching point. Specifically, explain that many stories refer to literary figures, such as characters from the Greek myths. Teach your students that powerful readers investigate these references in order to have richer understandings and deeper expectations as they read.

"Today I want to teach you that readers often come across allusions to mythological characters in the books we read. A book might say that someone was 'as greedy as Midas' and you'll understand that reference if you know Midas was the king who turned everything he touched to gold. We know that these references are there for a reason; they convey something meaningful. In time you will read lots of myths, coming to know famous characters, but meanwhile you can also do some research when you come to something that looks like it could be referencing a myth or another classical tale."

TEACHING

Using the read-aloud text, demonstrate how curious readers begin to investigate the antecedents of a reference.

"Readers, watch me start this work, then you'll have a chance to give it a try as well. So…first I notice the name itself—Icarus. That's definitely an unusual name, which is a clue. Then I think to myself—where have I heard this name before? If I'm not sure, I could look it up, or ask a reading buddy. I see a couple of you nodding—because you've read the Percy Jackson series, as I have, and Icarus is in that, or because you know Greek myths… Let's just talk to each other for a minute, ok, to show our classmates how we'd get started."

I had prepped one of these students to help me out. "Andrew, I seem to remember that Icarus is someone from the Greek myths, right? He has some story about him, about flying close to the sun or something?" Andrew nodded.

"Readers, do you see how I'm investigating this character, before I even get into the story I'm going to read? I expect that if the character is named Icarus, there's probably a reason. And I also know that the story is about a boy who flies in a spaceship, and now I'm remembering that Icarus flies. So it makes a lot of sense to find out more about the original Icarus—especially, reader, what kind of character he is. One thing I know is that the characters in Greek myths usually have strong character traits. So I might find that Icarus has those same traits in my story."

ACTIVE INVOLVEMENT

Invite your students to read a short version of the relevant Greek myth in order to develop ideas about the character referenced in your read-aloud text.

"In fact, this part we can do together. We can each find out something about Icarus, and then compare what we know before we start the story. Readers, when we want to find out about Greek myths, there are lots of versions. I've made some copies of a concise version. Let's take about ten minutes and find out more about Icarus. Why don't you and your partner join up with another partnership, or your club if you're in a book club. I'm going to give certain readers a copy of the story to read aloud. See what you find out about Icarus, and then be ready to come back with some ideas about what kind of character Icarus is."

They did so. I joined one club, and read the text aloud to that club. Then I reconvened the students to share their insights about Icarus's character traits. Children named that Icarus was daring, and reckless, and wild, and that he didn't listen to his father.

"Ok, readers, so we have a picture now of Icarus, before we even begin this book. Some stories are like this—they're modern stories but they make clear references, or allusions, to characters we're supposed to know. Sometimes we do already know the character, and we can call to mind everything we know and bring that knowledge to our book. Other times, we need to do some quick research. So far, we've said that the Greek Icarus was daring, reckless, and wild, and that he met an unhappy death when he flew too close to the sun. I think I'm not alone in already feeling somewhat anxious for our Icarus, right?"

Many nods.

LINK

Encourage your readers to continue their investigations of myths as literary antecedents, both for the pleasure of reading myths and for the knowledge they'll bring to modern literature.

"Readers, because we know something about Icarus now, we have expectations about how this story might go, and therefore we already have a sense of tension. As we read, one way we can think about our modern character is to compare his character traits and his situation to what we know about his antecedent (that means the character he's based on). We'll start reading our story now, and we'll see how it is similar to and different from the versions we just read."

"I imagine, readers, that one thing that might be helpful for us is to become more familiar with myths and other famous stories, so we're alert to references and retellings. Let's think about some ways to investigate these stories, and we'll start filling our classroom and parts of our reading lives with this inquiry. I'll make available, for instance, other versions of the Icarus myth, and many others."

Part Three, Lesson XI

GETTING READY

- Bring Lisbeth Zwerger's *Aesop's Fables* to class, and plan to read aloud from it "The Hare and the Tortoise."

- Prepare copies of "The Hare and the Tortoise" and from one or two other fables for children to read during the active involvement.

CONNECTION

Introduce children to Aesop's Fables. Explain that fables are short cautionary tales, similar to Greek myths, and that these tales often use animals to convey lessons or morals.

"Readers, you know how in some of the books you read, like *Poppy,* and *Fantastic Mr. Fox,* and *Charlotte's Web*, the animals are the main characters and they act and talk just like people? And then there are books like *Stone Fox* and *Because of Winn-Dixie*, where animals are like the ones we know in our world; they bark and meow and make other animal noises but they don't talk, right?"

"Some of you may already be familiar with stories like the ones we're going to begin reading today." I held up Lisbeth Zwerger's *Aesop's Fables* and said, "This is a book of fables. Fables are short stories that teach a lesson—or a moral. These particular fables were written by a man named Aesop who lived thousands of years ago in ancient Greece. I bet some of you have heard one or two or more of these fables before—maybe your mom or dad or a grandparent has read them or told them to you. The stories have lasted all these years, being passed down from generation to generation, because they are *teaching* stories. And here's the best part—these stories often use talking animals to teach! Some of the animals in fables make mistakes, like people do, and there are lessons in those mistakes. And other animals exhibit particularly good character traits, and because of this, they become models for how the rest of us should behave."

"Looking around I can see that this sounds familiar to you. It should! Fables are a lot like the Greek myths we read not too long ago. They are cautionary tales."

Name your teaching point. Specifically, tell children that readers who read expecting to learn a lesson know that even animals can deliver such a message. Readers choose to read fables to become even more aware of the lessons in stories, and we ask ourselves, "What lesson is this character teaching me?"

"Today I want to teach you that readers who expect stories to teach lessons keep in mind that unlikely characters, such as animals, teach lessons. In fables, each animal plays an important role in the overall message. So when readers see an animal playing the role of a character in a story, we ask ourselves, 'What lesson might this animal be teaching us?'"

TEACHING

Read aloud a fable with an easy-to-understand moral (we use "The Hare and the Tortoise") and then demonstrate how you extract the lesson that the animals in the fable teach.

"Readers, listen while I read one of the fables in this book. It's called 'The Hare and the Tortoise.' It's one of my favorites. As I read, see if you can guess what lesson Aesop is hoping to teach us through the animals in this tale."

> A Hare was one day making fun of a tortoise for being so slow upon his feet. "Wait a bit," said the Tortoise; "I'll run a race with you, and I'll wager that I win."
>
> "Oh, well," replied the Hare, who was much amazed at the idea, "let's try and see"; and it was soon agreed that the fox should set a course for them and be the judge. When the time came both started off together, but the Hare was soon so far ahead that he thought he might as well have a rest: so down he lay and fell fast asleep.
>
> Meanwhile the Tortoise kept plodding on, and in time reached the goal. At last the Hare woke up with a start, and dashed on at his fastest, but only to find that the Tortoise had already won the race.

- *We suggest you* first *demonstrate for children how you mull over the fable's possible moral(s) and* afterwards *read the moral that appears at the fable's end.*

Putting down the book, I looked up at the children and said, "Can you believe a slow-as-molasses tortoise beat a rabbit?! If you've ever seen a rabbit hop across the grass, you know that rabbits can move quickly! So what's going on here? What moral is Aesop trying pass on? What lesson might these two animals be teaching us?" I tapped my forehead as if deep in thought, then said, "I think the tortoise is teaching us that it can pay off to pursue something with some regularity, even if it takes a long time. Eventually, if we keep at it, we'll reach our goal just like the tortoise, slow-moving though he was, reached that finish line. At first, it must have seemed so far away to him! But he kept going…and going…and going…and ultimately, he got there. He even won the race!"

"Readers, in many of his fables, Aesop included the moral at the end. This is the moral of 'The Hare and the Tortoise':"

> Slow and steady wins the race.

I repeated the line slowly, for emphasis. "That goes with what I just said. The tortoise was steady—that means he was consistent. He kept plodding along. He was also stead-fast. That means persistent. He didn't give up. He was slow, but steady.

"The thing is, you know that books are often about more than one thing. So, let's think, what about the hare? What does he teach us? Hmmm. He's awfully sure of himself, isn't he? We could say he's haughty and maybe a bit too puffed up." (I puffed out my chest.) "Unlike the tortoise, he moves quickly…at first. And then, thinking he has all the time in the world, what does he do? He stops to snooze!" (I closed my eyes and put my hands behind my head, a smug grin on my face.) "That's awfully arrogant of him, don't you agree? I wonder if Aesop is cautioning us against being too prideful and too hasty, too. Although he doesn't spell this out, it seems as if he's saying that when we're too sure of ourselves in life, and when we aren't consistent, we don't come out ahead, but behind. That hare, though he might easily have won the race, came in second!"

ACTIVE INVOLVEMENT

Set children up to mine another fable or two for lessons that Aesop and his animals teach. If children struggle, call out little questions or coaching tips to help guide them.

"Readers, it's your turn. I'm going to pass out copies of this fable to each partnership. When you receive your copy, take a couple minutes to read it carefully with your partner, looking to see if you can find the lessons that Aesop and his talking animals teach us."

■ *You may want to hand out different fables to different partnerships. Your stronger readers will be able to discern the morals in Aesop's somewhat more abstract fables, such as "Town Mouse and Country Mouse" or "The Fox and the Grapes," whereas other readers will do better with fables that convey more concrete morals, such as "The Shepherd's Boy and the Wolf" or "The Fox and the Crow." Another option is for some students to read a fable aloud to a small group.*

As I handed out the copies, I added, "Fables are typically really short stories that convey really big lessons. That means that no words are wasted. Aesop was a real craftsman and he knew exactly what he needed to write to pack a punch. So read this carefully. Remember that Aesop uses animals to teach us about both good and bad behavior."

LINK

Remind children that talking animals in fables aren't the only characters who teach lessons. Encourage children to mine any text they read, modern or ancient, for lessons the author is hoping to convey.

"Readers, today we talked about how in fables, and in particular Aesop's fables, talking animals teach lessons. We're going to be reading lots more of these fun, famous fables over the next few days, and it won't be long before you'll be experts in how this sort of text tends to go. There's a rhythm and pattern to them, you'll see. But I want to remind you that other kinds of stories—and nonfiction books, too—teach lessons. Remember how we decided that the author of *Stone Fox* wanted to teach us an important lesson about generosity and selflessness? How Stone Fox did a really kind, altruistic deed by allowing little Willy to win the race when Searchlight died? Little Willy taught us something, too, didn't he, about how perseverance and hard work pays off. He's a lot like our tortoise. Come to think of it, *Fantastic Mr. Fox* also taught us about perseverance. He didn't give up even when those awful farmers with their big tractors plowed away at his home and his family—and by the end of the book, he won 'the race!'" I made quotation marks with my fingers. "Many, many modern books have roots in ancient tales—myths and fables and fairytales, among others—so be on the lookout for patterns across books.

"So, as you read, not just fables, not just today, but anything, any day, remember that authors are often out to teach lessons. They do this through major and minor characters and yes, even through talking animals!"

OTHER RESOURCES YOU WILL FIND ON THE *RESOURCES* CD-ROM

Letter to Teachers
Possible Books for This Unit

CONTENT-AREA STUDY
An Inquiry and Research Unit

By FJ DeRobertis

This unit invites children to research immigration at the end of the twentieth century, but I've designed the unit to be transferable to any whole-class social studies investigation. The emphasis is not only the specific topic but also on the reading and research processes that are part of learning social studies. I first taught this unit in May when my readers were reading at levels M through V.

The unit relies on students drawing from what I refer to as their "bag of reading tricks." I moved anchor charts from previous units of study front and center to remind readers of strategies and habits they learned earlier in the year. The unit especially draws upon prior work in a unit on character study, so the charts (and skills) from that unit are especially important here. Although the children are not in book clubs, they do engage in a lot of collaborative work, and they draw upon prior experiences in book clubs to do this.

Students learn from fiction as well as nonfiction and from videos, photographs, documents, and Web-based sources as well as from nonfiction books. The unit supports the skills of envisionment and empathy, questioning and critical reading, and interpretation. The unit begins with the proposition that one way to learn about an era in history is to learn about the people who lived in that era. Readers are channeled to study the people of a particular historical period, trying to understand the different perspectives of different people living in that historical setting. To do this, they use what they already know about reading in ways that allow them to put themselves in the shoes of other people—in this instance, of people living during the time period under study. Readers actually imagine that they are the characters, with the same desires and motivations, encountering the struggles of the people in the time period they're studying. The students learn to think about the people's choices to understand them in more complex ways. As they develop a stronger understanding of the historical time period, they think about who has power and who does not. This work on critical reading also affects the way readers think about the different perspectives that different people maintained.

After early teaching experience in urban New Jersey schools, FJ established his career at a suburban public school in Summit, New Jersey, where he currently teaches third grade.

As students study the motivations (or desires) and the obstacles (or struggles) of people from the past, they are encouraged not only to take in information about the people in that time and place but also to grow ideas about what they are learning. I encourage them to think, among other things, about ways in which the era has affected the lives of people living then and there. I teach children to revise and develop their ideas through continued reading, to synthesize what they are learning from varied sources, and to organize their learning journey. They'll be more adept at this if they notice the perspectives that authors put forth and think about how each author's point of view affects the way in which the author designs his or her text.

Of course, there is no such thing as one amalgamated "people of a time period." Always, different people (and groups of people) within a time period have different perspectives and experience different sides of the world. The third part in the unit especially shines a spotlight on this, although readers are aware of this throughout their reading, of course. Students also consider the choices an author has made in presenting the views of different characters.

Readers eventually get behind their own inquiry topics and narrow their research as they follow a pathway of thinking. Readers form their own opinions and ideas based on their research. To do this, it is important that the students read across different texts in the content area and use the accountable talk strategies they have been using in reading workshop all year while also learning new ones. As part of this, they write responses to their reading to prepare for their partner talk. These responses can be quick stop-and-jots on Post-its or longer entries in their notebooks. This helps them to shape their thinking so their talks are more substantive. The unit culminates with readers teaching others what they have learned.

Before starting this unit, I read aloud several books and articles about immigration during social studies lessons. The students also spent time in the computer lab researching on preselected websites that have information about immigration at the turn of the twentieth century. I hung posters and photographs in the room to give students some visual background for this era. In social studies, the students researched one of their own ethnic backgrounds and a country of origin. We also had classroom displays of artifacts from the time period, including bundles of things people might have carried with them as they journeyed to America. Students previewed vocabulary words they were likely to encounter across the various immigration texts in this unit.

Overview of the Unit: Teaching Points

Part One

Readers who want to learn about a time period use a whole variety of skills, but especially envisionment, so as to participate in a journey toward better understanding of a time period.

I. ▸ Today I want to teach you that readers learn about the historical time period by paying attention to the specific details of the landscape, clothing, and daily lives. We can pause after particularly descriptive passages and say to ourselves or to a partner, "I can see..." or "I am picturing...." We use these details to build our own mind pictures as we read. The details help us to develop a deeper understanding of what life was like for the people. *(See next section for the complete minilesson.)*

II. ▸ Today I want to teach you that readers re-create the world of the historical period we are studying by noticing the similarities and differences between our world and the world of that period. Sometimes these observations come in the form of surprises because people from the past can seem both very familiar and very strange to us. When information about life in the past surprises us, we can jot our thinking on Post-its or write quick entries so we can compare notes with others later.

III. ▸ Today I want to teach you that certain parts of texts especially help readers to envision another time period. Readers sometimes read those parts more slowly, taking note of the phrases that authors have provided that help readers create especially strong mental pictures. When readers notice that particular passages in texts bring a time period to life, it can help to think, "What did the author do to help me picture this time period?" because readers become writers and teachers, helping others picture a time period. We can get better at doing this if we study and learn from what other writers have done.

IV. ▸ Today I want to teach you that readers invent tools and techniques to hold on to what we are learning as we read so that we can, in turn, teach others. Sometimes it is helpful to draw a detailed picture of what we have read about the time period, including the landscape, the clothing, the transportation, and the way of life. Other times it helps us to simply jot quick notes and keep reading. The important thing is that whatever is recorded on the paper must spark the reader's mind so that the reader can look at the paper and think a ton of thoughts.

PART TWO

In fiction, readers get to know the characters by learning about what the characters want, the difficulties they encounter, and what they do to meet those difficulties. Readers can get to know people in history by thinking about what people in that time and that place wanted and what motivated them, and by thinking about the obstacles they encountered. We consider the desires and motivations and the struggles and obstacles of the people to get a clearer understanding of the historical time period.

V. ▸ Today I want to teach you that readers develop questions about the kinds of struggles that the people of a particular period faced, because we expect that by thinking about these difficulties, we will gain a better understanding of the people. We also ask, "What do these struggles reveal about the people during this time period?" Figuring out what makes people tick is never simple, so it helps to jot notes and to talk over ideas with others.

VI. ▸ Today I want to teach you that readers put ourselves in the shoes of the people in the time period. We do this so that we can empathize and imagine more realistically what it would be like to live in that time and place. Readers almost pretend to be the character while we read, experiencing what the character is experiencing in the time period.

VII. ▸ Today I want to teach you that readers develop a deeper empathy for the people who lived in another time and place by asking ourselves how we would deal with the kinds of obstacles or struggles they faced. We can also think, "What is it about this group of people that allows them to respond to obstacles so differently than we expect we'd do if we were in their shoes?"

VIII. ▸ Today I want to teach you that readers begin to develop ideas about the ways people of the historical period dealt with obstacles. We do this by putting Post-its on the text and doing quick jots on the Post-its about the big ideas, examples, and questions that strike us about how the people faced challenges. Sometimes we stop and jot as we read, thinking, "This part is mostly about…, and I am thinking…." Or we read through the chapter once and then reread it to jog our thinking. Either way, we plan to bring our quick bits of writing to share with partners.

IX. ▸ Today I want to teach you that readers study a different period in history by asking, "What were the desires and motivations of groups of people who lived back then?" Of course, we know that different categories of people tended to have different desires and motivations, so it helps to ask critical questions like "Which groups of people were more likely or less likely to get what they needed?"

X. ▸ Today I want to teach you that readers collect all of our thinking on what we have learned about the people who lived in another historical era, and we push ourselves to synthesize our learning by writing longer entries where we try to describe new understandings we now have about our learning. We might ask ourselves, "What have I learned about this time that makes me hopeful, concerned, sad, or angry?"

Part Three

Readers develop an understanding that similar events in a historical period are experienced differently by different groups of people and that the stories of those events will be told differently through different perspectives.

XI. ▸ Today I want to teach you that readers note the perspective from which a story is being told, or the perspective from which information is being given, by asking, "Who is telling the story? Whose voice is heard here? Whose voice is missing?"

XII. ▸ Today I want to teach you that readers begin to see how different people or different groups can perceive the same events in unique ways by paying close attention to their different descriptions of the same event. It often helps to make a mental movie of the different perspectives we read about, to really imagine how the experiences differed. Instead of trying to figure out which version is the "truth," we ask ourselves what those interpretations of the events reveal about the desires and struggles of each group. [See Resources CD-ROM for the complete minilesson.]

XIII. ▸ Today I want to teach you that readers develop big ideas about groups of people in a particular historical period by paying attention to how an event means different things to different people. We then ask ourselves, "How does this knowledge change my understanding of that time, those people?" and jot down our ideas.

XIV. ▸ Today I want to teach you that readers notice how one group of people views another group, because this can help us get a deeper understanding of the historical time period and the typical kinds of conflicts. When thinking about this, it is helpful to notice the stereotypes that people harbored about others within their community, and to notice what different people seem to think of as normal and not normal.

XV. ▸ Today I want to teach you that readers need to be aware that an author's perspective of an event or an era affects our understanding of that event or that era. It is helpful to ask, "Do I agree with the way this author has told this story? Are there places where I wonder if something is being left out?" Sometimes readers need to search to find texts that bring out the voices of people who might otherwise not be heard.

Part Four

Readers who want to understand an era in history often find it helpful to zoom in on a smaller topic, focusing our research like we focus on a piece of writing. Then, when looking at a smaller subject, we're more able to think about cause and effect by thinking about how the details of the time period affected that particular group of people.

XVI.
▶ Today I want to teach you that readers, like writers, know that if we want to become experts, it can help to focus our work a bit. One way to focus our research about a time period is to get to know a particular group of people and then to think more carefully about what accounts for their experiences. To think closely about one particular group of people, it can help to think about ways this one group's experiences were different from another group's experiences.

XVII.
▶ Today I want to teach you that once readers decide to research a subtopic, it is often helpful for the readers to get the lay of the land of that subtopic. Readers can do this by reading really easy books on the topic, if there are any, and by skimming and scanning across texts to try to construct a big-picture understanding of the topic.

XVIII.
▶ Today I want to teach you that readers understand the perspective of a particular group from the historical period by asking ourselves which details are left out from their accounts of their experiences and trying to figure out what accounts for the gaps in their stories.

XIX.
▶ Today I want to teach you that readers read not only to learn about what another group of people in another time was like but also to learn what that group may have to teach us. Readers can notice ways in which a particular group of people wrestled with problems that are not just specific to a different time and place but are also experienced today and can ask, "What can I learn from understanding those people's experiences?"

XX.
▶ Today I want to teach you that readers can rewrite our own lives in response to what we have read about the time period by noticing the collective action taken in the texts. We take note of the social action taken in our books and use it to work toward making our world today more just than the one we have learned about.

Part Five

Readers sometimes go from being readers to writers. We sometimes feel that we have learned things we want to share with others. This then ignites us to synthesize what we have learned to share with others. It is almost like readers become writers, although we may not actually write to share so much as outline, plan, organize, and prepare for teaching.

XXI. ▸ Today I want to teach you that readers skim and scan our notes to think, "What do I have to say about this topic that I can teach to others? What do I know about and care deeply about that I can inspire others to learn about? What are the main ideas I could put forward that could really spark discussion and new learning?"

XXII. ▸ Today I want to teach you that readers organize what we have to share by thinking about headings and subheadings and sorting our notes into piles that go with those headings and subheadings.

XXIII. ▸ Today I want to teach you that readers think about how we can use what we know about teaching to teach others. We think, "Are there pictures I can show? Are there things I can act out? Are there points I can list across my fingers?" We use what we know about teaching others to help plan our teaching.

XXIV. ▸ Today I want to teach you that readers think, "What do I have to say, and how can I best say it?" We plan a format that matches the content and helps us share our learning in ways that are clear to our audience.

Part One, Session I: Readers Visualize to Learn About a Historical Time Period

GETTING READY

- Student's immigration artifacts
- Immigration photographs and posters
- "Bag of Reading Tricks" chart
- *The Butterfly Seeds* by Mary Watson

CONNECTION

Remind students of the fascinating things we have seen in class so far about immigration at the turn of the twentieth century and how all of these things have built our background knowledge to help with our mental movies about the time period.

"Readers, it has been so much fun watching all of you get so excited about studying immigration. In the computer lab, some of you have watched video clips on YouTube, and some of you have read accounts by real immigrants on various websites. The bundles you brought in to display and share, along with the photographs and posters we have hung around the classroom, have made this time period begin to come alive in our classroom.

"In this past week, during our social studies lessons, I've overheard so many great questions related to the pictures and photographs that are hanging around our room. I've heard you ask things like, 'Why do some of the immigrants look so unhappy on the ship?' 'Shouldn't they be happy they are coming to America?' 'How come most of the immigrants look poor?' 'I saw photographs of children immigrants without their parents. Where are they?' 'Why did so many people come to America at the turn of the twentieth century?'

"Readers, today you are all going to have the opportunity to find out the answers to these and more questions because we will start reading books and texts about this amazing time period in our history!"

Name your teaching point. Specifically, teach children that we begin to learn about a time period by picturing the world and the people. We carry these pictures with us in our minds as we read other books.

"Readers, today I want to teach you that when readers begin researching and reading about a time period in history, we pay careful attention to the specific details of the landscape, clothing, and daily lives of the people. We pause after particularly descriptive passages and say to ourselves or to a partner, 'I can see. . .' or 'I am picturing. . . .' We use these details to build our own movies of the time period in our minds. Creating these pictures in our minds and carrying them forward with us as we read help us get a deeper understanding of what life was like back then."

TEACHING

Refer to pictures and photographs as well as the writing to get clues to help you visualize the landscape, clothing, and daily lives of the people.

"Okay, researchers, I am going to revisit a part of the story titled *The Butterfly Seeds* that we read together during our exploration period. Watch me as I use the pictures and words in the book to create a strong mental picture of the time period, pictures that lead me to understand life at this time better. What I want you to notice is how I read a little bit, look at the pictures, and then pause to create a mental image in my mind. Also, watch for how I *add on* to what I already know about the time period. As I create my mental pictures, you will also notice how that leads me to think of new questions and grow new ideas about the time period as well." I started reading.

> Jake looked out the dark narrow alley, cluttered with lines of drying clothes.

"Hmm, I know this story takes place in New York City, so it makes sense that I can see buildings that are close enough together to hang clotheslines between them. Look at the boy in the picture. He is wearing a newsboy cap, a long-sleeve button-down shirt, and suspenders. As a matter of fact, the kids playing ball in the alley are wearing the same thing, and the girls are wearing what looks like fancy dresses. I know kids today don't dress like that to play ball. Hmm, I'm wondering about the differences between the way people and kids dressed back then and now. I am going to continue to read part of the next page.

> The next morning Jake was up early. Below, he spotted a fruit vendor, in the marketplace, emptying a crate of apples into his cart.

Describe the mental images unfolding in your mind as you read about this particular place and time, using comparisons between then and now to grow ideas about the time period.

"Wow, I am picturing this busy street market with all kinds of vendors trying to get people to buy their goods. I'm noticing the old-fashioned carts, and I see one old-fashioned car parked on the street. Only one! Imagine! Today the streets are packed with cars!

"So let me go over all the things that I noticed so far. Immigrants lived very close to each other in apartment buildings. Kids dressed for all occasions in what we would probably consider dress-up clothes. People probably didn't have washers and dryers back then, so people had to hang their clothes on the lines between buildings to dry. Immigrants worked and shopped in a street market, not grocery stores and department stores like Target. Now that I have this picture in my mind, I'm also thinking that people must have worked really hard back then because they had to do so much on their own, without modern technology. They also had to move these carts full of goods to and from the marketplace each day. Because I see the one old car on the street, I also think that back then the streets were more crowded with *people* walking around, not with all the cars, buses, and taxis like we see today.

"Before you give this a try, quickly turn and tell your partner what you noticed me doing as I read this text."

Share the transferable skills that students noticed and could do in their own reading.

"Some of you noticed that I used what was in the *words* to make my mental movie, because some of the things I described were not in the illustrations. Some of you also noticed that I paid particular attention to the differences between our world today and the world of this story, which helped me grow some ideas about that time period. Now that we've done this, we can lock these mental images up in our minds and use them as we continue to read books about this time period. We will especially use these images when we read books with few or no illustrations."

ACTIVE INVOLVEMENT

Have children practice this work on another part of this book, discussing with their partners what they added to their mental images about the landscape, clothing, and daily lives of the people and how it helped them grow ideas about life during this time.

"Readers, now it's your turn to practice this. I am going to turn to another page in this book with you. It is the part where Jake's papa's boss helped Jake make hangers for his window box. As I am reading, I want you to listen carefully for the descriptions the author is providing. I would also like you to study the illustrations very carefully. You should be thinking, 'Now that I have some images in my mind about this time period, what am I *adding* to my mental images about the landscape, clothing, and daily lives of the people?' and 'What am I understanding better about what life was like because of this?'" I read:

> Jake hurried across the street to the blacksmith shop to show Papa. "I need a way to keep this crate from falling off our windowsill," Jake shouted over the ring of the anvil. "Maybe I can help you," someone hollered. It was Mr. O'Malley, the shop owner. He knew just what Jake needed. He hammered two bars of red-hot metal into a . . . .

"Okay, turn and talk to your partner about what you are envisioning and what new ideas you are growing about this time period."

As the students talk, voice over a reminder about adding on to their pictures and using these pictures to grow ideas about the time period.

"Readers, as you continue your partner talk, remember to discuss what you saw in the pictures and heard in the story. Make sure to add images to your mental pictures of the landscape, clothing, and daily lives of the people. See if this can help you grow some new ideas about the time period and the people who lived back then."

Name what you saw the students doing and what you heard them saying that you would like them to try doing as they read all of their books.

"You are doing such smart work using the words and pictures to make mental images in your minds that you will use to understand further reading and grow some ideas right away about this time period. I noticed that Julia paid particular attention to the clothing of the different characters and was surprised the father wore his pants tucked into his boots as he worked. Now that she has that image in her mind, she can draw upon it as she does more reading about this time period. I heard others of you notice the lack of machines in the pictures, which gave you the idea that people must have worked very hard to earn their money. Readers, you are off to a great start in trying to immerse yourselves in this world we are studying. I think it is time to begin reading on our own!"

Link

Send children off to read, reminding them to visualize the landscape, clothing, and daily lives of the people to help them understand what life was like at this time. Remind children to draw on other strategies from their bag of tricks.

> "Readers, today we learned that it is helpful to take time to grow our mental pictures by paying particular attention to the landscape, the clothing, and the daily lives of the people of the time period we are studying. Doing that also helps us get a better understanding of what life was like. So today be sure to look for pictures and clues the author provides that help us create as well as add to our mental pictures. And remember, when we build a strong mental picture in our minds of a particular time period, we also begin to grow some ideas about the time period and the people who lived in it as well. As we read today, don't forget to also keep in mind what you are using from your bag of reading tricks to help you."

OTHER RESOURCES YOU WILL FIND ON THE *RESOURCES* CD-ROM

Goals for the Unit

Anchor Charts
- Immigration Vocabulary
- Questions Readers Ask to Interpret Texts
- Bag of Reading Tricks
- Strategies for Understanding Text
- Ways to Grow Ideas, Theories, and Themes By. . .
- Accountable Talk
- Ways to Share My Research with a Partner
- Ways We Take Notes on Our Research

Read-Aloud Books

Immigration Text Sets

Part Three, Session XII

Works Cited

ASK CRITICAL QUESTIONS

By Tiffany Worden, Marianna Sanders, and Nora Jaramillo

Lloyd Alexander, a prolific writer for young adults, writes, "We learn more by looking for the answer to a question and not finding it than we do from learning the answer itself." Our unit titled "Ask Critical Questions" is a three-part unit that aims to raise the level of students' comprehension by using questions as a vehicle for close and critical reading. Embedded in the skill of questioning are many other skills, including inference, synthesis, prediction, and interpretation. The unit moves students from asking literal questions whose answers can be found in the text to critical ones whose answers require thought and discussion.

This unit was written for a class of students who read independently at levels O through W in March of fifth grade. These students had already completed two or three book club units and were well versed in the structures and routines surrounding book clubs. They were already able to use connecting phrases such as "I agree...," "So what you're saying is...," "I understand what you mean, but I disagree...," and "Here is a place in the text that...." They listened to each other and added on to what others have said, often by restating and offering additional examples rather than extending the idea.

In the first part of the unit, students learn how to ask questions that do not have straightforward answers. When students ask questions that begin with "Why?" "How come?" "I wonder?" they must engage in a variety of higher-order thinking skills. For example, imagine a student is reading *Maniac Magee*. The student asks the question, "Why does Maniac keep running away from families who love him?" To answer such a question, the reader must synthesize all she knows about Maniac's character—his traits, his hopes and fears, and his background.

In the second part, students ask critical questions of the author. This deepens their comprehension because it requires them to think about the author's message and purpose. All texts are ideological; they are representations of a particular worldview. When we teach students to question the author, we are teaching them to investigate various

Tiffany Worden taught sixth grade for four years in New Jersey, as well as students in kindergarten, first grade, and third grade in Brooklyn, New York. Marianna Sanders has taught across all the K–6 grades in settings as diverse as El Paso, Texas; Riverside, California; and New York City. After teaching in South Korea, Nora Jaramillo moved to New York City to attend graduate school. Nora currently teaches literacy to at-risk children at a public elementary school on the Upper West Side of Manhattan.

representations of the world. Imagine that the student who is reading *Maniac Magee* asks the question, "Did Jerry Spinelli write *Maniac Magee* because he thinks black people and white people should get along?" To answer this question, the student needs to gather evidence across the text, realizing that all texts are written with some sort of intent or purpose, and speculating as to what this specific author's intent might be. This sort of thinking requires students to see things from different perspectives, be reflective, and read texts closely.

In the third part, students move from questioning the word to questioning the world. They learn to apply a critical lens to their own actions and to the institutions in which they participate. Teaching children to call into question dominant perspectives and practices helps them imagine and reconstruct a more equitable and just world. It also conveys that they are the authors of their own lives. They have the power to question and alter the circumstances in which they live.

As Stephanie Harvey (2005) notes, it is important to "teach kids to ask thoughtful and insightful questions. After all, if we hope to develop critical thinkers, we must teach our kids to think about and question what they listen to, read, and view. Asking questions enriches the learning experience and leads to deeper understanding. Questioning is the strategy that propels learners forward." We found that this unit does just that by propelling students into a learning-rich journey of deeper understanding.

Two texts are integral to the minilessons in this unit. One of these is Sarah Weeks's *So B. It,* a coming-of-age story in which the protagonist, Heidi, goes on an adventure to learn about her mother's past. Another is Jerry Spinelli's *Maniac Magee.* These texts weave through many of our minilessons and are referenced often in our small-group work.

When the read-aloud is not embedded in minilessons, it supports book talks. Students alternate between talking about the read-aloud texts with the whole class and talking in small groups. We use read-aloud as a place to demonstrate and mentor children in asking critical questions that lead to deeper comprehension. We draw upon the following questions throughout our unit (McGlaughlin and DeVoogd 2004, and Jones 2006):

- Who is in this picture/story?
- Who is missing from the picture/story?
- What is missing from the picture/story?
- How come we never see. . . ?
- Who is doing the talking?
- Who are the most important characters in this picture? What makes you think so? Are the adults or kids more important?
- Are the characters good or bad? What makes them so?

- What kinds of people are in this book?
- What kinds of places do we find in this book? What places don't we see?
- What types of activities are the people doing?
- What does the author seem to be telling us about ____? How does the meaning of ____ change by the end of the book?

Instead of asking questions to which the students respond and then we evaluate, we tried to use the following kinds of phrases (Johnston 2004):

- "Let me see if I've got this right..."
- "That's a very interesting way to look at it. I never thought of it that way before."
- "Any questions? Let's start with these."
- "How can we check?"
- "Would you agree with that?"

Overview of the Unit: Teaching Points

PART ONE: ASKING QUESTIONS TO GROW IDEAS

Readers ask questions to grow ideas. Readers ask questions not only to clarify meaning but also to gain a deeper understanding of the text. During this week, we learn how to ask deeper critical questions, ones that fuel our conversations and grow our thinking.

I. ▶ Today I want to teach you that readers ask lots of questions as we read and use our Post-its and notebooks to keep track of our musings. We expect that the answers to some questions will follow in the text, but that the answers to other questions will require us to read on, write reflectively, discuss, and hold on to various theories about our characters and their world.

II. ▶ Today I want to teach you that when readers talk about books, it pays to collect "thick" questions. We can ask, "Why?" "How come?" or "I wonder?" (Harvey and Goudvis 2000, p. 90). *[See* Resources *CD-ROM for the complete minilesson.]*

III. ▶ Today I want to teach you that when we read, we keep our questions in mind and even carry them from chapter to chapter. We can do this by rereading our last entries in our notebook or by keeping an ongoing list of our thickest questions on a bookmark or Post-it.

IV. ▶ Today I want to teach you that often, when we try to answer a question or when we burst forth with an important realization, we wind up generating whole new thoughts and questions. We can push ourselves to articulate ideas and tuck new questions into those ideas by thinking, "Now that I understand. . . , this makes me wonder about. . . ."

V. ▶ Today I want to teach you that in book clubs, readers can push ourselves to talk long and think deep about one question. One way to do this is to pose a question and then to discuss a few possible answers. Accountable talk such as "On the other hand. . ." and "Another way to look at this is. . ." and "That's true, but. . ." can guide our clubs to entertain more than one theory and to thoughtfully debate. *[See* Resources *CD-ROM for the complete minilesson.]*

VI. ▶ Today I want to teach you that good readers notice when we have strong feelings or reactions to the text, and we take this opportunity to ask questions about our characters and their motives. Questions that emerge from intense responses to texts tend to be questions that matter. We can often grow some thinking from those questions. *[See* Resources *CD-ROM for the complete minilesson.]*

VII. ▸ Today I want to teach you that when good readers notice a turning point in the story (where the characters or events change), we know something dramatic will happen to the character or the direction of plot. We can pause at these turning points to ask, "What's the purpose of this turning point in the larger story? What is going to happen, and how might this fit into the whole story?"

PART TWO: QUESTIONING THE AUTHORS OF OUR TEXTS

As readers, we understand that texts are created by authors with individual experiences and perspectives on life. We can call into question the particular version of the world that an author has represented. We can try to make the author's choices, perspectives, and intentions visible, and we can question them to understand the text more deeply.

VIII. ▸ Today I want to teach you that readers think about the author's message by pausing at the parts of the story that feel important and asking, "What is the author trying to tell me here?" [See Resources *CD-ROM for the complete minilesson.*]

IX. ▸ Today I want to teach you that readers who want to think deeply can spy on the effect that different sorts of questions have on a discussion or a train of thought. Over time, we try to develop a felt sense for the sorts of questions that are (and are not) apt to pay off.

X. ▸ Today I want to teach you that strong readers remember that authors always write with purpose. We can question why the author may have included seemingly unimportant details or spent a long time describing particular scenes. This can be a way to explore what an author's intentions may have been.

XI. ▸ Today I want to teach you that readers pay attention to the message authors send about characters. We can consider that message by asking, "Why does the character act, think, talk, or dress the way he or she does? What might the author be trying to tell me through these choices?"

XII. ▸ Today I want to teach you that readers make theories about why the author chose to write the story from a certain character's perspective. We ask questions like "Whose voices do I hear?" and "Whose voices don't I hear?" and "How would the story be different if told from a different perspective?" and write reflectively from those questions.

XIII. ▸ Today I want to teach you that readers keep book club discussions going stronger and longer by playing the devil's advocate with prompts like "We may think..., but somebody else might argue that. . ." and "That's one way to look at the story, but another way is. . . ." Readers explore multiple sides of an argument by disagreeing with our partners' arguments, posing opposite views, and questioning assumptions that others may just pass by.

XIV. ▶ Today I want to teach you that good readers wonder if the author is writing to change the world in some way and ask, "What are readers supposed to think and feel during and after reading this book?" and "How might this book make me want to work toward social change?"

PART THREE: CARRYING OUR QUESTIONING INTO OUR LIVES

As readers, we carry this habit of questioning over to our lives. We can question our thoughts and actions as well as the social networks in which we participate. These questions lead us to change our perspective and realign our actions. In short, books change us.

XV. ▶ Today I want to teach you that when readers are done reading our books, we can go back into the books to trace our thinking about a certain topic. Specifically, we can choose a few Post-its about the same topic from the beginning, middle, and end of a book. We can compare them side by side and think, "How did my thinking about this topic change from the beginning to the end of the book?" and consider how that will carry over into our life.

XVI. ▶ Today I want to teach you that good readers don't stop thinking when we close our books. When we finish reading, we often have lingering questions. We can write about them, mull them over, talk to others about them, or do research on them.

XVII. ▶ Today I want to teach you that as readers finish reading our books, we sometimes ask ourselves, "Did I ever think or act like one of the characters? Has this book made me rethink any of my past actions?"

XVIII. ▶ Today I want to teach you that just as readers know how to question the author's plans and intentions, we can also question our own plans and intentions, those of our institutions, and those of the people around us. We can become more aware of how we position ourselves in different situations and how we sometimes have more power and sometimes have less power. When we talk or write about our observations, we try to extend our observations to our books, saying, "When I notice this in my own life, an idea I have about our character is. . . ."

XIX. ▸ Today I want to teach you that readers read books keeping an eye out for unfair situations. When we spot an unfair situation, we can ask, "Could this be something that happens in real life? Could I change it in some way?" *[See* Resources *CD-ROM for the complete minilesson.]*

XX. ▸ Today I want to teach you that just as readers can envision alternate endings and scenarios in our books, we can also envision alternate ways of doing things in our lives.

XXI. ▸ Today I want to teach you that just like readers think about different ways stories could go and different ways our lives could go, readers think about how book club conversations could go differently as well by looking closely at our conversations.

OTHER RESOURCES YOU WILL FIND ON THE *RESOURCES* CD-ROM

Unit Goals and Skills

Texts Used in Read-Alouds and Minilessons

Questioning Assessment Rubrics

Part One, Session II

Part One, Session V

Part One, Session VI

Part Two, Session VIII

Part Three, Session XIX

Works Cited

SOLVING THE MYSTERY BEFORE THE DETECTIVE

Inference, Close Reading, Synthesis, Prediction

By the Teachers College Reading and Writing Project Community

This is our all-time favorite unit for third graders, as almost every fiction book they read is actually a mystery, and the unit helps them create a through-line in a text, seeing cause-and-effect relationships, predicting outcomes, and reading closely. It's also a terrific hit with even middle-school readers.

When planning the unit, you'll want to decide whether children will be in book clubs. If they are, you'll need to alter the unit based on whether this is their first book club unit for the year or they've already received support with this social structure. This write-up overviews the work you may want to do with mystery. For help with book clubs read Chapter 20 of Calkins' *The Art of Teaching Reading* or *Unit 4: Tackling Complex Texts: Historical Fiction in Book Clubs*. In your own classroom, those two lines of work will need to be braided together.

This is a wonderfully straightforward unit, and the reason the unit works so well is that it is totally natural for readers of mysteries to be engaged in one gigantic enterprise, that is, trying to solve a mystery before the crime solver does. That is easy to say, but actually accomplishing this goal is as complex as all of reading. To do this, mystery readers need to be attentive and constructive readers. Mystery readers need to be close readers and need also to be the opposite, that is, we need to be readers who can pull back to think about the details we are accumulating and make something of them—a hunch, a suspicion, a prediction.

There are other advantages. First, in this unit more than in many others, there are lots of books for readers at diverse (and early) levels. Granted, we are not aware of mysteries that are easier than *Nate the Great* and *Cam Jansen* series, but there certainly are lots of mysteries for readers at levels M, N, and O, as well as lots of mysteries that you and I love to read.

Then, too (if you wish to do so), there are many television shows that can be used as touchstone texts. You may want to bring in an episode of a mystery show that your kids like and then use that episode as a touchstone, referencing it often in minilessons. Most of the skills you will want to teach readers in this unit are skills that can be illustrated with reference to any episode of a mystery series. Similarly, you may want to purchase the old-fashioned game of Clue and use that as a touchstone. You can teach readers that just as we need to keep track of all the possible suspects when playing Clue, readers of mysteries do this as well. We have little lists going in our minds, and when we learn new clues, we look back on those lists, sometimes eliminating one suspect or another.

You will also find that there are real-life mysteries in any classroom. Where did the hamster go? Where did I leave my glasses? You can use even just the tiniest of mysteries to convey that readers of mysteries first determine what the mystery is; then we all become detectives, gathering clues and speculating what those clues might suggest.

If you are teaching mystery to children who already experienced this unit during the previous year, be sure to clump together stuff they have already learned—don't parse out every little detail. For example, if your class is revisiting mysteries for a second or third time, you might start the unit by recruiting children to help you solve a real-life mystery. ("Before we start this minilesson, will you help me figure out what I did with my glasses? Let me think, where did I last have them?") If the class helps you tackle that mystery, you can use this to say, "You already know a whole lot about solving mysteries. Would you list across your fingers three things that we did right now to solve the mystery of my lost glasses— three things that mystery readers do all the time?" You can then say, "I heard you say that I first sensed something was wrong and realized my glasses were missing, and mystery solvers do this. We first figure out what the mystery is! Then we became detectives, searching for clues, replaying what the main character did. We became suspicious and slowed down, investigating more closely." The teaching point in this minilesson could be, "Today I want to remind you that whenever we start a book, it helps to think, 'What kind of book is this?' and to remember all we already know about how that kind of book tends to go, using this to help us be powerful readers."

If you start your mystery unit by reminding children of all that they know about how mysteries tend to go and the ways that mystery readers need to read, you may soon want to remind children that mysteries are also stories and that as readers they also need to draw on everything they know as readers of fiction. Most important, they need to grow ideas about characters. This, of course, becomes a way to help mystery readers realize that collecting clues and using these to grow theories are not just what one does to solve a crime; they are what one does to grow ideas about characters, too. When reading any novel, for example, we collect clues in order to think, "What kind of person is this?" and then we devise tentative hunches, which we consequentially add to or revise.

You could progress into teaching readers that whether we are collecting whodunit clues or clues about the sorts of people these characters are, we use those clues to predict. A weatherman uses clues to predict the weather; a fortune-teller reads the lines on a person's hand to predict what that person's life will hold. Readers are like, and also unlike, weathermen and fortune-tellers. Readers' predictions, like a weatherman's predictions, are based on detailed facts about what has already gone on, but unlike the weatherman, readers don't sum up our predictions in a single phrase ("cloudy").

Then, too, you could teach children that readers often entertain more than one possible prediction. One important thing that mysteries can teach us is to be flexible readers. Readers need to think about multiple possibilities, no matter the genre, and mysteries can help us to do this by holding on to various predictions and rationales for these predictions.

Certainly you will need to teach readers to read more closely. You might find yourself thinking that every time you watch *Monk*, you're dazzled by the way he spots details that turn out to be significant. You see the same things he sees, but you just pass over so many significant details. Great detectives are on the alert, seeing more and noticing more than the average person. We can use this to teach children the importance of reading more closely, with more alertness. Clubs can reread closely, trying to spot additional clues they may have missed the first time.

Skilled mystery readers not only search for clues, they also make something of those clues and use inference to do so. Phrases such as "I think this means…" and "I think this could show…" are the language of prediction and inference. We can teach students to point to particular parts of the mystery, to infer and predict by saying, "Because of this…, I think…" These predictions are based on the inferences that readers accumulate from the text.

As we're reading, we're on the lookout for information or behavior that seems out of place and for discrepancies that pose opportunities to ask questions such as "Why would…?" or "How could…?"

Of course, this unit also invites instruction on intertextuality. As children read one mystery and then another, they will develop a sense for how mysteries tend to go, and if they are reading mysteries within a series, they'll get a sense for this particular series. The knowledge of how mysteries tend to go can help children exercise their synthesis skills, so they not only read from chapter to chapter but also figure out how one chapter fits with the ones before it. Then they also read from book to book while synthesizing, or noticing common patterns between mystery books.

You'll want to read aloud a few mysteries, starting presumably with a short one (consider one of the books your struggling readers is reading) and then progressing to a more complex text. You'll support readers in higher-level thinking by supporting partner talk with prompts such as these:

> "That's weird! Let's reread, paying close attention to the description of this character." Then say, "Turn and tell your partner what's so weird."

"Oh my gosh—I think that's a clue! Turn and talk. What clue do we have, and what might that mean?"

"Let's figure out what's really going on. Partner A, be Jigsaw, and Partner B, be Mila. Act out this scene. Now talk about what's *really* going on."

"This changes everything! Now who do you think did it?"

"How does this part fit with your theory of who did it?"

Encourage children to extend each other's ideas with conversational prompts such as "I agree with…," "Another example is…," or "To add on…." They should value debate and be able to question each other's claims, asking, "Where do you see evidence of that?" and saying, "On the other hand…."

After children talk in their clubs about the excerpt you've just read aloud, you'll convene a whole-class conversation. It's not hard to teach children to stay with and elaborate on each other's ideas in a whole-class conversation. Try transcribing parts of their talk and then using the transcript as a teaching tool. During a minilesson, you can ask children to learn from a particular strength or a particular need in the transcript as well. Of course, as children become more skilled at talking about the read-aloud, you'll want to be sure they're talking in similar ways in their book club conversations.

You may ask children to sit with their book club members during read-aloud time. When they turn and talk in response to the read-aloud, they can now do so with their club members, getting yet another opportunity during the day to talk with each other. This also gives you another chance to coach them as they talk within their club.

Overview of the Unit: Teaching Points

PART ONE

When we read mysteries, we hold close to the story, looking for details that could help us solve the mystery.

I. ▸ Today I want to teach you that in the beginning of a mystery book, it's often helpful to read the title, the blurb, and the chapter titles and to ask ourselves: "What will be the big mystery in this book? Who will solve this mystery?" Then we read the first two chapters, gathering clues and suspects.

   ▹ Mid-Workshop Teaching Point: Today I want to remind you that mystery readers expect that the mystery will be revealed early in the story. After reading the title and the first two chapters, we usually have identified the central mystery.

II. ▸ Today I want to teach you that when we read, we pay close attention to the details in the story, and often we revisit those details. As we read mysteries, this means holding on to the clues and poring over them, wondering how we may have to revise our predictions. Just as the main characters in mysteries often go back to the crime scenes to revisit and study clues, we can go back and reread our books in order to study the information the author has given us to solve the mystery.

   ▹ Mid-Workshop Teaching Point: When we reread, we do so with our minds on fire, trying to notice and think about all of the information that we are getting and saying to ourselves, "This *might* be important because…." This helps us to talk about possibilities for how the story may go, and to revise our predictions because we may find details that we now think are important.

III. ▸ Today I want to teach you that it helps to write about a few different ideas for how a mystery might get solved, so that when we get to our club conversations, we are able to help our club mates think about the book in new ways.

IV. ▸ Today I want to teach you that mystery readers notice details that are surprising or that seem like they don't really fit into the story and ask, "Could these out-of-place details really be clues?"

PART TWO

Readers use what we are learning about how mysteries tend to go to become better detectives ourselves.

V. ▸ Today I want to teach you that when we read mysteries, we often read books in a series or mysteries written by the same author. Just as when we watch a series on TV, we come to know the characters (and their strengths and weaknesses), and to know that often the plotlines are similar from one book or show to another. We use what we know about how mysteries tend to go, and how the other books in the series have tended to go to help us solve the mystery.

VI. ▸ Today I want to teach you that as we read mysteries, we often change the pace of our reading. We notice when we come to a part of the story where we should slow down and read a bit more carefully, such as when the scene of the crime is visited or new characters are introduced. We read those parts slowly, scouring for clues, maybe even rereading them and making Post-its. *(See next section for complete minilesson.)*

VII. ▸ Today I want to teach you that when we finish a book, we think about the journey we've been on. When reading mysteries, it helps to return to our books and reread the parts we missed so that we can ask, "What can I do next time I'm reading a mystery so that I don't miss this kind of clue again?"

EXAMPLE MINILESSON
Part Two, Session VI

CONNECTION

Remind readers of what you have already taught them.

"For the last several days we've been talking and thinking about how we put all of the information in our mystery books together as we read. Yesterday many of you spent time talking in your clubs about all of the things you have learned about how your mysteries tend to go. You will want to remember to use that information to predict how your book will probably go.

"Today I want to teach you that as we read mysteries, we often change the pace of our reading. We notice when we come to a part of the story where we should slow down and read a bit more carefully, such as when the scene of the crime is visited or new characters are introduced. We read those parts slowly, scouring for clues, maybe even rereading them and making Post-its."

TEACHING

Tell readers that there are portions of books that need to be read slowly and give examples.

"I want to give you a quick example of this, and then we'll go back to our read-aloud book to think about some of the parts that are worth reading more slowly and maybe even rereading.

"Do you remember when we were reading the beginning of *Sammy Keyes and the Wild Things* and we got to the part when they discover the lookout has been broken into? Do you remember how we slowed down as we were reading and how some of you even asked me to reread the part about the things that had been stolen from the lookout? This is exactly what I want us all to pay attention to in our reading. There are often parts of our books that are important because there has been some big change or there is some new information that seems to relate to the big problem in the book. In these parts, we want to be sure that we slow down and read carefully or that we even reread these parts, thinking carefully about how the information we gather might be important to the whole book.

"I had a conference with Alex yesterday. He and his club are reading the *Third-Grade Detectives* series. Alex has realized that it's really important in the series to pay close attention to the clues that Mr. Merlin, the teacher, gives the class. Mr. Merlin's clues give the kids some information, but not too much, that helps to figure out the mystery. So now when Alex is reading, he slows down when he reads any of the clues Mr. Merlin gives. Alex has also put Post-its on each of these parts so that it's easy to go back and reread the clues.

"Again, one of the things we want to think about as we are reading is our pace. Often we realize as we read that a part of the book is important, so we slow down to gather as much information as we can and to be sure that we are paying close attention to everything in the scene. Often we'll also go back and reread scenes so that we can be more thoughtful and thorough about our predictions as we read."

ACTIVE INVOLVEMENT

Ask readers to think about sections of the current read-aloud that merit closer, slower reading.

"Okay, so as I said, those are just a few quick examples. Now I want us to think together about *Sammy Keyes and the Wild Things.* I want you to think about the book and all that we have read, and I want you to identify parts that you think we should revisit—these are parts that are worth rereading and parts that we should have read slowly if we didn't already.

"Put your thumb up when you have an idea of one of those parts.

"Turn and talk to your partner about the parts you have in mind."

After I listen in to the partnerships, I break in.

"Let's get together. I want to list the parts that you think are worth rereading or that should have been read slowly in the first place. I heard people saying they thought the part where Sammy and Casey find the boar near the campsite is worth rereading because it is like another crime scene. I also heard people say that we should slow down and pay close attention to the part with the professor—when he is introduced in the story— because Sammy didn't like him and maybe there are clues there about how he might be involved in the mystery.

"So I'm going to go back to the part with the professor and reread this part slowly. I want you to listen and pay close attention to see if you can pick up any new clues that may help to predict how the rest of the story might go. I'll reread starting on page 160 when Sammy meets the professor for the first time." (I did this.)

After reading the passage, I said, "Hmm, I saw a lot of your eyes light up at a few different points there. Turn and talk to your partner about what you are thinking now.

"Let's get back together and talk about a few things we learned. Some of you noted that the professor could not have been the guy on the horse because he's too small and he has a beard. Others mentioned that the professor did not seem very concerned about the condor because he was more concerned with Sammy, with finding out who she was, than he was concerned about Marvin's injuries. These might be very interesting clues. The big thing I want you to take away from this lesson is the idea that we often vary our pace as readers. We slow down when we come to parts where we recognize a change or where we get information that seems important."

LINK

Channel readers to scan their books, noting places that merit closer, slower reading.

"I'm going to ask you to take a few moments to think about your own books. Think about the places that seem particularly important. Did you read those parts slowly? Might it help you to reread those parts in order to be more thoughtful and thorough with your predictions? Take a minute to put a Post-it on any part that you think you should reread slowly. Then you can head off to your reading."

MID-WORKSHOP TEACHING POINT

"Readers, find a place to stop for a minute. You've been reading for fifteen minutes now, and I want you to take a moment to look back and think about the pages you have read so far today. Which parts did you read more slowly? Which parts did you read more quickly? Turn to your partners (perhaps within clubs), and tell them about your pace of reading today. Show the parts you read slowly and how that helped."

FROM PERSPECTIVE TO INTERPRETATION

By Anna Gratz

I designed this as a four-week-long unit of study to help sharpen my fifth- and sixth-grade students' awareness of perspective and to show them ways that being aware of perspective can help them read interpretively. I taught the unit at the end of the year as a culminating unit. I wanted the unit to draw upon the work my students had done both in social studies and in the yearlong reading workshop. The unit is for strong students who have already had the benefit of units of study on reading with volume and stamina; growing theories about characters; reading genre-based fiction such as mysteries, fantasy, and historic fiction; developing interpretations and critical readings skills; and the like.

Have you ever seen the ink drawing that appears to be a vase when it is looked at one way, and then when it is looked at another way, it appears to be two faces? That same drawing can be looked at in yet other ways and seems to be a face belonging to an old woman or, when looked at another way, seems to belong to a young woman. The lesson: what one sees depends not only on the object being seen but also on the mind of the viewer. The way that any one of us sees the world is shaped by our past experiences, our attitudes, our beliefs. If five of us attend the same wedding and later describe the same portion of the wedding—say, the exchanging of vows—we will each have seen something different.

A reader's interpretation of the events in a story will be shaped not only by the reader's past experiences and beliefs and personality but also by the perspectives of the characters who all have their own perspectives and contribute to the telling of the story. The narrator in John Steptoe's book *Stevie* describes Stevie, the child who comes to stay with the narrator's family, as a pain in the neck, but readers are supposed to know that this description reveals the narrator just as much as it reveals Stevie.

This unit tackles the relationship between perspective and interpretation. During the first two parts of this unit, I channel my students toward carefully selected texts that

---

After teaching in New Zealand and Honduras, Anna Gratz moved to New York City, where she settled into teaching fifth grade at a private school on the Upper West Side. She currently works as a literacy specialist for grades K–6 in Sydney, Australia.

have been written in ways that clearly reveal two (or more) differing points of view—texts such as Judy Blume's *The Pain and the Great One*, in which readers experience first the brother's side of the story and then the sister's. These texts function as scaffolds, helping readers become accustomed to thinking and talking about the different perspectives that different characters bring and helping them speculate on the reasons for those different interpretations. It is easier for a child to talk about the differences between the characters' points of view in *The Pain and the Great One* than for him to understand the differences between his perspective on that text and that of a classmate, but this is the journey that the unit will support. After talking about the different perspectives in the carefully selected texts, I encourage my students to note and to discuss the different ways that the readers in our classroom community will have perceived the book and to speculate about what, in their own experiences and identities, might have influenced their interpretations. During the third and fourth parts of this unit, readers will explore ways to apply this understanding of perspective to all fiction texts, particularly to ones in which only one perspective is explicitly presented. I've planned a unit that progresses, then, from more to less scaffolding and that brings readers toward some complex thinking.

At the start of the unit, most of my students were already adept at bringing a story frame to texts and analyzing characters by considering their motivations and their struggles. They had also become accustomed to reading with attentiveness to the relationships between primary and secondary characters. It had become second nature for them to draw on information that was both explicit and implicit in the text in order to grow theories about characters. My students had also already spent time analyzing nonfiction texts in order to ascertain the author's message and to recognize ways a text is angled to support the author's message. I designed the unit, then, with hopes of maintaining their learning curve and my own. I hoped it would be a natural progression for my students to go from the character work they'd been doing toward this new work, examining the role that the characters' perspectives have on the ways in which the story itself is told.

While teaching this unit, I made sure that my students' work in social studies was complementary. I coached them to see that the so-called factual, or informational, books they were reading on American history each had an angle and a purpose and that each was written to lead readers to reach a certain conclusion about the topic.

Overview of the Unit: Teaching Points

PART ONE

Readers study texts in which more than one perspective is given to understand that the same event can be experienced and recounted differently based on who is telling the story.

I. ▶ Today I want to teach you that readers understand that there is more than one way to perceive an image or an event and ask, "Who is telling the story?" Readers know that the answer to this question matters and think about how the story might be different had someone else told it. [*See* Resources *CD-ROM for the complete minilesson.*]

II. ▶ Today I want to teach you that readers are attentive to the perspective in a story and stop in the midst of reading from time to time to ask, "Who is telling this part of the story? Who is addressing the reader?" Readers who are attentive to perspective note when the perspective in a story changes—perhaps by watching for when a story "feels" different and then checking, asking, "Has the answer to the 'Who is telling this story?' question changed? Is that why things feel different?"

III. ▶ Today I want to teach you that readers notice ways in which language, including dialogue, is different depending on who is telling the story, and readers are aware that the way a character tells the story is worth pondering, as this is revealing of the character.

IV. ▶ Today I want to teach you that readers know that one of the great pleasures in life is to be able to talk about stories with each other. We usually read differently when we know we'll have a chance to talk with others who have read the same text. We read, saving up things to talk about. If we have been thinking about how different characters describe events or situations in the story differently, then we gather up our notes on our thinking so that we can share them.

V. ▶ Today I want to teach you that readers who get the chance to meet in book clubs love the chance to talk about whatever we've been thinking as we read. If we've been thinking about how the story changes when the perspective changes, then we talk about that with each other. It can pay off to talk about the details that are put in and those that are left out of a story as well as the relationship between this and the answer to the "Who is telling the story?" question. It can also be interesting to talk about how characters perceive each other differently and—always—why.

Part Two

Readers combine characters' perspectives in texts in which more than one perspective is given in order to fashion a more complete understanding of the story and of the characters.

VI. ▸ Today I want to teach you that readers notice that the details that are highlighted in the story (or that otherwise seem important) help us to understand characters' perspectives. We think about which details a character notices and we think, "Why is this character telling the story this way? What do I know about this character that might explain why this detail is important to him or her?" *[See* Resources *CD-ROM for the complete minilesson.]*

VII. ▸ Today I want to teach you that readers fill in parts of the story that are missing. For example, when reading about two characters who have a race, if we only know the thoughts of the one who won the race, we might think about what the thoughts might be of the character who didn't win the race.

VIII. ▸ Today I want to teach you that readers pay attention to the gaps and the silences in a story, to the left-out portions of a story. When we read about a character whose perspective is revealed to us, we can think about why that character is experiencing that event in this certain way. When we read about characters whose perspectives are not revealed, we sometimes think about how the story might have gone if it had been told from the missing perspectives. Either way, we ask ourselves, "What do I know about this character that makes me think he or she would tell the story in this way?"

IX. ▸ Today I want to teach you that readers mull over what some of the major factors in a character's life might be that influence the way the character experiences the world, realizing that each person brings to each event his or her own life history. A mother will experience an afternoon at a playground differently than will a child. Readers who have chances to talk together in book clubs sometimes prepare for conversations by noting which events in the story elucidate a character's perspective, coming to the discussion with clues in mind and expecting to fit our ideas with other readers' ideas in order to generate bigger theories.

X. ▸ Today I want to teach you that readers compile ideas about a character in order to construct bigger ideas about particular characters. Then readers mull over whether ideas about particular characters can be applied to other characters and even to people and situations outside of the text. Readers ask, "What can I learn from this that could apply even to my own life?"

PART THREE

Readers consider whose perspective is being given when reading all texts, not just when reading texts in which more than one perspective is given.

XI. ▸ Today I want to teach you that readers ask "Who is telling the story?" when reading all fiction texts. In many stories, the perspective does not change. Readers can track right away who is telling the story and think why it might be important that this particular character is telling the story. *[See Resources CD-ROM for the complete mini-lesson.]*

XII. ▸ Today I want to teach you that readers pay attention to ways in which the perspective in a story influences the descriptions readers are given of events and characters. We do this by thinking about which details are included in the story and which details may have been omitted. We also think about why the character who is telling the story is telling it in this way, wondering what influences from the character's past might shape the way the character experiences events and tells the story.

XIII. ▸ Today I want to teach you that readers think about the idea of "truth," aware that what seems to be real or true changes depending on who is telling the story. Readers notice that "perspective characters" (characters from whose perspective the story is told) often seem to tell a version of the story that seems to be what really happened, that seems as if it is the best way to explain what happened. Readers consider what other versions of the truth might be possible if someone else were to tell the story, opening ourselves up to the possibility that there is more than one viable version of the truth.

XIV. ▸ Today I want to teach you that when readers push ourselves toward deeper thinking and higher levels of understanding in our reading, we often find that we want to share our ideas with others. By doing so, our ideas change.

PART FOUR

Readers consider how the story might go if it were told from a different perspective and develop big ideas about the characters, the events, and the power structures in the story from this thinking.

XV. ▸ Today I want to teach you that readers identify characters whose perspectives are not revealed, and we try to bring out those voices, those perspectives. We take a secondary character and try to get to know him or her just as we have gotten to know a main character. We collect as much information as we can about the secondary character we've chosen to understand; we fill in missing information by making inferences about what this character might think, feel, or say; and we consider ways in which the character's background or role might lead the character to these conclusions. We may do this with a number of secondary characters.

XVI. ▶ Today I want to teach you that readers consider how non-perspective characters are portrayed by perspective characters, noticing how a main character talks about and interacts with a non-perspective character. We notice especially the power differential in this relationship. We look across many relationships that the perspective character has with non-perspective characters, again thinking about power. Do the non-perspective characters seem to have less power, and might this have something to do with the fact that they are not telling the story?

XVII. ▶ Today I want to teach you that readers imagine how non-perspective characters might tell the story differently. Readers think, write, and/or talk about how the story might go if told from the perspective of a non-perspective character, and we do this by putting ourselves in the character's shoes and imagining how he or she might experience life. We do this by thinking about what we know about a particular non-perspective character and thinking about how that character's background and life experience would influence the way he or she would tell the story. *[See the next section for the complete minilesson.]*

XVIII. ▶ Today I want to teach you that readers come to book clubs to talk not only about the stories that are told in our texts but also about the ones that are not told. We talk in book clubs about who is being heard in the story and who is not. We talk about how the story might be different if it had been told from a different perspective. We use both the "told" story and the "untold" story to construct big ideas about the text.

XIX. ▶ Today I want to teach you that readers reflect on work we do with each other like sojourners reflect on journeys to new lands. We ask not only "What did we learn?" but also "What did we do as individuals and as a club that led us to this learning?" *[See Resources CD-ROM for the complete minilesson.]*

EXAMPLE MINILESSON
Part Four, Session XVII

CONNECTION

Recall a trip the class took recently in order to evoke the image of characters who were present in a story but whose perspective we didn't know.

"On our trip to Colonial Williamsburg, we met a lot of characters. On our tour, we met Peyton Randolph, one of the wealthy landowners who had lived there. In Peyton Randolph's house, we watched as actors playing Mr. and Mrs. Randolph enacted what a dinner at the Randolph house might have been like in the late 1700s. Mr. and Mrs. Randolph took their places at the table, and immediately several actors playing slaves came to serve them dinner. The actors playing Mr. and Mrs. Randolph talked about the foods they were eating, about the Revolutionary War and whether George Washington would be able to lead the troops to victory. Remember how the slaves who served the dinner had to stand silently off to the side the entire time that Mr. and Mrs. Randolph were eating. They didn't say anything throughout the scene even though they were physically part of it.

"The scene reminded me of the work that we have been doing with perspective. We mostly experienced that dinner through the eyes of Mr. and Mrs. Randolph. They were the characters whose perspective was revealed to the viewers. There were other people at the scene who would have experienced the dinner very differently, such as the slaves who stood and waited for hours while the Randolphs ate. Yet their voices were absent from the story. They were completely silent. We don't know what the experience of the dinner was from their perspective. The slaves were the characters whose perspective *must be inferred.*"

Move into a different version of the story to highlight how the story might go differently if told from the point of view of the characters whose perspective had to be inferred.

"But remember that then the tour of the Randolph house continued. We moved from the dining room to the kitchen, where we met Aggy and Johnny, two of the slaves who had been standing in the dining room waiting on the Randolphs. This time, we got to listen in on the conversation that they had with each other. It turns out that the whole time they were standing and waiting for the Randolphs to finish their dinner, they were listening for information that might help them and the other slaves become free. This made me think that *everyone* has a story, even if it isn't revealed in a particular scene. We don't always hear everyone's side of the story in fiction books. Books won't always be like our tour, where we were able to hear two sides of an event and a story. As readers, we can learn to notice whose perspective is not revealed and try to *infer* how the story would go if it were told from the perspective of those characters."

Name your teaching point. Specifically, point out that imagining the perspective of characters whose voices are left out in a story helps us unearth greater meaning from a text.

"Readers, today I want to teach you that in order to gain even deeper insight into texts, readers imagine how the characters whose perspective must be inferred might tell the story differently. We think, write, and/or talk about how the story might go if told from the perspective of these characters."

TEACHING

Demonstrate how to consider the perspective of a character whose voice is not heard in a story. Have the students try to imagine how the story might be told differently from such a character's perspective using their read-aloud text *Freedom Summer*.

"Readers, watch me try this work with *Freedom Summer*. We've already determined that John Henry is a character whose perspective must be inferred. Even though he is a very important character in the story and Joe, whose perspective is revealed, talks about him throughout the book, we don't really get to hear what he is thinking. We don't experience the story through his eyes. I wonder how the story would go if it were told from John Henry's perspective. To show you how I might think about this, I am going to reread the section where Joe and John Henry are discussing the pool being filled in, and then I'm going to pause to think about how the story might go if it were told from John Henry's perspective:"

> We sit on the diving board and stare at the tops of the silver ladders sticking up from the tar. My heart beats hard in my chest.
>
> John Henry's voice shakes.
>
> "White folks don't want colored folks in their pool."
>
> "You're wrong, John Henry," I say, but I know he's right.
>
> "Let's go back to Fiddler's Creek," I say. "I didn't want to swim in this old pool anyway."
>
> John Henry's eyes fill up with angry tears. "I did," he says. "I wanted to swim in this pool. I want to do everything you can do."

"If John Henry's perspective was the one that was revealed, I think the story would feel very different. The story wouldn't *go* differently; the events that happened would still happen. The pool would still be filled in. But if John Henry's perspective was revealed, then we would know his thoughts and feelings, and we would understand the events of the story through his eyes. I'm going to try to imagine what he might be thinking. And I am going to use the 'I' voice, almost as if I was John Henry. I think he might say, 'I am so furious and just devastated that the pool was filled in. It is so unfair that Joe could swim in the pool because he is white, but I couldn't because I am black. And now they filled the pool in on purpose just so kids like me wouldn't have a chance to go swimming. Even though Joe says that's not true, I know it is. I think he knows, too, but he is too ashamed to admit it. Sometimes I get so jealous of Joe because he can do things I can't do. He is my friend, but he doesn't understand how I feel and he never will. I thought things were going to change, but this is just not right.'

"Readers, do you see what I did there? I didn't change the *events* in the story. I only changed the *perspective.* I told the story in the first person, and I told it the way I think John Henry might have told it. I also made sure to draw upon exact details from the text, like what the characters said and did, in order to imagine John Henry's words and feelings."

ACTIVE INVOLVEMENT

Set the students up to try this work on their own using another section of the text.

"Readers, I'm going to have you try this work on your own. I'm going to read this next part of the story, where John Henry and Joe go into Mr. Mason's store to buy ice pops. As you listen, use what you know about John Henry, and the details from the text, to think about what he might say and how he might feel in this moment. Then we'll stop and jot, writing what we think John Henry might say and feel in this moment." I began to read:

> We stop in front of Mr. Mason's store. I jam my hands into my pockets while my mind searches for words to put with my new ideas. My fingers close around two nickels.
>
> "Want to get an ice pop?"
>
> John Henry wipes his eyes and takes a breath. "I want to pick it out myself."
>
> I swallow hard and my heart says yes.
>
> "Let's do that," I say.

I give John Henry one of my nickels.

He shakes his head. "I got my own."

We look at each other.

Then we walk through the front door together.

After I read the section, most of the students began to scribble furiously. I asked a few of them to share what they had written. I highlighted how they used the details of the text and what they knew about both John Henry and Joe to tell the story using John Henry's perspective. I reminded them that this work isn't about creating a new version of the events. This work is about considering how different people experience the same events very differently and would use very different words and feelings to describe them.

"Readers, I'm noticing that you are all using what you know about John Henry through the words of Joe to think about what he might feel or say in this moment. Many of you thought John Henry might have talked about how important it was to him to go into the store, use his *own* money, and pick out his ice pop for *himself*. Others of you thought he might feel really nervous about going into the store but that he was going to be strong because he didn't want things to be so unfair anymore. Others of you thought that he was grateful to have Joe as a friend because he felt like he could face these tough, even terrible, situations with someone who cared about him."

LINK

Send off the students to try this work on their own, reminding them that the learning from today will deepen not only their reading work but also their ability to consider different perspectives in life.

"Readers, today as you go off to read, try this work in your own books. Think about what those characters whose perspective is not revealed might say if given the chance to tell the story. Doing this work can lead you to a deeper understanding about the characters and the relationships between them. It can also help you gain a deeper understanding of those ideas that are very important but hidden in the text. This is not simple work you are doing. In fact, this work is very complex. I think you are the kind of readers who are ready for it, though! Thinking about what characters who don't have a voice might say if they were voicing the story will help you deepen your understanding of texts, and of people in your lives, as you read today and always."

Conferring and Small-Group Work

One of the main points I wanted to cover during the conferring session was to make sure the students were telling their alternate versions of the story in a way that was consistent with the rest of the story. Doing the work of imagining how the story might go if it were told from the perspective of a different character does require some creativity, and I knew some of my students would have difficulty coming up with a different version of the story. But what I was just as—if not more—concerned about was that some students would take the story on wild tangents and wouldn't write from a different character's perspective in a way that was grounded in the text. I didn't want them to change the events in the story but to use these events as anchors to frame their new version of the story. I also wanted them to use as much of the information they already had about the character as they could and to keep the inferences they had to make solidly grounded in the text. One way I decided to help my students with this work was to push them to not just write *how* the different character would tell the story but also consider *why* they think the story would have gone this way.

I pulled up alongside Eamon, who was writing a very long passage in his reader's notebook. When I did a bit of research and found out what he had been writing about, I discovered that he had taken quite a few liberties with one section from *Tuck Everlasting,* the book he was reading in a club with Gabrielle and Hao Tong. Eamon was rewriting the story from the perspective of the man in the yellow suit, a character whose perspective is not revealed. He was writing about the moment when the man comes to tell the Tucks of his plan to take over the woods with the magic spring and thus take control of the spring of eternal life. Eamon was writing his story very creatively and with relish, but in the direction that he had taken, the story was too far removed from the events in the text. He didn't include any of the original dialogue, and he had written a strange scenario in which he suggested that the man in the yellow suit was really a police officer who had come to rescue Winnie.

I decided to pull Gabrielle and Hao Tong into the conference because I thought they could also benefit from this work. "Eamon, can I interrupt you for a moment? Gabrielle and Hao Tong, would you listen in as we talk? Eamon, I noticed that you quickly identified a character in your book whose perspective was not revealed and that you thought about what that character might say if the story were being told from his perspective. You chose someone to write about who is presented as sort of an enemy to the Tucks, and you told the story through his eyes in a way that shows maybe he's not such a bad guy after all. You clearly are thinking deeply about this character, and you are being considerate of his perspective. You are also writing creatively and passionately. Can I just give you a little tip?"

When Eamon nodded, I went on. "The thing is, when you write about how the story might go differently when told through a different character's eyes, it's so important that you use everything you know about the events in the story, including what characters say and do, using both the characters whose perspective is revealed and the ones whose isn't while you rewrite the version of the story.

"Just because we are telling the story through the perspective of the man in the yellow suit doesn't mean that this whole conversation between the man and the Tucks didn't happen. The man still makes the choices he made and says the things he said. And it's really important to include those in his side of the story. Also, I was just thinking about what I know about the man in the yellow suit. In another part of the story, we learn that his grandmother had told him the story of the spring and that he had spent his life searching for it. He talks about how rich he would become if he had control of the spring. So keeping those things in mind, I'm not sure it makes complete sense to me that he is a police officer and that what he really wants is to rescue Winnie. When you write his version of the story, you can write from inside his head and you can write *why* he said and did the things he did, but keep in mind what we already know about him. Does that make sense?"

Eamon nodded again, and I addressed the entire group. "I'm going to give you a strategy that you all can try to keep your writing grounded in the text. I'm going to give you a couple of prompts that you can use as you stop and jot about the character whose perspective is not revealed. Go back to one of the entries that you just collected. You all wrote how you think this character would tell the story. Next, think about what you know about that character that led you to your conclusions about how he or she would tell the story. Reread what you wrote, and then continue with the following prompt: I think (insert character's name) would tell the story this way because…."

I gave the students a few minutes to write.

"Okay, now continue writing with the following prompt: If (insert character's name) was telling the story, I think this part would be different…."

I gave them a few more minutes to write.

"The next prompt is: I think this part would be different because…. So, readers, when you write about a character, one way to keep your writing grounded in the text is to use prompts that push you to say why you think the character you are writing about would tell the story in this way. Then you can make sure you are using the parts of the story that do exist to infer what doesn't exist. In other words, you are using what you know from the book about that character, the setting and the plot, and the other characters—including the ones whose perspective is revealed—to infer how the story would go differently if told from that first character's perspective. You're not just making it up as you go. Go ahead and try this on your own."

Texts Used in Minilessons

Voices in the Park by Anthony Browne

When I taught this unit, the read-aloud that was especially important to the unit was Anthony Browne's *Voices in the Park,* which tells of a day at the park from the perspective of four different people. First, the story is told from the perspective of a young boy who has a controlling mother. Next, the story is told through the perspective of a father who is down on his luck and needs to find a job. Then that same day at the park is told from the perspective of the controlling mother, and finally it is told through the perspective of the father's daughter, a little girl. The characters interact with each other in different ways throughout the course of the day. What is really interesting is the way in which a character can be a main character, a focal point, in one version of the story and then essentially part of the background in another version of the story. Browne's illustrations are complex and intriguing, and the landscape he depicts is different for each character. Students get information about the way each character experiences the world based on the illustrations as well as the written text. For example, the background is bright and sunny during the little girl's scene at the park but dark and gloomy during the controlling mother's day. The mother and girl are at the park at the same time, so the different backgrounds are intended to show that the two characters actually experience life differently and that the same day can be experienced differently depending on what a character brings to the experience. This book can be used to introduce readers to the concepts of voice and perspective and to help them notice how the story changes when the voice changes. This book is especially important during the first two parts of the unit.

Black and White by David Macaulay

This is a picture book containing four stories told in four separate parts. I found that readers needed to read it several times in order to see how the stories fit together. It can help readers to collect clues to determine who is telling the story at a particular time. It can also be used to launch the unit in place of the famous black-and-white image.

Freedom Summer by Deborah Wiles (Level M)

This story is told from the perspective of Joe, who talks about the summer in which his best friend, John Henry, is not allowed to swim in the community pool because he is black. This read-aloud can be used to discuss whose voice is heard (Joe's) and whose is not (John Henry's) as well as what John Henry might say if he had a voice in the book. This read-aloud is especially effective for this work, as Joe tells John Henry's story pretty explicitly, and readers have many clues to draw upon when analyzing what John Henry might say if given the opportunity to speak.

Student Texts: Parts One and Two

Texts Written Using Multiple Voices

Ideally most readers will read one book a week, with those students working with easier texts reading more of them, of course. These books are arranged more or less in order of difficulty, from less difficult to more difficult.

The Pain and the Great One by Judy Blume (Level M)

This is a book told from the perspective of two siblings, a brother and sister, each of whom thinks that the other is loved more by their mother. The sister refers to herself as "The Great One" and to her brother as "The Pain."

Drita, My Homegirl by Jenny Lombard (Level Q)

This book tells about fourth-grader Drita, who has come to live in New York City from Kosovo because her family is seeking asylum from her war-torn country. The other voice in the story is Maxie, Drita's classmate at their predominantly African American elementary school. The story switches between each girl's perspective and shows how eventually they learn to understand each other and become friends.

Ernestine and Amanda Series by Sandra Belton (Level U)

These series books tell the story of Ernestine and Amanda, two African American girls growing up in 1955. They have a bitter rivalry, and to make matters worse their older brother and sister are high school sweethearts.

Never Mind! A Twin Novel by Avi and Rachel Vail (Level T)

This story is told from the perspectives of twins Edward and Meg, rivals who realize through their struggle that they are more alike than they thought.

If a Tree Falls at Lunch Period by Gennifer Choldenko (Level Z)

This book is written from the point of view of an overweight girl who has issues both with her mother and with friendships, and an African American boy who comes to her private school.

The Wanderer by Sharon Creech (Level V)

This book is the story of a journey across the ocean told from the perspectives of Sophie and her cousin Cody. Both Sophie and Cody learn lessons about letting go of the past and facing their fears during the journey. They also learn that they are not as different as they thought they were when they first met.

Flipped by Wendelin Van Draanen (Level U)

This story is told from the perspectives of Bryce and Juliana. Juliana has a crush on Bryce but then gets over him, and he can't understand why she stops paying attention to him.

Salem Witch: My Side of the Story by Patricia Hermes (Level T)

This is a story presenting two very different viewpoints of the Salem witch trials told through the perspectives of two children who witness the events.

My Side of the Story Series, by various authors (Levels S/T/U)

This series would be excellent used during this unit or during a social studies unit. It asks readers to consider such questions as "Is there one true version of history? Is there a 'good' and a 'bad' side?" The series is historical fiction and recounts events told from two very different perspectives. Typically, the main characters are children. For example, the book *Journey to Jamestown* tells the story of establishing the colony at Jamestown from the perspectives of both a young boy who is an English settler and a Native American girl who is living in the area when the settlers come.

Bull Run by Paul Fleischman (Level Y)

This is a heartbreaking Civil War tale told from the perspective of sixteen different people who experienced the war. The people are male and female, black and white, Northern and Southern.

Seedfolks by Paul Fleischman (Level W)

Thirteen voices tell the story of a vacant lot turned into a neighborhood garden and the impact this transformation has on their lives.

Good Masters! Sweet Ladies! Voices from a Medieval Village by Laura Amy Schlitz (Level Z)

This book is historical fiction about the medieval era told in twenty-two monologues. This is a shorter text, so students reading this text might read three books during this phase of the unit. This could also be a great book to use for Reader's Theater.

The Whale Rider by Witi Ihimaera (Level V)

This is the story of Kahu, an eight-year-old Maori girl who is the sole heir in line to become the leader of her tribe, a tribe descended from the legendary "whale rider." She struggles to gain attention from her great-grandfather, who is the current chief and has no use for a girl. The story is told from the perspectives of both Kahu and the whales with whom she can communicate.

The Music of Dolphins by Karen Hesse (Level V)

Mila is a girl who has been raised by dolphins and finds it difficult to integrate into the human world after she is rescued by the Coast Guard. She must learn to communicate with humans as she has learned to communicate with dolphins. Her love of music is what allows her to become part of the human world but remain part of the world of the dolphins, as well.

Witness by Karen Hesse (Level Z)

This story, written in free verse poetry, is told through the voices of different townspeople who are divided over the arrival of the Klu Klux Klan in their small Vermont town in the early 1920s. A young Jewish girl and an African American girl are two of the witnesses who see the effect of prejudice on people.

Because of Anya by Margaret Peterson Haddix (Level Q)

This story is told through the perspectives of two ten-year old girls: Anya, who wears a wig due to her alopecia areata (a condition that causes her hair to fall out), and Keely, a popular girl who befriends Anya after she loses her wig in gym class.

Morning Girl by Michael Dorris (Level S)

This story takes place on a Bahamian island in 1492 and is told through the perspectives of two Taino siblings, Morning Girl and Star Boy. They describe what family life and daily life were like before the arrival of Christopher Columbus.

Student Texts: Parts Three and Four

During the next two parts, students can choose virtually any fiction book in which to do this work. The books that work best will be ones that have a strong central character and that reveal relationships that character has with minor characters. I've seen readers do incredible work with *Maniac McGee, Esperanza Rising,* and *Holes.* I listed a couple of books here that I think could lead to particularly provocative thinking and discussion, but again, this work really could be done with virtually any fiction book. The texts below would also make excellent read-alouds if you would like to use a longer text than *Freedom Summer.*

The Daydreamer by Ian McEwan (Level S)

This is the story of Peter, the title character, who spends his life in a fantasy world. The book contains several vignettes in which Peter imagines himself to be different characters while in the midst of everyday situations, leading to him being seriously misunderstood by other characters. For example, in one vignette, he daydreams about being a mountaineer and saving his sister from a pack of wolves while on the bus to school, consequently leaving his sister on the bus. Students could consider what the perspectives of those close to Peter might be and how Peter's version of reality is most likely very different from those around him. This book leads to particularly provocative thinking about perspective because Peter's version of reality is so outlandish and different from versions of those around him, and his perspective is strongly favored.

Tuck Everlasting by Natalie Babbitt (Level W)

In this story, Natalie Babbitt tells of a family, the Tucks, who drank from a spring over one hundred years before the story of the book began and became immortal. The story is told from the perspective of Winnie, a girl whose family now owns the woods in which the spring is located and who stumbles on the Tucks' secret. This story works well for the second half of this unit for two reasons. First, because the text does not make it crystal clear who the perspective character is at the beginning, it pushes students to really think about how to determine whose perspective is favored; second, each character has such a different feeling about the idea of immortality. Students can think and talk about what in each character's background shaped his or her thinking about immortality. Miles, the older brother, hates his immortality because he was starting a family when he became immortal and his young wife and children left him when he stopped aging. But Jesse, the younger brother, sees his immortality as being exciting and as freeing him from the burden of responsibility.

OTHER RESOURCES YOU WILL FIND ON THE *RESOURCES* CD-ROM

Goals for the Unit

Reading Skills Addressed by the Unit

Texts Used the Unit

Instructional Structures

Sample Schedule

Assessment

Part One, Session I

Part Two, Session VI

Part Three, Session XI

Part Four, Session XIX

Works Cited

READING FOR JUSTICE AND POWER: A SOCIAL ISSUES BOOK CLUB UNIT

By Mary Coakley

This four-week social issues unit helps young people develop the reading strategies and the identities that enable them to read critically and to think deeply, especially about power, relationships, and social issues. The social structure of book clubs runs throughout the unit, and students are taught ways to engage in collaborative intellectual work. The skills students will use to improve their reading of texts—empathy, critical reading, and interpretation—are skills they can also use to "read" their worlds and to inform the way they live their lives.

I developed this unit with and for a fifth-grade class and taught it during the month of April. The students in my class range from reading levels M through T. By the time we launched the unit, students were already able to write detailed Post-its in response to books, predict elaborately, envision the details of scenes in a book, make sense by connecting several parts of a text, and examine story elements. Students also could identify and interpret character development, character relationships, conflicts, and aspects of the author's craft. They didn't yet create many big ideas about their reading that connected with authors' intended or unintended messages. They had not yet developed a strong vocabulary for, or many ways of talking about, social issues found in the stories they read.

During book clubs prior to this unit, students used accountable talk phases such as "I hear what you're saying, and I see it differently…," "I agree with the statement that …," and "Another place in the text that supports that idea (or doesn't support that idea) is…." With these starters, they showed evidence of listening to each other's ideas as they summarized their peers' statements. I wanted to work with them to find ways to build new ideas that were illuminated by the combined perspectives of the group, to use the discursive power of conversation to reduce repetition of isolated ideas, and to support them in arriving at webs of new connections. I also devised this unit because I wanted my students to begin to observe the way relationships and power work in books and in the world without preaching to them about one particular right way to think. As my students' teacher, however, I mold their experiences, and these experiences, in turn, frame their thinking.

During her seven years as an elementary classroom teacher in New York City, Mary Coakley taught second and third grades in Harlem and fifth grade on the Upper East Side. She designed this unit of study while teaching fifth graders at a school for girls. Mary has had the opportunity to study literacy and social studies education internationally through two summer travel fellowships.

As my students reach the end of fifth grade and prepare for sixth grade and as they begin to notice more cliques and bullying among their peers, I thought that reading and discussing books through a social issues lens would provide them with powerful language and insights for examining their own lives and actions. All of these key words—control, unfair, demeaning, dollars (money), wish, force—relate to power. They describe power in and across various contexts: physical, mental, emotional, financial, and ideological.

Social issues book clubs provide students with texts about which they feel passionate while providing me with an opportunity to teach strategies that will boost their talk through minilessons, small-group work, and conferences. This will include talking long about ideas and connecting personally to specific events, language, and messages in the book while staying close to the text and using "and" instead of "but" more often in conversations when that might be appropriate.

Major goals in this book club unit center around building competence in the following reading skills: empathy, interpretation, and critical reading. Empathy, interpretation, and critical reading can each stand alone as reading skills, but they also can each rely on the others. In order to build competence in these three areas, students also need to build on other skills that intertwine with them, such as making sense of the text, using inference, making personal connections, and envisioning. These are skills we have worked on in the past, and while they are not the main skills addressed here, they show up nonetheless. More specific goals include learning the following:

- To use clues stated in a text to understand what is not explicitly stated in a text (inference)

- To use clues stated in a text, along with our prior knowledge about life, to draw conclusions about what is not explicitly stated in a text (inference, empathy, interpretation, personal connection)

- To use clues stated in a text to draw conclusions about the author's intended and unintended messages (critical reading, interpretation)

- To reveal characters by studying their relationships to individuals and to groups (interpretation, critical reading)

- To revise our inferences, interpretations, critical reading, and personal connections (which may all be related) as we add new details to previous details

POSSIBLE TEXTS FOR A SOCIAL ISSUES UNIT

These are the texts I use for read-alouds, small-group work, strategy lessons, and conferences:

Creativity by John Steptoe
The Black Snowman by Phil Mendez
The Other Side by Jacqueline Woodson
Freedom Summer by Deborah Wiles
Thank You, Mr. Falker by Patricia Polacco
How Many Days to America? A Thanksgiving Story by Eve Bunting
My Best Friend by Mary Ann Rodman

Other suggestions for possible read-aloud texts for this unit and for book club books are included on the *Resources* CD-ROM.

USING FILM AS A TEXT

You may want to show your students the short film *Binta and the Great Idea* by writer-director Javier Fesser, an Oscar-nominated short film in 2007. It is about an eight-year-old girl named Binta, whose uncle does not allow Binta's twelve-year-old cousin, Soda, to attend school. Soda must stay home and care for her little siblings. The children at school put on a play to try to get the uncle to change his mind and send Soda to school. This film is a child-friendly social narrative in which lots of social issues pop up. You can access this film for free on the Internet at www.spike.com/video/2771644. If you do not have access to this particular film, you can easily use part of another film, a TV commercial, a TV show, or a book that can be shared with the whole class in order to highlight social issues. Film and TV are great resources for examining social issues as a class and for practicing the reading skills students will use while reading books.

CLASSROOM CHARTS

Students often refer to charts in my classroom to remind them of what we have studied and some of the language we have used to discuss their work. Decide how detailed you want your charts to be. The goal is to have them be easy references for students. Each of these charts could support work on social issues; however, add each new question as you teach students to use that strategy. The charts are meant to grow from the work the class is doing, not as assignments for them. For example, here are some of the charts in my classroom.

Questions Readers Might Ask When They Read Critically

- Who or what has power in the story?

- How is that power shown?

- What seems fair in the story? What seems unfair? Why?

- What are the rules around being a girl or boy for this character?

- What pressures does the character face? How does he or she respond?

- Whose voices or perspectives are heard in this story? Why might this be so?

- Whose voices or perspectives are not heard in this story? Why might this be so?

- What do the main characters believe to be true about life? Why?

- What does the author want you to feel when reading this text? Why do you think so?

(These questions were inspired by Katherine Bomer, Randy Bomer, and Mary Ehrenworth.)

Questions Readers Might Ask to Help Them Empathize with Characters

- How is the character feeling at this point in the text? Why is he or she feeling that way?

- How would you feel if you were the character?

- Can you imagine being in the character's shoes right now? What do you imagine?

- What does this character believe to be true about life? Why? Do you believe anything similar?

- What might the character say in this situation? Why do you think so?

- What might the character do in this situation? Why do you think so?

Questions Readers Might Ask to Grow Big Ideas About a Text

- What's <u>really</u> going on here? What is this story <u>really</u> about?
- What is a message that you could take from this story/text?
- What do you think the author intended the message to be?
- What themes are present in this story? How can you tell? What evidence is there?
- After looking at many clues about a theme in the story, what idea do you have about that theme in this story/text?
- Do you notice any symbols in the story/text? How do the symbols connect with important ideas from the story/text? What do the symbols show?
- Why do you think the author chose to write in this way/structure/style?
- Why do you think the author chose to represent this character in this way?

The next chart displays examples of accountable talk that students will learn to use over the course of the unit. These accountable talk phrases are meant to support students' development in learning discussion skills, reading skills, and critical reading content. I am also trying to teach students to use the word "and" to grow conversation instead of the word "but," which can feel threatening.

- What I hear you saying is that...
- This is an interesting observation because...
- What I think is important about what you said is...
- I agree with what you're saying because...
- I see it differently because...
- What you said made me think that...
- This part fits with this other part because...
- Can you show me in the book where...?
- These two (three, four, several) parts connect because...
- We know that the character is _____ because...
- This part makes me feel uncomfortable or relieved because...

Overview of the Unit: Teaching Points

PART ONE: IDENTIFYING SOCIAL ISSUES

Critical readers often identify social issues that weave through the texts we read. This is important because as we keep track of the details of these issues, we can braid them together to inform and create bigger meanings from the text. The beginning of Part One is intended to rally kids around looking at social issues in books and in the world—seeing these everywhere.

I. ▸ Today I want to teach you that critical readers choose the lenses through which we wish to view texts—and life. When we decide to read critically, we put on lenses that allow us to see social issues as they thread through books (and also through movies and the world). Reading for social issues can help us understand people in books, movies, and our world. *[See the next section for the complete minilesson.]*

   ▹ Mid-Workshop Teaching Point: Critical readers sometimes decide to think more about a social issue or two as we see them threading through a book and might decide to use Post-its on words and phrases that we think might be helpful in explaining that social issue or to collect the Post-its in our reader's notebooks, giving us a vocabulary to use when discussing, thinking about, and writing about social issues.

   ▹ **Strategy Lesson:** Social issues are often present when we notice that something feels unfair in a text. One way readers can identify social issues is by noticing where something feels unfair in the text and trying to name what issue is at work there.

II. ▸ Today I want to teach you that when readers are onto something as readers, we bring whatever it is we are thinking to conversations with other readers. If we're in book clubs, for example, and we've been reading a share book critically, we're apt to talk about issues of fairness that we see in that book. We say things like "I think that is fair because..." or "I think that is unfair because..." and "This fairness/unfairness matters because...."

   ▹ Mid-Workshop Teaching Point: Critical readers—readers who think about social issues and fairness in books—think about these issues also in our own lives, and that includes in our own book clubs. We "read" our book clubs through the lens of fairness and try to respond to each other fairly. In part, this means hearing each other and showing that we are hearing each other.

> ▷ Mid-Workshop Teaching Point: "Hearing each other" happens internally, but there are external things we can do that show we are hearing each other. Sometimes it helps to say things such as "What I hear you saying is…," "That is an interesting observation because…," or "This seems important because…." Summing up what another person has said or referencing what another person has said allows us to check that we heard the other person right and also lets the other person know that we are listening and care about what that person has said.

III. ▸ Today I want to teach you that critical readers can collect additional clues about social issues as we read on in a text. Braiding clues together about a social issue can help readers grow big ideas about the book. As readers, we can ask ourselves how new details about social issues fit in with other details we have already noticed in order to understand the bigger ideas of the text.

> ▷ **Strategy Lesson:** Readers may have to reread to find connecting parts. We reread to look more closely at the details of the story, perhaps using Post-its to mark and jot why those details seem important upon a second a reading, and then look and talk across the Post-its to grow our ideas.

IV. ▸ Today I want to teach you that book club members find parts of a story where the social issues remind us of other parts of the story and then we discuss how the two parts fit together because this can help us grow ideas about what is important in the text. We might say, "This part fits with this other part because…" or "These two parts connect because…."

V. ▸ Today I want to teach you that critical readers construct big ideas about stories by braiding together clues about social issues and creating a message from the clues. In order to grow a big idea, readers can ask ourselves what message can be taken from these clues. Readers sometimes jot down big ideas in our reader's notebooks. *[See Resources CD-ROM for the complete minilesson.]*

> ▷ Mid-Workshop Teaching Point: Readers often find ourselves wondering if an author's messages may have been intentional or unintentional. We may never know the answer, but we share our ideas with our book clubs. We can say, "I think the author was intentional/unintentional in creating this message because…."

Part Two: Experiencing Characters

Critical readers recognize that the characters in our stories are complex and that the characters experience social issues in a variety of ways. Readers can seek connections and disconnections between our lives and the lives of characters as we read.

VI. ▸ Today I want to teach you that powerful readers are always searching to understand our characters in deeper ways. We look carefully at characters' words and actions and ask ourselves why the characters might talk or act in that way. Readers sometimes jot clues about how characters talk and act on Post-its to keep track of them.

   ▹ Mid-Workshop Teaching Point: When readers are mulling over particularly interesting dialogue and actions, we tend to ask ourselves how characters' words and actions might point to or highlight social issues in the story.

VII. ▸ Today I want to teach you that when book club members are sharing what characters' talk and actions reveal about them, we are likely to ask each other and ourselves, "What do we know about the characters?" and "What did the characters do or say to make you think that?"

VIII. ▸ Today I want to teach you that critical readers study a character's desires, wondering why a character might want or long for those things. Readers sometimes collect details from the story on Post-its to support our thinking about a character's desires. *[See Resources CD-ROM for the complete minilesson.]*

   ▹ Mid-Workshop Teaching Point: Readers might notice that sometimes characters are aware of a desire and sometimes characters are quite unaware about a desire, even though their desire seems obvious to us. We can track a character's wants, showing our book clubs how what a character wants affects how a character acts.

IX. ▸ Today I want to teach you that when book club members are striving to build our level of talk, we might role-play a scene while acting as the characters. If we are having a conversation with our club mates from the perspective of a character, we might say, "I want _____ because..." and include examples that illustrate the character's desires from the text. Other group mates might respond to our character with "I hear that you want _____, and (but) I think your next step should be...."

   ▹ Mid-Workshop Teaching Point: Readers notice the emotions we feel while "getting into the shoes of the characters." We name these emotions and ask ourselves how feeling that way in the characters' shoes can help us identify where social issues exist for the characters.

X. ▶ Today I want to teach you that critical readers can understand the characters in our books better by looking at what pressures the characters face. Readers examine the pressures characters face because these pressures are often related to social issues in the book. Then we ask ourselves how the characters resist or respond to the pressures and why we think they resist or respond in that way. *[See* Resources *CD-ROM for the complete minilesson.]*

▷ **Strategy Lesson:** Readers can draw sketches to show pressures on characters and how characters resist or respond to these pressures (inspired by Mary Ehrenworth).

XI. ▶ Today I want to teach you that book club members sometimes ask ourselves how we might have resisted or responded to the pressures the characters encountered.

▷ Mid-Workshop Teaching Point: Readers remember to take into account the contexts and constraints of the characters when we contemplate our own responses. It can be difficult to evaluate a character's response if we don't understand how his or her situation is different from our own.

XII. ▶ Today I want to teach you that critical readers often ask ourselves which characters are heard or not heard by other characters in the story. Readers find details in the story to show when characters have been heard or not heard. Then we ask ourselves, "Why might characters be heard or not heard by others?"

▷ Mid-Workshop Teaching Point: Readers notice how silence might have power in a text. Readers might ask ourselves, "Does silence empower a character or take power away in some way?"

XIII. ▶ Today I want to teach you that critical readers think about the rules placed on characters. We might ask ourselves, "How 'are characters allowed to be' (Bomer and Bomer, 2005) in the world of the story? What are the rules placed on them by groups, individuals, themselves?"

PART THREE: UNDERSTANDING POWER

Critical readers can examine social issues by observing and interpreting the way that power works in the text. Readers can also observe the way that characters use, celebrate, and resist power in a text.

XIV. ▸ Today I want to teach you that critical readers often ask ourselves, "Who or what has power in this story/text?" and "How is that power shown?" Readers sometimes write Post-its when we notice power in a text. We do this in order to understand characters and their relationships better. *[See* Resources *CD-ROM for the complete minilesson.]*

▹ Mid-Workshop Teaching Point: Readers notice that sometimes characters have power in some ways and do not have power in other ways. Characters can simultaneously have power and not have power—it isn't an either/or situation.

▹ **Strategy Lesson** (for advanced students): Classifying power as "power to do something" or "power over something else" can help develop more theories about the author's message.

XV. ▸ Today I want to teach you that book club members might discuss power relationships in a text by using the prompt, "She/he/it has power in _____ way. I know this because...." Book club members push each other to talk long off the "because" because this helps us to grow ideas about texts.

▹ Mid-Workshop Teaching Point: Critical readers might notice that when we talk about the power characters have, we sometimes think about the power they could potentially have and the power they actually have.

XVI. ▸ Today I want to teach you that once critical readers identify ways that power is shown in a text, we can connect that power relationship to a social issue within the text (for example, gender, money, friendship, dictatorship). How a critical reader identifies, names, and interprets a power relationship in a text indicates what kind of lens the reader is using to read.

XVII. ▸ Today I want to teach you that book club members can create skits about a scene where we think a lot of power is shown. Acting out a scene and getting ourselves into the "shoes" of characters can help us to understand how power might work in obvious and hidden ways. Acting out a scene can also help us understand big ideas about power in the text better.

XVIII. ▸ Today I want to teach you that critical readers understand how characters experience power by asking ourselves, "In what ways do characters resist or respond to powerful forces in the story/text?" and "In what ways could they resist or respond?"

    ▹ Mid-Workshop Teaching Point: Readers might recognize that given the circumstances or setting of a character, it might be difficult for the character to resist or respond differently. It is important to recognize the constraints on a character in his or her responses to power.

PART FOUR: GROWING PLANS FOR SOCIAL CHANGES

Critical readers often grow ideas for social change from their reading.

XIX. ▸ Today I want to teach you that when powerful readers finish a book, we keep asking questions and thinking about our characters. We might find ourselves asking other readers, "Could we have done anything to change life for this character in the book? Would we have been able to do anything realistically? What constraints might we need to have changed to make a difference?"

XX. ▸ Today I want to teach you that book clubs become so invested in the social issues in which we have lived that we are likely to find ourselves proposing solutions to those issues we discuss in our groups. We might continue to collect as much information on an issue as possible, looking in other informational resources. We might even decide to take action. For example, sometimes we raise money for a certain cause or do a "teach-in" for our peers, parents, and/or teachers about a particular issue. We might write letters to the editor of a newspaper or propose guidelines for dealing with a certain social issue in our schools.

XXI. ▸ Today I want to teach you that when we take a critical lens to our books, we find ourselves bringing that same lens to our daily lives. When this happens, we write about our new or changing observations of the world, sometimes writing descriptively and sometimes writing reflectively about our ideas for social change.

EXAMPLE MINILESSON

Part One, Session I

GETTING READY

- My students have a collection of bumper stickers, T-shirts, stickers, pins, flyers, bags, posters, and advertisement slogans that we collected when I was teaching students how to create a "bumper sticker" phrase in order to summarize a main idea from a book (Laminack March 2008).

CONNECTION

I laid out all the bumper stickers, T-shirts, stickers, pins, flyers, bags, posters, and advertisement slogans in a display in the front of the meeting area so that all the students could see them.

"Readers, I have noticed recently how you really seem to care about fairness in our classroom and in our world. You have collected all of these artifacts—bumper stickers, T-shirts, stickers, pins, flyers, bags, posters, and advertisements—that highlight and give a message about various social issues. When you presented them to the class, you each seemed to notice what the social issues were. We have a bumper sticker that says, 'Make Levees, Not Bombs,' and Kell told us that that bumper sticker is about the social issues of war, violence, and natural disasters, like floods, that really affect people. She really noticed what all of the underlying issues were. This canvas bag says, 'Plastic bags are so last century,' and Lisako explained that it means we need to stop using disposable plastic bags because they create too much garbage and are not recyclable. Lisako even suggested that we make canvas bags made from recyclable materials with environmental messages on them to sell at our school craft's fair. We have this T-shirt that says, 'Practice random acts of kindness,' which Tara pointed out is a reminder to us to be kind to others and to not bully them. A group of you sorted the artifacts and found out that most of our bumper stickers, T-shirts, and bags addressed the social issues of violence and war. You noticed that that particular social issue came up a lot.

"Readers, today I'm going to teach you that you can use this same skill of noticing social issues when you are reading books or even watching TV or movies. You can notice when social issues pop up in books a lot and can mark where they pop up."

"Today I want to teach you that critical readers notice social issues when they pop up in texts. We sometimes jot down when we notice social issues, to see which ones pop up and how often. Jotting down where social issues appear helps us to keep track of which issues seem to be present and where we see signs of them."

Teaching

"Social issues are themes and problems that pop up as a result of humans living and interacting together in this world. We have already listed some social issues that we found in our collection of artifacts: war, violence, pollution, recycling, bullying. There are so many more social issues to name and so many ways to label and talk about each of them. Many social issues are also intertwined with other social issues as well. We often see clues about social issues in books that we read and in the world around us.

"Listen and watch how I notice that as I'm reading or rereading a text and making sense of it, I might also notice when a social issue appears. In this case, I will reread the start of *The Black Snowman* so that we can notice some of the social issues that pop up here."

Read-Aloud/Think-Aloud from *The Black Snowman* by Phil Mendez

Page	The Text Says	What I Say as I Think Aloud About the Text
4	Invaders capture the villagers and seize their property. The prisoners are loaded onto ships that cross a vast ocean to the continent called America, where the African people are sold into slavery. The magic kente is sold, too.	"Hmm, the text says that invaders capture the villagers, and in the picture the man is shackled. I think that *violence* and *captivity* are social issues at work here, so I will put a Post-it that says those words right here. The text also says that the African people were sold into slavery, so *slavery* is definitely a social issue here. I'll jot that one down, too. I think that *ownership* is an issue here as well. How can one person think they can own another one by buying them? People shouldn't be bought or sold! Oh, that word sold—both the people and the kente cloth are sold. Selling involves money. I think that *money* can be a social issue because humans use it. Even on this one page, I notice all of those social issues and jotted them down on Post-its: *violence, captivity, slavery, ownership, money.* Wow! All of those issues have to do with the way people live in this story."

"Did you see how I noticed some of the social issues present on this page? Some of the words on the page were clues that social issues might be present there. I marked where I saw the social issues pop out of the clues. As I read on, I'll continue to notice if I recognize clues about these same social issues and if I see clues for new social issues popping up."

Active Involvement

"Now it is your turn to practice noticing where you see social issues pop up. I'm going to give out a copy of another page of *The Black Snowman.* I will read it aloud while you read it to yourselves. While I read, jot down where you see social issues pop up. You will probably mark the social issue, like I did, next to a particular clue."

Page	The Text Says	What I Say as I Think Aloud About the Text
8	Can we go Christmas shopping today?" Peewee asked. "Well, not today," Mama said. "Not today or any day," Jacob interrupted. "Poor folks like us can't afford Christmas." "Now Jacob..." Mama spoke, trying to smooth over the hurt she saw rushing into Peewee's eyes.	"Wow, I see several clues about social issues here. Jacob seems so upset about things. He seems really upset about.... Jot down your ideas." "I see you all had ideas about social issues present on this page. You wrote down *money* as a social issue next to the clue "Christmas shopping," *poverty* next to "Poor folks like us," *fighting* next to "Jacob interrupted," and *anger* next to "Not today or any day." The list could go on and on. *Family relationships* seem like a social issue here because we see Peewee, Mama, and Jacob all having this discussion together." "You really noticed social issues and problems by looking at clues in the text. By finding places where social issues pop up, you are also learning about the characters."

Link

"Readers, as you read or reread a book, notice where social issues pop up. There will be clues that will point you toward certain social issues. Usually you will not read expecting to find certain social issues, but looking at the clues in the story that make a certain social issue pop up for you. You might notice clues about these same social issues throughout a story or just in one part of a story. Keep jotting on Post-its or in your notebooks about where you see these social issues pop up in different ways."

MID-WORKSHOP TEACHING POINT

"Readers, let me interrupt you for a moment! I want to tell you a really smart strategy I saw Ana and Dilara doing today. Not only were they writing down social issues on Post-its and placing them near where they read clues about the social issues in the story, but they were keeping a list of "social issue" words, thoughts, and phrases in their reader's notebooks. They have the words *meanness, self-esteem, divorce, different opinions,* and *brother/sister rivalry* on their list. Their plan was to remember what kinds of words and phrases are helpful for discussing social issues and to share them with their book clubs tomorrow to help with their discussion. We'll have to create a class chart of these words and phrases that have helped us discuss social issues. Great idea, Ana and Dilara!"

STRATEGY LESSON

Some students may struggle with finding places where social issues pop up in texts. I might pull a small group of students to teach them the following strategy for identifying social issues. In book clubs the next day, I will have students use the prompts "That seems fair because..." and "That seems unfair because...." I will teach students who are struggling with identifying social issues to notice where they feel something is unfair in the text and try to name what issue might be at work there.

"Social issues are often present when we notice that something feels unfair in a text. One way readers can identify social issues is by noticing where something feels unfair in the text and try to name what issue is at work there. Let's look at *My Best Friend,* an old favorite of ours, and notice where things seem unfair. Then we'll try to name the issue that is causing the unfairness."

Page	The Text Says	Unfairness	Social Issue at Work
4	"Hi Tamika," I say. Tamika wrinkles her nose and sticks out her tongue. Then she jumps into the pool with Shanice. Tamika is my best friend. She just doesn't know it yet.	"Tamika totally ignores Lily when she says hello. She meanly sticks out her tongue, which is very rude. It doesn't feel like Tamika is very nice at all. It seems totally unfair that Lily is nice but Tamika is mean back to her."	Bullying Meanness Friendship

OTHER RESOURCES YOU WILL FIND ON THE *RESOURCES* CD-ROM

Other Texts for a Social Issues Unit

"Words that Might Be Useful for Thinking About Social Issues" Chart

Part One, Session V

Part Two, Session VIII

Part Two, Session X

Part Three, Session XIV

Works Cited

AUTHORING CURRICULUM

By Lucy Calkins

This series will have done its job well if it not only helps you to teach the units described herein but also helps you and your colleagues author your own units of study. In this chapter, I'll help you do that curriculum development work.

As I do this, I'll be drawing on my experience teaching a graduate course every year designed to help people author upper-grade reading units of study and my experience working in schools where it is commonplace for the teachers on a grade level to develop one or two brand-new units of study each year, while also returning to other familiar units.

Suggestions for Beginning to Plan Your Own Units of Study

Before reading this chapter, it will help if you have studied some of the alternate units of study in this volume. You'll see plans for units of study on all sorts of topics—critical reading, humor, tackling of complex perspectives, content-area reading, social issues, and mystery. The unit plans are elaborated upon within the *Resources* CD. Those units are not entirely fleshed out, so one possibility for your curriculum development work will be to start by taking one of those units as a starting place. You can borrow the parts of the unit that work for you, develop other parts that seem to you to be missing, and in general use the work that has already been done as training wheels to help you and your colleagues gather momentum as developers of reading units of study.

Alternately, you can take a topic that has not been addressed and aim to produce a plan for a unit that resembles the plans we've included in *Constructing Curriculum.* Notice that these plans aren't fleshed out yet. Yours probably wouldn't be either until you and your children actually live your way into those plans. Even then, they'll be revised multiple times as you cycle through the units in subsequent years, learning ways to anticipate challenges your students encounter, to tuck in more tips, to differentiate more thoughtfully.

Before you embark on this curriculum development work, I should point out to you that the process is a recursive project, requiring enormous amounts of revision. You will not be able to progress through one step, the next, and the next in sequence, finishing one step once and for all before continuing to the next step. Realize, too, that if you spend five days on this effort, you probably won't write your first minilesson until day three because there are many decisions to make and work to accomplish before writing even the first minilesson.

Decide on Your Content and Goals

Of course, the first thing you will need to do is decide what you will teach. This is no easy decision, especially because you'll need to decide both what the kids will think you are teaching and what you are, in fact, teaching. For example, the children will think of the fourth unit as one on historical fiction; to us, it is really a unit on tackling complex books, on interpreting, and on reading critically. We could just as easily have taught historical fiction in a way that highlighted the skills of close reading and envisionment. (After all, readers need to be able to create a whole other world as they read, and to do this, readers need to read extremely closely.) So when thinking about what you are teaching, keep in mind that although kids may think that the unit of study teaches them to read a certain kind of book, chances are good that you know that this is actually a unit on a certain kind of skill, or on several skills.

There are lots of wonderful units of study that are begging to be written. For example, I think it would be wonderful to develop a unit of study on the following, among other topics:

- Personal response
- Voice of a reader
- Intratextuality (finding connections within texts)
- Reading to nourish independent writing projects
- Rereading great books to see more in them

If you and your colleagues author one of these units or any other one, please consider sharing what you do with the community by sending it to me to be included on the Teachers College Reading and Writing Project's website.

What Can Your Students Do and Almost Do?

In thinking about what you will teach, it is important to think about what your students can do and can almost do. You'll no doubt recoil from the question, thinking, "My students are all different. I can't talk about what 'they' can do as if there is some amalgamated 'they.'" Of course I understand that, but it is also the case that students are very amenable to instruction and that most of the readers in a class will learn to do roughly similar work—some with a bit more finesse, some with less—and with the work always being something they do with whatever the text level is that they can read. The fact of the matter is, you can probably generalize about the sorts of predicting work that most of your readers do or the sorts of theories that most of your readers grow about characters.

In other words, the kind of thinking work that students can and cannot yet do with texts is often a function of prior instruction and history. For example, as a class, many of your readers may have grown accustomed to reading the dutiful half hour a night at home, and many may not yet carry books everywhere, finding stolen moments throughout their days when they can catch ten minutes for reading. Some of your students may be accustomed to jotting Post-its as they read, but for a majority of your class, those Post-its might at this point tend to capture what the students saw in the text that was significant, and may not yet capture the students' thoughts in response to what they saw.

To think about lines of development or about skills and strategies that might pertain to your unit, it helps to think about reading skills. Here is one (of many) possible list of reading skills:

- Decoding
- Monitoring for sense
- Predicting
- Envisioning or building a mental model
- Using a knowledge of story structure or text structure to construct meaning
- Making meaning through personal response
- Inferring
- Synthesizing
- Asking questions
- Interpreting
- Reading critically
- Making meaning through inter- and intratextuality

Remember you will also need to teach life habits to your readers. You'll want to teach habits such as these:

- Reading with stamina
- Developing relationships that support their reading
- Talking and thinking in response to reading
- Developing and revising theories as they read
- Talking and writing about their theories in persuasive ways
- Learning about a subject through reading
- Developing an understanding of literary terms and concepts
- Noticing and learning from an author's craftsmanship

Which Texts Will Your Students Need and at Which Levels?

As you think about your students and what they can and can't quite do, think also about the texts that you have available related to the area in which you are designing a unit. For example, if you are considering writing a unit of study in which you channel students to read nonfiction texts pertaining to a particular topic, such as the Civil War, then you will want to think about the texts you have available in that genre, on that topic, with the text levels that your kids can handle. Remember Richard Gentry's research that suggests that if a student is reading a book such as *Stone Fox*, the student needs to read three of those books a week, twelve in a month. For readers who are reading level S texts, it is somewhat unlikely that you have twelve nonfiction books on the Civil War (let alone more than that so that readers can make choices from among them).

One solution might be for students to do lots of work with texts that are easy for them, thereby spending some of the month reading the books you have for less proficient readers. Another solution might be for students to read relevant historical fiction; a third solution might be for the unit to channel students to read nonfiction texts that are related in peripheral ways to the Civil War, such as books on race or on war or on American geography. Then again, you may simply decide your resources can't sustain a unit that is focused in that way.

You will also need to make some decisions about specific kinds of texts. For example, if you are teaching a unit on interpretation and believe that interpretation is best done when a reader is reading the second half of a text, then you start the unit by asking readers to reread the final portion of books that they already know well.

You will also need to decide on the read-aloud texts you will use to demonstrate throughout the unit. Typically you will select two short texts and a chapter book to use in the unit. You'll need to read aloud parts of the chapter book outside of reading workshop time. You might, for example, read Chapter 1 and Chapter 2 of the novel outside the reading workshop in read-aloud time and then use the start of Chapter 3 in the reading workshop minilesson. Next, you might read the rest of Chapter 3 and Chapter 4 outside the reading workshop and then bring the book back in, relying on reading Chapter 5 in the unit's next minilesson. Typically about half of a unit's minilessons will be built around the chapter book that threads through the unit.

How Will You Support Kids' Ongoing Reading?

It helps to keep in mind that as important as your unit will be, children's ongoing reading is even more important. Above all, you need to be sure your teaching doesn't *hurt* students' reading. For example, if you are thinking of designing a month-long unit involving something like reading poetry, you probably need to angle the unit so that you teach students that reading poetry can alter how they read any well-written piece of literature—or you'll need some other way to make sure that your unit doesn't constrain the volume of reading that children do. This same issue comes up if you consider a unit of study on reading fairy tales (see *Constructing Curriculum*) or reading the newspaper. Keep in mind also the research from Gentry that suggests kids need at least ninety minutes of actual eyes-on-print reading every day; make sure that your unit doesn't channel your students to read such short texts that the volume of their reading takes a giant hit. Usually you can get around this problem by angling the unit so that you show students that intensive work reading the shorter texts can affect the way they read longer texts.

The larger point is this: you must have humility and common sense enough to keep in mind that your teaching is not as important as your kids' reading work. Above all, your teaching needs to support your students doing the reading and thinking and talking about texts that they need to do. I'm suggesting that you plan a unit by focusing less on the question of "What will I say in my first minilesson? My second minilesson?" and more on the question of "What will my students be reading and doing across this stretch of time?"—at least as you start planning.

More specifically, this means focusing first and most importantly on designing structures that enable your kids to read up a storm, reading tons and tons of texts they can and want to read—and to read as thoughtfully as possible.

How Will You Structure the Reading Workshop?

As you plan a unit, then, think about the ways in which you will structure the entire reading workshop. Will the workshop end with ten minutes for sharing and will that time include partnership work, or will those ten minutes be for reading clubs? Will that final time for talking about reading need to be longer? Will you want to give your students five minutes to reread and jot in preparation for their clubs? Will the clubs meet daily? Twice a week? Will every club meet on the same day, or will they be on different days? Will your minilessons support reading and your mid-workshop teaching points support clubs, or will club days be structured so that minilessons support clubs and students go from minilessons to clubs, reading afterwards? Will kids be reading the same books at home and at school, as is usually the case, or are there reasons to alter that? Will your partnerships be same-book partnerships, or will it only be your strugglers who are in same-book partnerships? Will the other partnerships be swap-book partnerships? What sort of writing about reading do you envision kids doing, and how will you make this work as thoughtful as possible without letting it overwhelm reading? How will you differentiate instruction, and especially how will you provide your strugglers with the regular support they need? How will you make use of extra adults if you have access to them? How will after-school work or interventions support the unit?

As you think about the structures that you'll provide your students, you'll be thinking about ways in which structures can evolve over time to support increasing rigor and also about ways in which structures can be differentiated to support diverse learners. So, for example, children might read books at home and in school for three days without discussing them and then meet for a twenty-to-thirty-minute discussion. Then again, you might worry that children won't make good use of a twenty-to-thirty-minute time block for conversation. It is much easier to read books for twenty minutes, meet to talk for five minutes, resume reading for another twenty minutes, and then talk for another five minutes and do that every day. Work that encompasses more time, more texts, more people, and more independence tends to be more difficult to do well.

Draft and Revise Multiple Plans for the Progression of Your Unit

After thinking through the content and goals of your unit, you'll be ready to think about the sequence of instruction you'll provide. You definitely will not want to begin by writing a minilesson! Instead, think about the specific goals your teaching will aim to accomplish and the journey of work and study that the unit will support.

For example, if this is a unit on asking questions and thinking deeply about texts, you need to decide if you want to begin by showing kids the sorts of questions they might ask as they read.

Will you approach this by showing them the questions they could ask at the beginning, the middle, and the end of stories? Or will you move them from asking questions that allow them to grasp the surface level of the story toward asking more provocative and deeper questions? Will you plan your unit so that readers work at first to ask and carry questions on the run as they read, and progress towards them learning to ask questions that support sustained rereading and cross-text comparisons?

It is almost inevitable that when you approach a topic, one progression of study springs to mind fairly quickly. Delay deciding on that pathway so as to entertain other options. In the end, many of the possibilities that you consider and reject will end up giving you ways to enrich your strongest readers, to support your most struggling ones, and to give nuance and depth to whatever route you select.

Challenge Your Own Plans

The process of weighing and rejecting options requires that you challenge your own ideas for your teaching. I encourage you to learn to be hard on your wonderful ideas:

- **Are you reteaching?** For example, oftentimes you'll find that you invent teaching plans that essentially reteach what many students can already do instead of finding a way to tap those capacities and then extend them. Be willing to see that your plan doesn't take your students beyond what they already know how to do.

- **Are you telling, not teaching?** On the other hand, if you are really teaching students to do something that many of them cannot yet do, you need to remember that telling will not be teaching. Telling students to ask deep questions will not mean that suddenly they can do this! Whereas you may have imagined that work requiring a few days, it may in fact require a few weeks, and planning for this teaching may require you to think much more deeply about the smaller steps that you'll need to help your students take.

- **Do students have enough time to read?** You'll also want to guard against your fancy unit doing students harm as readers. That is apt to happen if your good ideas crowd out their time for reading. If you are asking students to devote a lot of their reading time to something other than reading—even if it is something related to reading like writing about reading or dancing about reading or painting about reading—be sure you check yourself. Is this truly what your kids most need?

- **Are you assigning work on teaching readers to know how to do things, now and always?** One of the most common problems teachers encounter is that they often realize in retrospect that their minilessons are actually attempts to assign work. Instead of teaching readers a skill that he or she will draw on repeatedly, their minilessons ask readers to jump through the hoop of the day.

Decide on the Parts of Your Unit and Begin Drafting Teaching Points

Once you've begun to think about a progression for your unit, I'd suggest you study the way other units of study progress. Look over multiple units, including those in the final section of *Constructing Curriculum: Alternate Units of Study*. Try to get a sense for the parts in the units of study that others have designed so that you can internalize the text structure for this unique sort of text. When you study other people's units of study, you will probably see that there is a certain way that units go.

The next thing you will probably do is begin to plan your own parts of the unit and start the long process of generating possible teaching points. I'd plan a good deal of this before starting to write a single minilesson, although once I do start writing minilessons, I'm generally back at work on the sequence of teaching points.

When you begin to hone in on what your teaching points might be and how those teaching points might fit into the parts in the unit, you'll quickly find that the first lesson or two in a unit poses special challenges. These first lessons need to rally kids to the new work. This is sometimes tricky because the unit may actually require students to recall some stuff they already know and can do, but asking readers to recall previous work isn't necessarily the most exciting way to create a drumroll for new work. I try to find ways for the first minilessons to invite kids into the exciting work of the new unit. Often the first minilesson involves a short text—a picture book, a short story, a poem, a book written for much younger kids, a snippet of video—so that it can give students an intense overview of the new work.

Then minilessons two and three might be the ones that remind students of relevant work they learned earlier, perhaps bringing old charts forward and showing students how to use these previous lessons in this new context. The message during the first few days of a new unit tends to be "Give this a go! Try it!" I tend to invite kids to approximate the new work, doing it as best they can with enthusiasm and confidence.

You won't be surprised that after a generous "Give this a go!" the minilessons tend to slow down so as to ratchet up the level of what students are doing and to address the fine points of how to do this work. At this point, the unit will tend to take a turn toward a second part, suggesting that readers can actually aim toward more, do more. Then at some point, the unit will start to head down its final stretch.

Often this final stretch involves work that goes across several texts or across larger social configurations, or work that encompasses more of students' time (as in work that extends beyond the reading workshop). There is usually less scaffolding provided and more independence expected. The message is, "You can do this work for the rest of your lives, even when this unit is over."

Integrate the Read-Aloud Text into Your Plan

Once you have a general plan for the way the parts in your unit might conceivably go, try reading the read-aloud text and other texts that your kids will be reading, spying on the mind work that you find yourself doing.

Note what seems to you to be essential mind work that almost any proficient reader would be apt to do.

Try to think of the tiny individual steps that you take in order to do that mind work.

Think, too, about how your students would be apt to do this differently than you.

In this way, you are uncovering some of the skills and strategies that you'll probably teach in the unit.

As you imagine the progression of work that might unfold across the unit, remember that kids will not proceed in sync with your progress through the read-aloud book. For example, you may read a mystery aloud over ten days. You can't, on day ten, teach the class how to read the end of a mystery as if they're all doing this in their books on that same day. Those who are reading easier mysteries will have reached the end of their first mystery on the second day of the unit! Usually, remembering that readers will not progress in sync with you will nudge you to teach what readers do at the end of books much sooner than you might otherwise teach this, which often supports the decision to start the unit by reading aloud a short text.

Draft Teaching Points, Craft Anchor Charts

Most of us work very hard on our teaching points, hoping to make them memorable and helpful. This work is done concurrently with an effort to think about anchor charts. What are the big skills you'll be helping kids to work toward, and what are the specific strategies you'll suggest they could choose between? What charts might thread through the entire unit?

Draft the Minilessons

Now you will be ready to plan your actual sequence of teaching points and to plan the minilessons themselves. Remember as you do this that you can usually teach two or three teaching points in a day—one through the minilesson, another through the mid-workshop teaching point, and a third through the teaching share.

You are ready to write some minilessons. I've described the architecture of a minilesson in the chapter on minilessons, and that chapter will serve you well with this portion of curriculum development. But here are a few general words of advice.

First, plan to actually write your teaching point, working with the wording of it a bit while keeping some exemplar teaching points close at hand. It is extremely easy to forget ourselves and shift from teaching readers strategies readers can use often across books toward assigning them an activity to do for the day. There's a world of difference between the two.

Second, try composing your minilessons by saying them aloud to a pretend group of kids rather than composing while sitting at the computer. You'll find your teaching is more vital and alive if you plan with your kids foremost in your mind, thinking above all about reaching them, teaching them. If you think of this as a new kind of writing, you may get too writerly. Realize that usually the times when you demonstrate a strategy by thinking aloud need to be kept extremely brief. Kids do not want to sit and listen to you yammer on and on and on and on about whatever free associations come to mind as you read. If you are going to think aloud in front of the kids, usually two or three sentences of this will suffice to make your point; then stop and freeze-frame what you have done.

Finally, plan on discarding whatever you work so hard to plan, because when we teach we take our cues from kids. You'll approach teaching with your best laid plans and kids will surprise you. They'll struggle in ways you couldn't have imagined possible, and they'll generate insights that turn your thinking upside down. Expect the unexpected and embrace it.